METH WARS

ALTERNATIVE CRIMINOLOGY SERIES

General Editor: Jeff Ferrell

Pissing on Demand: Workplace Drug Testing and the Rise of the Detox Industry
Ken Tunnell

Empire of Scrounge: Inside the Urban Underground of Dumpster Diving, Trash Picking, and Street Scavenging
Jeff Ferrell

Prison, Inc.: A Convict Exposes Life inside a Private Prison
by K. C. Carceral, edited by Thomas J. Bernard

The Terrorist Identity: Explaining the Terrorist Threat
Michael P. Arena and Bruce A. Arrigo

Terrorism as Crime: From Oklahoma City to Al-Qaeda and Beyond
Mark S. Hamm

Our Bodies, Our Crimes: The Policing of Women's Reproduction in America
Jeanne Flavin

Graffiti Lives: Beyond the Tag in New York's Urban Underground
Gregory J. Snyder

Crimes of Dissent: Civil Disobedience, Criminal Justice, and the Politics of Conscience
Jarret S. Lovell

The Culture of Punishment: Prison, Society, and Spectacle
Michelle Brown

Who You Claim: Performing Gang Identity in School and on the Streets
Robert Garot

5 Grams: Crack Cocaine, Rap Music, and the War on Drugs
Dimitri A. Bogazianos

Judging Addicts: Drug Courts and Coercion in the Justice System
Rebecca Tiger

Courting Kids: Inside an Experimental Youth Court
Carla J. Barrett

The Spectacular Few: Prisoner Radicalization and the Evolving Terrorist Threat
Mark S. Hamm

Comic Book Crime: Truth, Justice, and the American Way
Nickie D. Phillips and Staci Strobl

The Securitization of Society: Crime, Risk, and Social Order
Marc Schuilenburg

Covered in Ink: Tattoos, Women, and the Politics of the Body
Beverly Yuen Thompson

Narrative Criminology: Understanding Stories of Crime
Edited by Lois Presser and Sveinung Sandberg

Progressive Punishment: Job Loss, Jail Growth, and the Neoliberal Logic of Carceral Expansion
Judah Schept

Meth Wars: Police, Media, Power
Travis Linnemann

Meth Wars

Police, Media, Power

Travis Linnemann

NEW YORK UNIVERSITY PRESS
New York

NEW YORK UNIVERSITY PRESS
New York
www.nyupress.org

References to Internet websites (URLs) were accurate at the time of writing. Neither the author nor New York University Press is responsible for URLs that may have expired or changed since the manuscript was prepared.

Library of Congress Cataloging-in-Publication Data
Names: Linnemann, Travis, author.
Title: Meth wars : police, media, power / Travis Linnemann.
Description: New York : New York University Press, [2016] | Series: Alternative criminology series | Includes bibliographical references and index.
Identifiers: LCCN 2016023893| ISBN 978-1-4798-7869-7 (cl : alk. paper) | ISBN 978-1-4798-0002-5 (pb : alk. paper)
Subjects: LCSH: Methamphetamine abuse—Social aspects—United States. | Methamphetamine abuse—Press coverage—United States. | Minorities—Drug use—United States. | Police—United States. | Drug control—United States.
Classification: LCC HV5822.A5 L56 2016 | DDC 362.29/950973—dc23
LC record available at https://lccn.loc.gov/2016023893

New York University Press books are printed on acid-free paper, and their binding materials are chosen for strength and durability. We strive to use environmentally responsible suppliers and materials to the greatest extent possible in publishing our books.

Manufactured in the United States of America

10 9 8 7 6 5 4 3 2 1

Also available as an ebook

CONTENTS

contributions to the book and for years of humor and friendship. A special thanks is due Tyler Wall, whose contributions here are crucial and many. Lastly, I would like to thank Judy Linnemann, and Jessica Jones, for their unwavering love and support and for listening patiently as I have droned on about this project for years.

Introduction

The Methamphetamine Imaginary

You are normal. It's the speed that made you a freak.
—Jerry Stahl, "Bad"

February 2014: According to local news broadcasts, the Benson family of Union County, Illinois, got the "scare of their lives" when "drug agents" raided their home expecting to find a methamphetamine lab. Laura Benson described the scene and her surprise, explaining, "I heard the dogs barking. And I knew that meant somebody was outside the house. And I looked out the windows and I seen a truck coming up the driveway fairly fast. And an Anna police car right behind it." Apparently a few blue plastic barrels and tubing near some of the trees on the property had led one of the Bensons' neighbors to alert police. "I think my neighbors on their way to church see the buckets and stuff and think we've got a meth lab operation going on here," Benson explained. Much to the chagrin of the "drug agents," the barrels and tubing had nothing to do with methamphetamine and instead were used by the Bensons to collect tree sap to make maple syrup. "They [the police] pointed to the buckets and I told them my husband has a hobby of making maple syrup. Of course they realized it once they seen it," Benson explained. "But I was quite startled this morning."[1]

A few months later and several hundred miles away, another misguided raid driven by the anxious desire to police methamphetamine unfolded. This time, a nineteen-month-old boy was permanently disfigured and nearly killed by a "flash-bang" stun grenade carelessly tossed into his crib by a member of the Habersham County (Georgia) Sheriff Department's Special Response Team. Earlier, a confidential informant sent to the home by police had purchased approximately fifty dollars' worth of methamphetamine from one of its residents, Wanis Thonetheva. Because of a previous weapons charge, when the Special Response Team returned to arrest Thonetheva, they entered the home behind a battering ram and assault weapons in the familiar no-knock fashion. Not only did they ignore signs that Thonetheva's relatives were visiting from out of town, terrify the family, and maim a young child, but police also failed to make an arrest or find any illegal drugs.[2] Even more troubling is that a Justice Department investigation into the circumstances leading up to the raid found that a Habersham County Sheriff Department investigator falsified information in order to obtain the initial search warrant.[3] Neither these cases nor the hundreds similar, however absurd or tragic, should be dismissed as simply the unfortunate outcome of corruption or as human error or even regarded as all that unusual. Rather, all emerge from a shared political and cultural history stretching back decades, leading to a present in which police, politicians, and well-meaning neighbors see the risks and dangers of drugs like methamphetamine everywhere.

For the better part of two decades, I too have been looking for and perhaps seeing methamphetamine everywhere. For most of my childhood, I called Marysville, a small farm town in northeast Kansas, home. Of the nine small towns in Marshall County, Marysville is by far the largest, with a population of around 3,000. These are working-class communities, where most folks manage small family farms or look to the service industry, light manufacturing, and the Union Pacific Railroad for a paycheck. The county has been home to my family since the turn of the last century, and the farm that sets a mile or so off the west bank of the Big Blue River has been worked by my family since the 1920s. In the 1960s, when my mother was in high school, the county population was around 16,000. By the 1990s, when I was in high school, the population had dipped to 12,000 and now sits around 10,000. Leaving for college, I intended to be one of the many out-migrants never to return. But just a few years later, I found myself back home, working as a probation officer covering the four-county judicial district stretching across the top-right-hand corner of the state. This was the late 1990s, and widespread social anxieties over home-cooked methamphetamine were on the rise. At state-mandated trainings, I heard from doctors and dentists who graphically described how the drug literally dissolved the brain, flesh, and teeth of users and from "proactive" narcotics officers and social workers who described how meth was dissolving communities like my hometown, one family at a time. None of this was much of a surprise. Growing up in the small farm town, I had heard whispers of older kids taking "speed" to perform on the football field or wrestling mat and of bikers and rough locals who peddled "crank" out of local taverns. Because meth moves through the body so quickly, to "catch" probationers using it, my supervisors instructed me to drug test as much as possible, alternate routines, and "surprise" them whenever I could. As I was still learning the job, one of my supervisors led me on several dead-of-night excursions to visit probationers living in the tiny farm towns dotting Nemaha and Brown Counties. One night, after relentlessly banging on the doors and windows of a small run-down trailer home set yards off a muddy road, we managed to rouse a supposed "meth head" out for his court-ordered drug and alcohol tests. Because the home did not have electricity or running water, I collected the urine sample in a similarly run-down lawnmower shed, shining a flashlight on the man as he straddled a five-gallon bucket. As I read the results of the field test aloud—marijuana, cocaine, opiates, phencyclidine, methamphetamine—all negative, my supervisor could hardly contain his disappointment, offering the man no encouragement for passing, no apologies for forcing him out of bed, just an acerbic "better luck next time" as we packed up and moved on to the next home.

Encouraging, in fact demanding, such tactics while simultaneously ignoring years of the state's own data showing that only a tiny fraction (2.7 percent) of "high-risk" probationers are "caught" using methamphetamine, we might say that Kansas, like my supervisor and I, stubbornly refused not to see methamphetamine in the lives of probationers.[4] The same would hold for the citizenry of Kansas and other states across the country. In the coming years, nightly news broadcasts were overrun with reports of lab seizures and meth-fueled violence, while everyday journeys to work or the grocery store were interrupted by shocking antimeth billboards and checkout-counter bulletins warning to "be on the watch" for customers buying meth-making ingredients. After nearly fifteen increasingly frustrating years of work in criminal justice and social welfare, I left for a career in academia, as methamphetamine skulked in the background, not far from sight.

Seeking advice on my fledgling research agenda from a highly re-garded criminologist, I explained my interests in the consequences of mass imprisonment for rural America, to which he replied, "Well, you're going to have to get to know methamphetamine then." However quick and misguided his rural + crime = meth calculus may have been, I still took it seriously, setting out to situate the so-called methamphet-amine epidemic within a broader culture and politics of drug control and mass imprisonment. Toward the project's beginning, I returned to the family farm curious if my aunt or her neighborhoods had meth-lab trash dumped on their land or had anhydrous ammonia stolen. Though neither she nor her neighbors had any such experiences, my aunt did provide a particularly interesting anecdote. One afternoon a man iden-tifying himself as a Kansas Bureau of Investigation (KBI) agent drove up her mile-long dirt lane and asked my aunt's permission to hunt on the farm. As they made small talk, the agent remarked that he could not believe how many "meth heads" he had spotted as he passed through a nearby town. As he saw it, "nearly every other person in town" looked as though they were on meth. Perhaps the agent had mistaken a few, par-ticularly rough-looking characters on their lunch breaks from welding at the trailer factory for burned-out junkies. Perhaps he was just trying to curry the favor of my aunt and uncle so he could hunt their land. It could even be that he truly believed he had encountered ground zero of the meth epidemic. And though the state's own records show that police in the county have encountered just three meth labs in the past twenty years, the agent saw methamphetamine, and because of that, my aunt saw it too, retelling the story as certain fact.[5]

This sort of conjuring, searching for, and seeing methamphetamine, whether it is there or not, continues in rather interesting ways. As the criminologists Rodanthi Tzanelli and Majid Yar describe, a cottage tour-ist industry has sprung up in Albuquerque, New Mexico, around the hit television series *Breaking Bad*. Here "televisual crime tourists" mind-walk through the city, imagining important scenes and characters, map-ping them and the broader narrative of meth-fueled crime and violence onto its landscapes. Not unlike police who raid homes hoping to seize drugs, only to come up empty-handed, *Breaking Bad* tourists produce a distinct sort of materiality, projecting fantasy onto Albuquerque's streets—experiencing the imaginary as real.[6]

All of this cultural work serves as a conceptual reference point for what I call the *methamphetamine imaginary*. To be clear, invoking the imaginary in no way suggests that the problems associated with drugs are not real and thus without consequence. Rather, *imaginary* describes important yet often-overlooked mediated dimensions of social life. Taking a cue from the philosopher Charles Taylor, who understands the social imaginary as "the ways people imagine their social existence, how they fit together with others, how things go on between them and their fellows, the expectations that are normally met, and the deeper normative notions and images that underlie these expectations,"[7] we can say that the methamphetamine imaginary encompasses the many ways in which methamphetamine mediates the social world—how individuals imagine themselves and their relations to one another through this particular drug.[8] A dynamic generative practice, the methamphetamine imaginary encompasses the taken-for-granted, commonsense knowledges and everyday affects that surround methamphetamine, its users, and those who are concerned with controlling, treating, and punishing both.[9] Mapping the imaginary then helps to explore the materiality of methamphetamine and the innumerable sites where meaning is made, remade, consumed, and contested. As I will show, the methamphetamine imaginary and the broader drug-war imaginary of which it is a part are circumscribed and animated by literature, television, film, news media accounts, public-service ad campaigns, word of mouth, and the pronouncements of police and politicians. So, for instance, in a speech designating October 1986 Crack/Cocaine Awareness Month, President Ronald Reagan uttered the rhetorical template that has structured the imaginary dimensions of the drug war for decades. He pleads,

> Cocaine poses a serious threat to our Nation. Long masquerading as glamorous and relatively harmless, cocaine has revealed its own deadly truth—cocaine is a killer. It can cause seizures, heart attacks, and strokes. It is indifferent in its destruction, striking regular users and initiates alike. . . . Despite the best efforts by law enforcement officials, cocaine continues to come into our country at alarming levels, supplied by ruthless criminals who draw their power from public acquiescence. Bigger supplies and lower prices have put cocaine in the hands of people who were never before tempted to use it.

Today an even more devastating form of cocaine—"crack"—has appeared. Crack is smoked, producing immediate effects in the user. It is relatively inexpensive, but is so powerfully addictive that the user, even a first-time user, feels an overwhelming compulsion for more. Crack is used by people of all ages. Tragically, it is sold to and used by even 11 and 12-year-olds. To mothers and fathers, boys and girls at this age are children. To a cocaine dealer, they are just another market.[10]

While a month dedicated to broadcasting the ills of crack/cocaine may now seem odd, Reagan's logic, language, and grammar are all too familiar. The warning goes, because of the irresistible laws of supply and demand, a "new" drug, somehow more potent, dangerous, and deadly than the last, threatens the very fabric of American social life. Its spread must be stopped and its peddlers punished. We know now, of course, that regardless of the veracity of this warning, the American public heard it loud and clear, roundly supporting a vicious narcopolitical project[11] the consequences of which are still uncounted and unpaid. Looking back through nearly four decades, Crack/Cocaine Awareness Month is one of many sad, ultimately futile moments in a history of disastrous, indifferent social policy. This is of course no revelation. It is no longer a radical position to cite the many failures of the drug war,[12] advocate for some form of harm-reduction strategy, or call for outright legalization of some drugs or all. Even among mainstream commentators, it is now conventional practice to describe the drug war as a literal war[13] or Jim Crow oppression born anew.[14] A history replete with contradictions, falsehoods, and failures makes the next and more recent chapter all the more disquieting. Twenty years and one month after Reagan's proclamation, George W. Bush named November 30, 2006, National Methamphetamine Awareness Day. While the drugs had changed, the panicked and desperate language had not. Bush pleads,

Methamphetamine abuse shatters families and threatens our communities. On National Methamphetamine Awareness Day, we underscore the dangers of methamphetamine and reaffirm our collective responsibility to combat all forms of drug abuse. Methamphetamine is a powerfully addictive drug that dramatically affects users' minds and bodies. Chronic use can lead to violent behavior, paranoia, and an inability to cope with the ordinary demands of life. Methamphetamine abusers can transform homes into places of danger and despair by neglecting or endangering the lives of their children, spouses, and other loved ones. Additionally, methamphetamine production exposes anyone near the process to toxic chemicals and the risk of explosion.[15]

Bush, like Reagan before him, confronts an epidemic driven by a new powerfully addictive drug that elicits violence, paranoia, and dependency from its users, shatters families, and destroys communities. Unsurprisingly, large swaths of the American public again took these warnings seriously, enlisting in the "meth war" taken up here. Yet, given the outcome of the "crack panic," perhaps another bit of Bush's sage advice—"Fool me once, shame on—shame on you. Fool me—you can't get fooled again"[16]—would have been more apropos. When it comes to illicit drugs, it seems as though the American public is indeed fooled and fooled again. This is particularly the case if we look beyond the Nixon administration, the point that many commentators mark as the drug war's beginning. If the historian Kathleen J. Frydl is correct, we should instead mark the 1930s and the proto-drug-warrior Harry Anslinger's Bureau of Narcotics—if not 1914 and the Harrison Anti-Narcotic Act—as the drug war's beginning.[17]

So the question persists: If the American public knows its history, why does it seem that it is not only condemned but perhaps committed to repeating the mistakes of the past? Of course, I do not mean to suggest that the American public is monolithic or that each and every citizen secretly supports the drug war. Rather, I simply suggest that the drug war is something *we* (and hence the world) in the United States suffer to varying degrees, whether *we* like it or not. Is it that the drug war is simply the will of a state too formidable to oppose? Recent progress made by grassroots movements toward decriminalizing marijuana might suggest otherwise. What if the coercion, dispossession, and violence so often decried by people on the left and right as altogether avoidable products of bad policy are not the fault of the drug war at all? Could it be that we attach everyday violence, social exclusion, and death to the drug war because the alternative is much more terrifying?

What If We Need the Drug War?

Consider a question posed by the radical philosopher Slavoj Žižek: "Who among us would be able to continue eating pork chops after visiting a factory farm in which pigs are half-blind and cannot even properly walk, but are just fattened to be killed?"[18] Žižek believes that once people witness a system of such brutality, suffering, and injustice, few could continue to participate in it. And though the horrors of factory farms are no closely guarded secret, animals are still mistreated, slaughtered, and consumed en masse. Why is this? For Žižek, it is not that we are blind or indifferent to the suffering of others. On the contrary, it may be that out of some sense of powerlessness to intervene in the horrors that surround us, we have developed a way to forget or ignore what we know to be true, if only so that we might continue to live our lives as we wish. Žižek calls this cultural-cognitive process the "fetishistic disavowal." Here we say, "I know, but I don't want to know that I know, so I don't know."[19] Could it be that the drug war operates in this way? This is not to suggest the American public is simply mystified, in denial, or willfully ignorant of the drug war's causes and consequences. Rather, the objects of the drug war, drug users and the drugs themselves, operate as fetish objects— symbolically articulated knowledge ignored by the subject—permitting the public to disavow and endure the many, in Žižek's words, "dirty compromises of American life."[20]

The drug war du jour, an inexhaustible reservoir of constituents— marijuana, heroin, crack, meth, "bath salts," "krokodil"—helps displace that which we know to be true. It is our participation in the violence, coercion, dispossession, and inequality of late-capitalist life that is denied. Displacing these inequalities onto methamphetamine or another from a veritable menu of fetishes permits the American public to act as if it did not know. With that, we can perhaps better understand why, even though it probably knows better, the American public seems ever willing to entertain the dangers of the next drug epidemic. And because the fetishistic disavowal obscures more immutable inequalities, we might also predict that so long as capitalism is the fundamental organizing principle of American social life, there will be a war—drugs, crime, terror—or several. It is no coincidence, then, that the American experiments with prohibitionist and punitive drug-control strategies did not begin with the Nixon administration but rather grew in lockstep with the inequality, unrest, slums, and ghettos[21] of early industrial capitalism.[22] Much like Marx's understanding of religion, the drug war is not the cause of human misery but a symptom, the "sigh of the oppressed creature, the heart of a heartless world and the soul of soulless conditions."[23]

Methamphetamine, Epidemic, Emergency

Or course, methamphetamine is very much a part of this broader drug-war history and hence not all that unique. Like all drugs, illicit or otherwise, methamphetamine is really distinct only in terms of chemical composition and its effects on the human body. This might seem terribly obvious, but we should be clear from the outset about what methamphetamine is and what it does, so that we can better understand what it is not, what it does not do and, ultimately, for what it should not be blamed.

First synthesized in 1919, N-methyl-alpha-methylphenethylamine is just one of a number of stimulants in the amphetamine family.[24] Like the others, it improves concentration and wakefulness and increases blood pressure and heart rate in users to levels that are similar to those produced by vigorous exercise. Methamphetamine-hydrochloride, sold under the brand name Desoxyn since the early 1940s, has a number of legitimate medical uses. For decades, militaries have used it to keep soldiers awake and flying and fighting longer. Even in methamphetamine's illegally produced, "street" form, it is nearly identical in chemical structure to the prescription drug Adderall, widely used to treat ADHD and narcolepsy.[25] Yet it is not the composition or physiological effects of particular drugs but rather their culture and politics that offer a unique lens through which to view the social world.

In the United States, illegal manufacture of methamphetamine in clandestine laboratories began in the early 1960s. Long thought to be the purview of outlaw bikers, "speed" or "crank" was a relatively common street drug throughout the 1970s. Perhaps because it was supposedly only consumed by working-class whites, available in similar forms legally, and not imported in large quantities into the United States, meth remained somewhat off the radar of the Drug Enforcement Administration (DEA), which at the time focused its attention on heroin, cocaine, and marijuana. It was not until the supposed emergence of "ice" or "crystal" meth in the late 1980s, according to the historian Philip Jenkins, that federal authorities began to take notice. From the late 1980s until the mid-1990s, what Jenkins has dubbed the "ice age," a variety of politicians and journalists pushed the crystal meth issue despite the lack of a significant change in either production or consumption in the United States, outside of Hawaii and some parts of California. These observations led Jenkins to predict that the methamphetamine problem would reemerge from time to time regardless of how much of the drug was actually used by the American public.[26] Jenkins's predictions in 1994 proved true in the coming decade, as politicians like George W. Bush and New York senator Charles Schumer began to sound familiar warnings. As Schumer once claimed, "It's 1984 all over again. Twenty years ago, crack was headed east across the United States like a Mack Truck out of control, and it slammed New York hard because we just didn't see the warning signs. Well, the headlights are glaring bright off in the distance again, this time with meth. We are still paying the price of missing the warning signs back then, and if we don't remember our history we will be doomed to repeat it, because crystal meth could become the new crack."[27]

Borrowing Jenkins's metaphor, like a glacier's steady creep, the methamphetamine problem in the United States has advanced over decades, perhaps exceeding that of crack cocaine but not in terms of use and users. If there has been an "ice age" or methamphetamine epidemic in the United States, it has been one of culture, discourse, and imagination. Everyday news reports that frame the issue in dire terms as "a matter of life and meth,"[28] as well as aggressive policing and reactionary legislation, fix the broken language of war and epidemic in the public's imagination. Known colloquially as "poor man's cocaine," "redneck coke," "white man's crack," and so on, meth appears frequently in popular culture and everyday discussions as the "white trash" cousin of cocaine.[29] My own ethnographic work bears this out. For instance, when I asked a small-town Kansas police officer why meth seemed so resilient in out-of-the-way rural towns, he explained, "I say its economics. Cocaine is an expensive drug by comparison to meth. Meth is a poor man's drug. If you look at what we've been talking about and what we're dealing with, we're dealing with the disabled, welfare, those types of folks. They have limited resources." Following this thinking, the poor, mostly white, rural folks said to be the primary producers and consumers of meth, like 1980s "crack heads," are seen as the cause or consequence of all manner of social change—job loss, withering populations, and unequal economic development.[30] In a recent documentary on the drug war, David Simon, the writer and producer of the critically acclaimed television crime drama *The Wire*, echoes this sentiment, offering this comment on the political economy of methamphetamine:

> A funny thing happened on the way to the twenty-first century, which is that we shrugged off so much of our manufacturing base, so much of our need for organized labor, for a legitimate union wage, for union benefits, for the types of jobs with which you could raise a family and be a meaningful citizen. We got rid of so much of that, that oops, we marginalized a lot of white people. And lo and behold, white people, when they are marginalized, when they are denied meaning, when they are denied meaningful work, they become drug addicts too. They become involved in the methamphetamine trade, they start turning themselves over to the underground economies, the only ones there to accept them. Capitalism is fairly color blind, in the end. Our economic engine, when it doesn't need somebody, it doesn't need somebody, and it doesn't give a damn who you are. White people found out a little later than black folk, but they found it out.[31]

While Simon's attempts to link crack and methamphetamine to growing class inequality are admirable, we should be cautious of adopting a causal logic that holds that when work disappears, the jobless instinctively turn to drugs, either as vocation or escape. Other than not necessarily being true, the problem with this sort of thinking is that the drug, the gang, or whatever the pathology linked to economic decline quickly becomes the focus and fetish. Perhaps even more fundamentally, given that the federal government's own data suggest that just a sliver of the US population uses the drug regularly, it would seem that alarmist warnings of "meth epidemics" are largely misplaced. For instance, the National Survey on Drug Use and Health (NSDUH) estimated the number of regular or "past month" methamphetamine users in 2013 to be 595,000, or 0.2 percent of the US population over twelve years old. Similar rates were estimated for 2012 (440,000, or 0.2 percent), 2011 (439,000, or 0.2 percent), and 2010 (353,000, or 0.1 percent). In fact, estimated rates of regular methamphetamine users have not exceeded 0.5 percent since the government began making such estimates. By comparison, the most recent estimates place regular marijuana use at 7.5 percent, cocaine at 0.6 percent, and the nonmedical use of prescription drugs around 2.5 percent of the population over twelve years told.[32] Even if the estimated number of regular methamphetamine users is grossly inaccurate, we could double it and double it again and still come nowhere close to the estimated number of people who abuse prescription drugs. Of course, this is not to suggest that we should refocus our attention on another drug but rather simply to build some context in which to confront persistent warnings of "epidemics."

Critical of meth's mythology, researchers such as David Erceg-Hurn have pointed to the ways in which state drug-control agencies and non-state intervention programs keep meth's dangers alive in the public's imagination as part of broader ideological and market-based projects.[33] In keeping with many of the themes taken up here, the anthropologist William Garriott's ethnographic work in rural West Virginia shows how methamphetamine control helps order social life outside the usual drug-war terrains. For Garriott, the narcopolitics of methamphetamine control are not concerned with crime or law but with the potential threats the drug is thought to represent. The shift to threats, risk, or "precrime" is a significant perversion of the criminal law as he sees it. No longer concerned with redressing grievances, the police power[34] focuses on "prevention and incapacitation,"[35] or what I would describe as policing insecurity.[36] In the United Kingdom, the criminologists Tammy Ayers and Yvonne Jewkes have documented claims of a coming "meth epidemic" that are nearly identical to those in the United States. Appropriating the mug shots of suspected meth users, British news media warn, "these horrifying pictures reveal the ravaging effects of the dance-sex drug poised to sweep Britain."[37] As I have done, Ayers and Jewkes are quick to note that the British Crime Survey shows methamphetamine use to be quite low, with about 0.05 percent of people surveyed having used the drug in the past year. Nevertheless, they recognize that this sort of claims making—part propaganda and part myth—helps solidify "deadly crystal meth" as a lived reality of everyday British life.

But what of *epidemic*, a word that is almost always included in any discussion of illicit drugs? The US Centers for Disease Control defines *epidemic* rather ambiguously as "the occurrence of more cases of disease than expected in a given area or among a specific group of people over a particular period of time."[38] Given the numbers of regular users described earlier, most people would be hard-pressed to validate notions of a meth epidemic. However, if we see the problem as the state does,[39] that is, through the desire to impose outright prohibition of any unauthorized drug use, legal or otherwise, then the threshold of epidemic is quite easily satisfied. Since the prohibitionist state expects, in fact demands, no unauthorized drug use of any kind, any sort of transgression in this regard can be seen as an epidemic. And so the methamphetamine epidemic spreads, not in the number of initiates but in the imaginary, the pulsing background of social insecurity, animated by newspaper editorials, news broadcasts, investigative journalism, documentary films, and the word on the street, all of which speak of the drug in dire and spectacular terms.

Drug War, Real and Imagined

Returning to the idea of the imaginary, my aim here is to broadly theorize the ways in which the methamphetamine and drug-war imaginaries are at work within a boundless governing strategy encompassing foreign and domestic, local and global. What the book does not provide is a detailed history of methamphetamine or an analysis of contemporary use patterns. While it is critical of current policing practices, it also does not systematically evaluate particular strategies, nor does it offer specific policy remedies. Likewise, the book does not spend a great deal of time contemplating why people use methamphetamine or exploring the various avenues for drug treatment. Though it draws widely on political and cultural theory, the aim is not to document or define subcultural traits unique to methamphetamine users. And while cultural representation is a primary concern, the book does not aim to adjudicate the real or objective facts of methamphetamine. In other words, this book is not intended to be a work of empirical social science or one that abides by particular disciplinary boundaries. The focus here is on the ways in which the methamphetamine imaginary animates the politics of fear and insecurity across a variety of seemingly unrelated social fields.[40] From the environmental dangers of discarded chemicals and volatile clandestine laboratories,[41] the corporeal and racial insecurities provoked by the drug's effects on the body, and coalitions mobilized to protect children, families, and the boundaries of traditional morality to the politics of mobility, border, and nation, produced and reproduced by police who hunt traffickers across landscapes of all kinds, as part of a broader politics of security, the methamphetamine imaginary links small-town streets to distant battlefields, setting out homeland battle-fronts in a global drug war.

To more fully elaborate what this means, it is perhaps a useful exercise to explain my approach through a brief comparison to recent sociological/criminological writing on methamphetamine. In the fine book *The Methamphetamine Industry in America: Transnational Cartels and Local Entrepreneurs*, authors Henry Brownstein, Timothy Mulcahy, and Johannes Huessy aim to describe how "methamphetamine markets evolved in the United States over more than a decade given changes in public policies and practices and changing public opinion."[42] One chapter in particular sets out to document all that goes into the meth-amphetamine industry—local recipes, knowledges, languages, tastes, preferences—in short, its culture:

> We live in a world that is made up of stuff. . . . The stuff also includes the words and actions you use to communicate, maybe to describe or explain something. The point is that all this stuff has shared meaning for the people who use it and the people around them who share the world they live in. In that way they can be part of a group or collective of people that shares the same time and space and has the ability to collaborate or even cooperate to accomplish things, or at least work around each other. Every society and every subgroup of people has their stuff. This is also true for the subgroup of people who participate in the methamphetamine industry.[43]

Conceiving the culture of the methamphetamine industry as the "stuff" of this particular "subgroup of people" is in keeping with long-standing sociological understandings of culture. However, one of the many problems with this approach is that it understands culture as rather fixed and uniform—a deterministic structure—something that just is.[44] The view of culture as something discrete and distinct to a particular group ultimately defines the boundaries necessary to exclude members of that particular group as separate, alien, *Other*. This becomes all the more apparent in the authors' discussion of modes of "communication in the methamphetamine industry": "The developments in modern communication technology have been as important for doing business in the methamphetamine industry as they have for most other areas of social life. Respondents as far apart as Atlanta, Georgia, and Salem, Oregon, told us about cases of meth deals being set using code transmitted during an online game involving Xboxes. Others mentioned iPods and Skype for communicating information to set up meth deals."[45] Here it seems as though Brownstein and colleagues are surprised to learn that people in the "methamphetamine industry" communicate in the same ways as those in "other areas of social life," an assumption that subtly upholds the view of a distinct and separate "methamphetamine culture." As I argue here, in theory and application, this could not be further from the truth. One way around this is to view culture not as fixed and determined but as a collection of resources or a repertoire, a dynamic ongoing process and accomplishment, rather than something to which one takes part or is born into.[46] As researchers and writers, Brownstein and colleagues draw on methamphetamine culture to understand and accomplish things in the world, while also helping to shape how others understand it. In fact, having much to say about methamphetamine, the book and its authors are as much a part of its culture as are the police, dealers, and users whom they describe (the same is true for this book as well).

The view of culture—dynamic, performative, produced, consumed— taken up here is very much in keeping with the views advanced by the sometimes-disparate collection of writers gathered under the edifice *cultural criminology*. Simply put, cultural criminology is a perspective aiming to critically engage with and intervene in the politics of meaning surrounding crime and crime control.[47] Whereas scholars from a functionalist perspective might hold the rather-contradictory view that the very existence of a "methamphetamine culture" actually signals an absence of culture, a pathological failure of socialization into collective meaning, cultural criminologists see such transgressions as a way to more fully understand and challenge social inequalities. As the cultural criminology stalwarts Jeff Ferrell, Keith Hayward, and Jock Young are careful to explain,

> The two ways of understanding culture are not irreconcilable; both high-light the collective construction of shared meaning, if in different do-mains, and both suggest the ongoing, contested negotiation of morality and cultural identity. For some, this negotiation calls forth a collective *belief* in tradition, an emotional embracing of stasis and conformity, and the ideological mobilization of rigid stereotype and fundamental value. For others, it calls forth against this conformity a gnawing *disbelief* in the social order itself, and so a willingness to risk inventing collective alterna-tives. For cultural criminologists, both are of interest—and the moments when the two collide around issues of crime and justice form a significant subject matter for cultural criminology itself.[48]

Tensions between the two views of culture outlined here lead to an-other key point that must be untangled. Just as we cannot break the "culture of the methamphetamine industry" cleanly from the broader culture from which it emerges, neither can we so neatly separate the facts or an objective reality of methamphetamine from the innumerable ways that it is imagined, represented, and understood. Here we can say that human behavior and actors themselves determine social worlds and social reality. Always conditioned by the past and shared histories, the present and future are active processes, an unfolding narrative or script, written and rewritten through social interaction. This does not mean the aim here is to theorize culture and representation to the point of the hyperreal, where there is no shared meaning and hence no future. On the contrary, the aim is to understand the self as a constellation of representations and constructed meanings conditioned by the broader society. As Majid Yar puts it, "Representations cannot and should not simply be dismissed as instances of ideological misdirection or 'false truths,' but should instead be taken seriously as socially situated and contextually relevant forms of sense-making that both reflect and shape our shared world views. It is precisely in their resonance with com-mon existential and moral concerns that they find their purchase in the imaginations of their audience and offer us an important window into collective sensibilities."[49] Observing Yar's warning, the imaginary as I conceive of it here is distinguished from the traditional Marxist view of ideology, which is a sort of false consciousness that can be dispelled by truth or supplanted by revolutionary politics. In other words, we should be concerned not with finding an objective reality of methamphetamine but rather with how its representations are put to use by people in order to understand and create their social worlds. So, for instance, as the philosopher Louis Althusser set out in his famous *Ideology and Ideological State Apparatuses*,[50] state power and authority operate through what he called repressive state apparatuses (RSAs), institutions such as the police and military, which dispense violence in order to maintain the position of the ruling classes. Ideological state apparatuses (ISAs) also do the work of repression on behalf of the bourgeois classes and state power, but rather than through direct coercion and violence, they do so by means of an active process Althusser called "interpellation." The act of interpellation or becoming a subject of state power, according to Althusser, occurs at the moment one responds to or recognizes state authority. So when the policeman addresses the citizen, "Hey, you there!" at the precise moment of recognition, the citizen is interpellated by the police power and thus actively creates his own subjectivity. And so Althusser understands ideology not simply as false consciousness but as a dynamic political and cultural process of habitual subjection—in which individuals reaffirm their subordination to state power and authority. By engaging in particular social and cultural practices—education, religion, economy—we become the subjects of particular institutions, while simultaneously reconstituting them. Yet in order to be addressed by state power, one must understand that one is always already subject to it. Here we might again draw on the work of Žižek, to expand on the Althusserian understanding of interpellation. Building on the Lacanian "big Other," Žižek asks how ideology might prefigure or predetermine interpellation. For Žižek, the "very positing of the big Other is a subjective gesture, that is, the big Other is a virtual entity that exists only through the subject's presupposition."[51] Whereas Althusser's aim was to describe the material relations of ideology as interpellation between state and subject, Žižek would add another level of abstraction, a third figure, and argue that the state as "big Other is, on the contrary, ultimately virtual and as such, in its most basic dimension, 'immaterial.'"[52] Also through the example of the policeman, Žižek explains, "The 'third figure' which intervenes between us ordinary citizens and the policeman is not directly fear but the big Other: we fear the policeman insofar as he is not just himself, a person like us, since his acts are the acts of power, that is to say, insofar as he is experienced as the stand-in for the big Other, for the social order."[53] So for Žižek, the "third figure" or big Other represents a totality of Althusserian ideological state apparatuses, which is to say immaterial relations internal to the individual, which prefigure the police and state power. This returns us to the imaginary.

Police and state power do not exist in a vacuum, nor do they emerge naturally; there is always a preexisting internal and imaginary dimension. As Žižek puts it elsewhere, "ideology is not constituted by abstract propositions in themselves, rather, ideology is itself this very texture of the lifeworld which 'schematizes' the propositions, rendering them 'livable.'"[54] The drug war is enacted and thus made livable not only by state coercion and propaganda but also by the background of routine symbolic cues, signs, habits, narratives, actions, and immaterial utterances that structure the ways people imagine their social existence and their relations with others—*the imaginary*. So when a shopper buying a box of over-the-counter cold medicine inquires as to why the clerk needs his identification card and learns that it is because "people use it to cook meth," the methamphetamine imaginary is invoked, rendering the drug war a livable part of everyday life. Likewise, when police announce major busts, complete with trophy-shot photos triumphantly displaying large amounts of seized cash, drugs, or guns, and online commentators gleefully join in, offering praise without questioning the legalities of civil asset forfeiture, "policing for profit," and primitive accumulation, the drug war in its most problematic, ideological form is reproduced. This is at least a starting point. By dispelling the false dichotomies between consent and coercion and the real and represented, we move away from a simple top-down ideology/propaganda model of drug control and better understand how subjects put methamphetamine and the drug war to work as part of a dynamic repertoire of everyday life.

Understanding the methamphetamine imaginary as a collection of images, gestures, cues, utterances, and dispositions that can be put to work in the material practices of everyday sense making returns us to what we might call the act of *pretending to pretend to believe*. Here,

Žižek's oft-used example of the relationship between parents, children, and Santa Claus is useful. Žižek insists that children, beyond the youngest and most naïve, know that Santa Claus does not exist, but continue to play their part in the myth well past the point of realization as part of habituated ritual and custom. For adults, performing the Santa Claus myth "for the sake of the children" actually helps disavow, for a time, their need to believe in the existence of innocent and gullible children, making the adults themselves, not the children, the true subjects of ideology.[55] This sort of disavowal—pretending to pretend to believe—helps us better understand why the drug war exists in spite of a perpetually expanding collection of evidence speaking to its deleterious effects and impotence.

Thinking in crude binaries for a moment, we might imagine how people from the left and right understand the drug war. On the right, a conservative politician might be dedicated to the drug war, wholly believing the consumption of illicit substances to be the cause of many social ills, crime, violence, dependency, unraveling moral order, and so on. And so the conservative politician supports aggressive policing, draconian punishments, and the politicians who peddle them. Whereas on the other side of our crude binary, a more liberal politician might be suspicious of official doctrine and instead understand the drug war as rooted in the legacies of racism and divisive politics and choose to work toward undoing the consequences of bad policy and toward the restoration of civil liberties. What both share in common is a collection of social ills—crime, violence, poverty—associated with drugs and the drug war. Regardless of how one chooses to address these problems, positioning them as things to be solved by solving the drug war divorces them from the much-larger systems of violence and inequality in which they both participate. Though crime, violence, and poverty are preexisting conditions, drugs and the drug war enable people from the right and left to disavow their embeddedness and thus their complicity in the inherent social inequalities of life under capitalism. It is therefore not enough to search for and find the objective reality of methamphetamine on which to build a better drug war; rather, we must map its immaterial dimensions and apprehend how it fits within existing structures of power and inequality, in order to begin to imagine a world not only without the drug war but unfettered by the vicissitudes of predatory capitalism.

***

Through an exegesis of perhaps the best-known contemporary meth story, AMC's wildly popular *Breaking Bad*, chapter 1 outlines the form, force, and effect of the methamphetamine imaginary and the place of the drug war in contemporary American social life and begins to theorize it, not only as governing logic or racial caste but as death wish, a compulsion arising from a disavowal of the many inequalities of the present social order and the certainties of human mortality. Rather than simply seeing *Breaking Bad* as an entertaining program about methamphetamine, we might better understand it as part of a cultural imaginary of spectacular self-destruction, which permits the voyeuristic public to live through and reproduce the drug war in the real and everyday.

By way of two well-known antimeth advertising campaigns, chapter 2 engages the burgeoning field of visual criminology to show how crime-control projects use the image to draw on and reproduce disparate subject positions and social relations. I describe how the popular Faces of Meth program and the Meth Project's "Not Even Once" campaign actively (re)produce meth's powers of monstrous transformation. Structured by and embedded within already-existing cultural anxieties about the figure of "white trash," these crime-control projects produce meth's visualities, the ways of seeing the supposed ills of meth use, and carve disparate race/class hierarchies from relative homogeneity.

Focusing on one year and an antimeth legislative campaign in Kansas, chapter 3 details the political problematization of the methamphetamine imaginary and the ways in which a seemingly disparate group of political actors engage it as part of broader governing strategies. Relying primarily on news media accounts, the chapter illustrates how by overstating the realities of meth use, politicizing official statistics and reframing key events, authorities link local meth control to the wars on drugs and terror, themes that are taken up in earnest in subsequent chapters.

Treating police as important cultural producers, chapter 4 asks how the drug war is made a livable part of everyday life in small towns across the rural Midwest. Drawing on ethnographic fieldwork and interviews focusing on police officers' attitudes about community and their beliefs about the causes of crime and drug use, the chapter identifies a narrative of rural decline attributed to the producers and users of methamphetamine. This narrative, it is argued, reproduces punitive and authoritarian sensibilities making the drug war a lived reality for small towns far removed from what is considered typical drug-war terrains. As such, the cultural work of rural police provides important insight into the shape and direction of late-capitalist crime control beyond the familiar terrains of the city and its "ghettos."

Focusing on the cultural production of space and particularly longstanding notions of idyllic rural landscapes, chapter 5 shows how the methamphetamine imaginary, crime control, and police power combine to fabricate the affective landscapes of the rural United States. Beginning with a critical reading of the *New York Times* best seller *Methland: The Death and Life of an American Small Town*, the chapter aims to expand cultural criminology's urban focus and to work toward a cultural criminology of the rural.

Engaging the emerging concern for "Mexican meth," chapter 6 shows how the methamphetamine and drug-war imaginaries, interlaced with the terror war as "narcoterror," bolster nationalistic arguments for "border security" and lay the ideological framework for economic and military intervention beyond the United States' borders. Positioning current counternarcoterror projects in Mexico within a longer history of counterinsurgency and pacification in Central America and Southeast Asia, the chapter describes the drug war as an ideological gesture obscuring and justifying neoliberal trade policies and capital accumulation by dispossession.

1

Walter White's Death Wish

I have spent my whole life scared, frightened of things that could happen, might happen, might not happen. Fifty years I spent like that. Finding myself awake at three in the morning. But you know what? Ever since my diagnosis, I sleep just fine. What I came to realize is that fear, that's the worst of it. That's the real enemy. So get up, get out in the real world, and you kick that bastard as hard you can right in the teeth.
—Walter White, *Breaking Bad*

In 2008, viewers became acquainted with and quickly enamored by a mild-mannered high school chemistry teacher turned methamphetamine kingpin, Walter White. In the AMC hit television series *Breaking Bad*, Walt is a devoted father and teacher who supplements his meager income working a second thankless job at a car wash. Skyler, his wife, put her dreams of being a writer on hold to help raise a family. She manages the chaos of the family's finances and scrapes together some extra money selling garage-sale finds on the Internet. Their son, Walt Jr., is in high school and suffers the awkwardness of his teen years with the added burden of cerebral palsy. Already stretched dangerously thin, Walt and Skyler are expecting their second child. The indignities the Whites shoulder as they scratch out a barely middle-class life are familiar, and their courage despite it all is endearing. In the series pilot, Walt is diagnosed with lung cancer, and the outlook is grim. Accompanying Hank, Walt's DEA agent brother-in-law, on a raid of a small, clandestine meth lab, Walt has a chance meeting with a former student and low-level meth cook, Jesse Pinkman. This meeting sets the stage for Walter's entrée into the meth business as a way to provide for his family should his cancer win out. The everyday problems of a typical American family, combined with the menace of the drug trade, made Walter White's descent into criminal megalomania riveting television, earning the series, its cast, and its producers widespread acclaim and adoration.

However realistic *Breaking Bad* seemed to its viewers, the key to its popularity is its resonance with broader social anxieties over crime, violence, and economic precarity. That is, *Breaking Bad*'s take on the madness of addiction and the violence of the drug trade reflects, shapes, and reaffirms the already deeply held worldviews of much of the American public. This is uniquely illustrated by the burgeoning *Breaking Bad* tourist industry and the popular news media's interest in documenting instances when the program bleeds into "real life." In late 2012, for example, police in Linden, Texas, arrested William Duncan, a junior high chemistry teacher, after he allegedly sold methamphetamine to undercover officers in the parking lot of the school where he worked.[1] The reporting on Duncan's case highlights the tangle of reality and representation, with fantastic headlines such as "Breaking Sad: East Texas Chemistry Teacher Busted for Selling Meth"[2] and "Life Imitates Breaking Bad—Again—as Texas Chemistry Teacher Charged with Cooking, Selling Meth."[3] Of course, interest in cases in which "life imitates *Breaking Bad*" does not end with William Duncan. Another report describes how police arrested the seventy-four-year-old math professor Irina Kristy for "running a meth lab" with her son.[4] Another "real-life Walter White,"[5] the Massachusetts resident and seven-term state representative Stephen Doran, was arrested on the grounds of the charter school where he worked as a tutor, after he accepted a package containing 480 grams of methamphetamine. Doran, who like Irina Kristy was an educator, drew further comparisons to *Breaking Bad*'s protagonist, as he was undergoing cancer treatments at the time of his arrest.[6] But the case that drew the most of this sort of media attention was that of an Alabama man named Walter White, whom *Vice* magazine labeled one of the state's most successful meth cooks. According to *Vice*'s short documentary film, simply titled *The Real Walter White*, "Ten years before *Breaking Bad* premiered in 2008, Walter White of Bessemer, Alabama, was already building a meth empire, and the drug was becoming an epidemic nationwide." Beyond the coincidence of name, the film draws a number of other connections between Alabama's Walter White and his small-screen doppelganger. In a conversation between the film's narrator and the director of a faith-based drug-rehabilitation program that Walter had completed, the importance of the cook and product are elaborated:

> NARRATOR: Walter wasn't a low-level meth cook; he knew what he was doing.
> TREATMENT CENTER DIRECTOR: He very much knew what he was doing. In fact, I guess if you can classify as a high-ranking meth cook, he would be up there. He may even be a meth chef, because he's just good at it.[7]

This anecdote fits with ethnographic work detailing how meth cooks are often set atop methamphetamine cultural hierarchies.[8] This is an important point underlying both the fictional program and the broader imaginary—methamphetamine's exceptionality. Like Alabama's version, who drew local acclaim as a top "meth chef," what helped transform television's Walter White into his ruthless alter ego, "Heisenberg," was the ability to produce high-quality methamphetamine, dubbed "Blue Sky" because of its color. Unsurprisingly, as early as 2010, drug-control agents across the United States began to encounter blue methamphetamine, leading them to speculate that local cooks dyed their product in order to tap into the program's popularity.[9] Not only does this document the myth of a particular drug's exceptional purity and potency; it also details the reciprocal fluidity of objective realities and cultural representations. As the burgeoning *Breaking Bad* tourist industry observed by Rodanthi Tzanelli and Majid Yar demonstrates, everyday actors draw on the methamphetamine imaginary, using it as a way to confront broader inequalities or to adorn the mundane spaces of everyday life with the affective wash of meth-fueled crime and violence. Here, in the words of Keith Hayward and Jock Young, "the street scripts the screen, and the screen scripts the street."[10] In the case of *Breaking Bad*, once Blue Sky hit the streets, it unleashed a torrent of market-based competition and violence that ultimately cost Walt and those around him dearly.

Like the myths advanced by Ronald Reagan, George W. Bush, Charles Schumer, and countless others, the myth of the new drug's devastations is central to the series. This is evident in the episode "Negro y Azul,"[11] which opens with a music video for the *narcocorrido*[12] "The Ballad of Heisenberg":

Among the gangsters,
His fame has greatly spread
'Cause of a new drug
That the gringos have created.
They say it is colored blue
And that it's pure in quality,
That powerful drug
That is running through the town.

Sung by Los Cuates de Sinaloa (the twins from Sinaloa), these lines perfectly characterize the terror of the methamphetamine and drug-war imaginaries—that is to say social life weighed down by the violence, death, and destruction of a "new," or rather the next, drug epidemic. As we know, however, it is generally not innovations in production or changes in chemical structure but the meanings attached that make a drug "new." Again, the hysteria that formed around crack cocaine in the 1980s is particularly instructive here. Cocaine hydrochloride (powder) and cocaine base (crack) are for all intents and purposes chemically identical and produce the same, predictable effects on users' bodies.[13] Despite minor differences between the two, in the response to the so-called crack epidemic, it was cultural, not chemical, differences that mattered most to policy makers and the public.[14] The idea that crack was an altogether "new," more powerful and addictive form of cocaine materialized as real policing and punishment practices that continue to affect poor communities and people of color more harshly than the upper-middle-class whites commonly associated with powder cocaine.

Despite claims of police, educators, and users that methamphetamine "takes everything good in your life,"[15] it is not supernatural. Even in the imaginary world of Breaking Bad, Blue Sky can never be more than what it is—methamphetamine. As a matter of fact, imagined in the series as 99.1 percent pure, Blue Sky is of slightly lesser quality than Desoxyn, which, following United States Pharmacopeial (USP) standards, is 99.99 percent pure methamphetamine. In other words, Blue Sky, the "new" drug on which Breaking Bad's entire plot hinged and the catalyst of all manner of obscene violence and horror, was less potent than a drug licensed and sold legally in the United States for more than seventy years. What is more, because Walt cooks a P2P formula that Hank calls "old-school biker meth," we might say that even within an imaginary illicit-drug market, Blue Sky is not new but actually *old*.[16]

Nevertheless, embedded within Blue Sky's crafted novelty are assumptions of its purity, potency, and addictiveness. Again, the series follows a standard drug-war template that can be fitted to a variety of drugs throughout history—that is quality begets demand, demand leads to use, use leads to addiction, and addiction turns casual users into subhuman "zombies."[17] As absurd as this trajectory and the drug-zombie trope might seem, it is also in no way new. For instance, in 1980, Canadian news media reported on an "epidemic" of spectacular violence in Chicago attributed to the "new" drug PCP. As one reporter claimed, "Zombie murders committed by heavy drug users were rare in the 60s but now appear to be increasing sharply."[18] While daily meth users are curiously underrepresented in *Breaking Bad*'s story line, a few of its characters access and reproduce this trope, thereby animating the "meth zombie" in the contemporary imaginary. The first we meet is Wendy, who, living and working out of a seedy hotel dubbed the Crystal Palace, trades sex for meth's fleeting rush. With an emaciated body, sunken cheeks, discolored rotten teeth, and a lifeless blank stare, Wendy is the small-screen approximation of the widely discussed Faces of Meth project of Multnomah County, Oregon, which sought to deter meth use through graphic before-and-after mug-shot images. Wendy first appears, as a matter of fact, when Hank introduces her to Walt Jr. in order to "scare him straight." It is quite likely that the widely circulated Faces of Meth mug shots inspired *Breaking Bad*'s writers, whether directly or indirectly. In fact, the series's creator, Vince Gilligan, admits to knowing very little about the drug initially, and the casual conversations that eventually led to the series were sparked by a news report of children made sick by a Brooklyn meth lab.[19] The point is that this wildly popular program probably did not have its origins in some objective lived reality but was drawn from news media accounts, crime-control projects, and word of mouth, making up an always-already-existing social imaginary.

A couple of other "meth zombies" appear early on in the series. "Spooge" and his girlfriend, "Skank,"[20] live in utter squalor with their young son, whose obvious developmental disabilities no doubt result from years of abuse and neglect. As we learn, the diseased, emaciated pair support their habits through petty theft, robbery, and if need be, murder. The couple's crime spree ends only after Skank, in a fit of drug-driven rage, drops a stolen ATM machine on Spooge's head, killing him. Like Wendy, Spooge, Skank, and their neglected son seem to have stepped right out of one of the (Montana) Meth Project's incendiary "Not Even Once" public-service advertisements, which warn of how the drug wrecks whole communities one family at a time.

Of course, meth zombies did not begin with, nor are they confined to, *Breaking Bad*. Take for instance the episode "San Francisco's Meth Zombies" of the television series *Drugs Inc.* Serializing drug scares an episode at a time, *Drugs Inc.* is little more than tabloid television pawned off as serious investigative work under the guise of the National Geographic Society. In the episode in question, a parole officer working the city's tough Tenderloin district has this to say about meth and the meth users under her care:

> We've seen an increase in our clients that are addicted to methamphetamine. A new strand is on the street that is very addictive, and it's causing them to have extreme paranoia. They'll come in convinced that someone is following them, trying to kill them, and there's really no calming them down. So it's really difficult to navigate that psychosis. Some of our clients develop sores on their face from scratching. Physically it's a very damaging drug. Their hair gets brittle, and they've lost their teeth. They're literally like zombies.

The narrator then adds, "And like zombies, the denizens of the Tenderloin come alive at night."[21]

As do the characters of *Breaking Bad*, the work and everyday pronouncements of state agents represented in salacious tabloid television animate the zombie as a distinct part of the methamphetamine imaginary. Not unlike with Blue Sky or PCP, the officer believes a dangerous "new strand is on the street" and is set to unleash "extreme" effects. And like Wendy, Spooge, and Skank, drug users become zombies—the violent, undead offspring of the boiling methamphetamine epidemic—in the imaginative minds of television writers and street-level state agents. This sort of *zombification*[22]—the mediated transformation of a human being into a disposable object—is part of a larger ideological frame that normalizes state violence and conceals the fundamental inequalities of late capitalism. That is, in the eyes of police and an uncritical public, meth zombies are an indicator of an unraveling moral order and, as such, do not merit even the most basic rights, pity, or compassion. They are in a very real sense the *walking dead*. As they are imagined here— lumbering, rotting bodies with insatiable appetites—these decimated drug users bear close resemblance to the postwar horror-fiction zombie most commonly attributed to the imagination of the pop-culture luminary George Romero. In the foundational movie of the genre, *Night of the Living Dead* (1968), radioactive contamination from an errant space probe summoned the dead from their graves. Released in the thick of civil unrest and at the height of the Cold War, Romero's film was a powerful critique of violent American militarism, racism, and sexism. But *Breaking Bad* bears no such critique. Despite all the critical acclaim it won for its dark narrative and the watercooler debates over Walter's spinning moral compass, *Breaking Bad*'s central premise is simply that *drugs are bad*. I will have more to say on this later, but first it is important to address some of the series's other fundamental components.

The senseless meth-fueled violence that guides *Breaking Bad* is perhaps no better represented than by Tuco Salamanca, the local boss of the Ciudad Juárez Cartel. Habitually snorting meth and rambling at an unintelligible, manic pace, Tuco approximates the "tweaker" or "speed freak" of old. Yet it is his unpredictable violence that sets him apart from pitiable characters like Wendy and Skank. In his first appearance, Tuco earns his reputation for violence, snorting huge bumps of meth off a large bowie knife just before beating Jesse nearly to death. After Tuco brokers a partnership with Walt and Jesse, his violence escalates, beating his henchman "No-Doze" to death for some perceived slight. Predictably, this violent meth-fueled trajectory leads to Tuco's demise in a high-desert shootout with Hank, reminiscent of the death scene of Tony Montana (Al Pacino) in *Scarface*. In this way, Tuco stands in for the drug's violence-inducing effects and the market-based skirmishes between users, dealers, producers, and police.

In the imagined world of *Breaking Bad*, Blue Sky is the catalyst of all manner of chaos and violence. Of course, this assumption reaches well beyond popular television and cinema representations and is advanced by well-positioned politicians, police, and media personalities. In the book *The Gang and Beyond: Interpreting Violent Street Worlds*, Simon

Hallsworth develops the concepts of *gang talk* and *gang talkers*. As he describes it, *gang talk* is free-floating discourse that operates independently of the lived realities of actual gang life. On its face, Hallsworth writes, gang talk "can be considered a *conspiracy discourse* produced by those who do not live gang realities but have a vested interest in gang lives and gang worlds."[23] Gang talk, then, is the discourse that legitimizes the work of *gang talkers*—those who are removed from the lived realities of gang and street life, such as state agents and academic criminologists, who nonetheless position themselves as authorities in the business of treating, controlling, and punishing those whom they classify as gang members.

Borrowing from Hallsworth, we might describe *meth talk* as the language, grammar, and free-floating discourse of *meth talkers* interested in methamphetamine control. The cultural work of meth talkers, in no small part, shapes the methamphetamine imaginary. And while Hallsworth is clear to point out the differences between the lived realities of gang life and the talk of academics and state agents, this is not to suggest that we refocus our efforts here on the search for an objective reality of methamphetamine. Rather, the aim is to situate the cultural work of meth talkers of all sorts—police, educators, researchers—within a critical analysis of the methamphetamine and drug-war imaginaries. In the same way that Tuco Salamanca characterizes the violence of the drug's pharmacology and market, meth talkers produce and reaffirm commonsense links between methamphetamine use and violent crime. So, for instance, at a 2012 hearing of the House of Representatives Committee on Oversight and Government Reform, its chair, Trey Gowdy, Republican of South Carolina (meth talker), offered the following testimony (meth talk) on meth's violence-inducing effects:

> I know the witnesses are at the ready with statistics on methamphetamine and the problems permeating our country. When I think of methamphetamine, my mind doesn't go to statistics. It doesn't go to a debate between pharmaceutical companies and law enforcement. It goes to a couple named Ann and Ray Emery in the Drayton community in Spartanburg County, South Carolina. Ann and Ray Emery were a beautiful couple. They were active in their community, active in their churches, deeply in love with one another, and full of life.

They had a next-door neighbor named Andres Torres. Andres Torres was a troubled person with a long criminal history, and an addiction to methamphetamine. He knocked on their door one afternoon and said he needed a ride to the grocery store to get some food, so Ray Emery, being the decent, kind, human being that he was, stopped what he was doing, and took Andres Torres to the store. And he even did one better than that; he bought the groceries for Andres Torres. That was the kind of person Ray Emery was, kind, selfless, always ready to help a neighbor, even a neighbor as troubled as Andres Torres.

About a week later, Andres Torres came back to the Emery home, but this time, he didn't come in the afternoon. He came in the middle of the night under cover of darkness. He crept in through a side door. He walked into Ann and Ray Emery's bedroom and began to bludgeon Ray Emery with a hammer. Nineteen times he raised the hammer and struck the face or the head of another human being. Ray Emery's face was unrecognizable as a human face in the crime scene photos. He is laying there in a pool of blood on his bed with his skull fractured and his left arm is reaching out toward his wife. His body is on the floor. She too had been bludgeoned with a hammer, both of her eyeballs were absent. The bridge from her mouth was down into her neck, having been beaten there by a hammer, and she was raped postmortem. So statistics are fine. They certainly have their place. If you want to see the carnage of methamphetamine, I invite you to come look at the crime scene photos with me from the State of South Carolina v. Andres Torres.[24]

Written into the official and cultural record by an expedient politician, the testimony animates the horror of the methamphetamine imaginary in all its bloody violence and gore—a kindly, unsuspecting couple bludgeoned and butchered in their own bed, a mangled corpse raped by a ghoulish intruder high on methamphetamine. A more horrific crime or fate is unimaginable. While the story of the Emerys' violent deaths drove home the dangers of the drug in dramatic form, the veracity of Gowdy's meth talk should not escape careful scrutiny. In hearings appealing Torres's death sentence, the court heard evidence, from both the defense and the state, that Torres had been diagnosed bipolar at an early age; suffered from intermittent explosive disorder; had abused alcohol, methamphetamine, and the prescription drug Clonopin; and at the time of the murders had been awake for more than two days.[25] Despite a number of conditions that may have also precipitated the crime, Gowdy chose only to focus on methamphetamine as its cause. In this case, we might say that like a '60s horror-fiction film, methamphetamine is the singular disaster that crashed in from the ether and destroyed the lives of two innocent people. Gowdy's sort of apocalyptic, meth-obsessed myopia reveals an important and reciprocal dynamic. On the one hand, the drug provides a useful and believable cause for all manner of crimes, no matter the mitigating and contradictory evidence. On the other, might it be that very little evidence is necessary to link a horrific crime such as the Emerys' murders to methamphetamine because meth talk is so potent and the imaginary so concrete? Just as Gowdy ignored the other drugs Torres abused and a biography littered with mental, physical, and social difficulties only to focus on methamphetamine, might it be that some people choose to fetishize methamphetamine in order to avoid more complicated explanations or to reaffirm already-existing worldviews?

There are, after all, other ways to imagine methamphetamine. In controlled laboratory experiments, the neuroscientist Carl Hart and his colleagues at Columbia University Medical Center administered one single large dose of methamphetamine to volunteer participants who were regular users.[26] The team found that meth elevated the heart rate, body temperature, and blood pressure of participants to levels similar to those achieved by vigorous exercise. It also improved the mood and concentration of study participants.[27] While the tests did show that participants' sleep decreased on average from eight to six hours, even this finding is hardly in keeping with the myth that even a single dose "keeps people up for days." Perhaps most importantly, Hart and his colleagues' research casts some serious doubt on the "not even once" logic of instant addiction. Replicating their previous studies with cocaine users, the group offered participants the choice between one large dose of high-quality methamphetamine or five dollars cash.[28] On average, about half of the participants chose the money. When the researchers raised the cash amount to twenty dollars, almost all of the participants chose the money. This, they argue, is tangible evidence that meth users are able to make rational decisions and delay gratification, seriously challenging commonsense assumptions of the drug's addictiveness and the "not even once" logic of instant addiction peddled by drug-war activists.

Another federal program, the Office of National Drug Control Policy's Arrestee Drug Abuse Monitoring Program (ADAM), offers an interesting challenge to the drug's links to violence. In order to explore links between drug use and criminal behaviors, ADAM conducts urine analyses of people arrested in several American cities.[29] In its most recent reporting year, the program screened 3,229 people for illicit drugs (alcohol not included), of which 71 percent (2,300) tested positive for at least one drug. Among those tested, about 10 percent (322) tested positive for methamphetamine, and about 15 percent (484) were arrested for acts of violence. Of those arrested for violent acts, only 13 percent (64) tested positive for methamphetamine. In other words, of 3,229 people arrested across five cities, only 64, less than 2 percent, of them fell into the violence/methamphetamine category.[30] Again, this is not to say that methamphetamine does not lead to chronic use or that it is not associated with violence, only that these links are more complex and tenuous than often imagined. Invoking these surveys is also not meant to suggest that the data are infallible. Indeed, all social surveys should be interpreted within the context in which they were created. It is worth stating, however, that meth talkers routinely cite these very surveys in furtherance of broader drug-control projects. And while I have offered some nuance by way of research and government surveys, I do not mean to refocus our attention to a search for the objective truth of methamphetamine. Rather, the focus is on the very narrow understanding of the drug and its users, an understanding that is reflected and reinforced through the cultural work of programs such as *Breaking Bad*. It is the composition of the methamphetamine imaginary and the beliefs that win out over others that offer important insights to the production and maintenance of the drug war and a window into broader political, social, and cultural sensibilities.

Though the violent, broken lives of drug users and drug dealers have long been a staple of network television, *Breaking Bad* offers something more. Returning to "The Ballad of Heisenberg," we catch a glimpse of a broader narrative:

> And the owners of the market
> Couldn't stop it, though they tried.
> The cartel's running hot because

They were disrespected,
Talking 'bout some "Heisenberg"
Who now controls the market.
No one knows a thing about him
Since they haven't seen him yet.
The cartel's about respect
And they never forget.
This homie's already dead.
He just doesn't know it yet.

Wealth, fame, and death, Los Cuates remind, await those who through skill, violence, or blind luck win control of the market. This warning is central to each of *Breaking Bad*'s five seasons. From bumbling through transactions with local dealers like Tuco and "Krazy 8," distributing across the southwestern United States under cover of Gustavo Fring's restaurant franchise, to Madrigal Electromotive's global distribution network, Walt and Jesse's rise to the heights of their field is the consummate capitalist success story—Horatio Alger born anew. As such, the ensuing competition and market-based violence, entangling police, street-level dealers, white-power gangs, Mexican cartels, and shadowy multinationals alike, should be seen as the expected consequences of the capitalist imperatives of expansion and accumulation. This dark heart pounds to the surface in one of the most memorable and widely discussed scenes of the series. Walt laments the fortune lost by selling his interest in an earlier business, explaining, "Jesse, you asked me if I was in the meth business or the money business. Neither. I'm in the empire business." Here we learn that Walt's concern is no longer his family; perhaps it never was. His desire is respect and recognition. He wants to stand atop a heap of vanquished enemies and crushed competition. Walt's power-hungry aim of empire reminds that in the drug war's American Dream, there is never *enough*. Police arrest and cage wave after wave of low-level dealers hoping to win the war one street corner at a time. Prison gangs fight to control institutions, and cartels bits of territory. All the while, the materials of war—drugs, weapons, money, bodies—circulate through byzantine webs of electronic wire transfers, shipping lanes, and smuggling routes mapped onto "High Intensity Drug Trafficking Areas" by state power. This is neoliberal predation par excellence and the sublimated horror of the methamphetamine imaginary. It does not honor convention, custom, border, or boundary. It expands, consumes, and destroys.

In the final lines of *Fear and Loathing in Las Vegas*, the quintessential tale of American drug-addled nihilism and excess, Hunter S. Thompson describes himself as "a monster reincarnation of Horatio Alger: A man on the move, and just sick enough to be totally confident."[31] Part self-aggrandizing yarn and part hallucination, Thompson narrates his obscene exploits in a "savage journey to the heart of the American Dream"[32] through Raoul Duke, his thinly disguised alias. Duke and his companion Dr. Gonzo, believing they will never have to settle up with the house or suffer any real consequences, veraciously consume drugs, rental cars, and hotel rooms with sheer abandon and disregard for those whom they encounter. As with Duke, drugs seem to have obliterated Walter White's social, moral, and ethical boundaries. But Walt does not use meth; he is intoxicated by the freedom from the pains of his old life, high on freedom from conventionality. On these emancipatory possibilities, the theorist Avital Ronell writes, "More so perhaps than any other 'substance,' whether real or imagined, drugs thematize the dissociation of autonomy and responsibility that has marked our epoch since Kant. Despite the indeterminacy and heterogeneity that characterize these phenomena, drugs are crucially related to the question of freedom."[33] Whereas drugs simply enable Hunter S. Thompson's most depraved and obscene desires, Walter White characterizes another sort of freedom that is richly foreshadowed in the series pilot. Walter poses the question "what is chemistry?" to his mostly disinterested students, adding, "You see, technically, chemistry is the study of matter, but I prefer to see it as the study of change. Electrons change their energy levels. Molecules change their bonds. Elements combine and change into compounds. That's all of life, right? It's the constant, it's the cycle. It's solution, dissolution. Just over and over and over. It is growth, then decay, then transformation. It is fascinating, really." A short time later, Walt's cancer ushers in, as Gilligan put it, the transformation of "Mr. Chips into Scarface."[34] In the imagined world of *Breaking Bad*, producing and selling methamphetamine transformed a mild-mannered teacher into a ruthless drug impresario. A monster reincarnation in his own right, Heisenberg *is* the dream of freedom, that envied soul able to shake the fetters of late-capitalist life—anonymity, monotony, the stifling impotence of conventionality—and embrace, without fear of reprisal, a darker side, a destructive *jouissance*. Yet in *Breaking Bad*, freedom is always tethered to methamphetamine. Had Walter used his considerable intellect and skill to produce another, more conventional product, say a particularly effective fertilizer, Heisenberg would have taken an altogether different form. There is no Heisenberg or *Breaking Bad* without methamphetamine, a point to which we will return shortly.

For all the emancipatory potentials of Ronell's "question of freedom," the dissociation of autonomy and shirking of stifling responsibilities, it is important to consider how this freedom cuts both ways. Intoxication, in her words, is both sacralized and Satanized. In the aptly titled series finale, "Felina," Walt seeks out Skyler to say his last goodbye:

> WALT: Skyler, all the things that I did, you have to understand . . .
> SKYLER: If I have to hear one more time that you did this for the
> family . . .
> WALT: I did it for me. I liked it. I was good at it. And I was really—*I
> was alive.*

It may be that Walt started down the path that led to Heisenberg with the noblest of intentions, but at the end of it was the truth. To be Walter White, an unappreciated, underpaid high school chemistry teacher was to be frightened, bullied, and hopeless. Walter White was dead long before his cancer diagnosis. His was a choice. He chose the joy of destructive freedom. He chose to lie and murder. He chose Heisenberg.

Absolved of guilt and no longer haunted by memories of a kind, generous man and the unspeakable things he did in order to care for his family, Skyler too is granted a freedom, but hers is a freedom to hate Walt's choices and what they revealed. Embodying all that he gave away and destroyed in his epicurean dream, Heisenberg represents the pleasures that ordinary people must deny themselves and the evils they must suppress in order to participate in conventional society.[35] Emerging from the depths of a mild-mannered teacher, Heisenberg is the eternal foe of conventionality, a Satanized demon, a monster, as of yet banished from capitalist modernity. And so we might say that Walt's transformation is not one of freedom but of destruction and death. On this, Gilligan adds, "When you give your lead character a terminal illness, usher him into the underworld and embroil him in ever bolder and more ambitious criminal plans, you create a man who is rushing toward the ultimate change—*from being alive to being dead*."[36] Life and death—production/consumption, solution/dissolution, growth/decay—the ultimate change: they are, in Walt's words, *the constant*. The narrative of transformation was indeed the constant. Of course, even the name *Breaking Bad* suggests rupture, a change from one state to another. Herein lies the question. Could it be that Walt's suicidal abandon, his willingness to destroy all that he loved in his self-gratifying rush toward death, finds resonance with the mounting insecurities and anxieties of modern life and the certainty of human mortality? Might the death that Walter White engineered and met on his own terms, however inevitable and violent, offer some consolation? That is, might a death of our own choosing be preferred to a death forced upon us? The soundtrack, which often operated as a character in its own right, offers a hint. In the final shot of the series, as Walt lies gasping in his last strained breaths, the camera drifts away from his face, invoking a dreamlike incorporeality, as the lyrics "I guess I got what I deserved . . ." of the Badfinger song "Baby Blue" waft in. Perhaps the song is meant as a nod to the death that Walt orchestrated for himself, the final punctuation on an elaborate antidrug message, a reminder of a world governed by rational choice, where even a man with the best intentions must pay for his sins. We might also read the later lines, "Didn't know you'd think that I'd forget or I'd regret the special love I have for you, my baby blue," as Walt's last overture to his creation Blue Sky and a final reminder of his meth-obsessed megalomania.

With the cancer back, money gone, and law closing in, Walt's options were few. Yet, as he had throughout, Walt has used his considerable genius to exercise his will. He goes out on his own terms: not before coercing his old business partners into delivering the last of his money to his children, rescuing Jesse, and killing an entire white-power gang. Given the utter totality of his victory, perhaps the Hank Williams song "You Win Again" might have been a more fitting soundtrack for his departure.

The transformation is complete, the break is clean—solution, dissolution, growth, decay—*victory in death!* And with that, could it be that it is Walt's death drive or death wish that makes *Breaking Bad* so enticing? Here the certainties of human mortality and the freedom of death find, as Yar puts it, purchase in the imaginations of the program's audience, offering a useful window into collective sensibilities, the many contradictions of life under late capitalism, and the certainties of human mortality.[37] And while Walt may have been able to claim final victory and freedom in death, within this act is also the compulsion to repeat. So it might be useful to understand the drug war's baffling series of repeated failures, its history of death and destruction, in the same way—that is, the *drug war as death wish*. The drug war is thus not a series of episodic moral panics but a choice made purposefully and repeatedly.

On this, it is useful to recall Žižek's description of our fetishistic disavowal, of that which we know but choose to deny. It is true that Walter White made his own choices and perhaps got what he deserved, but even this reveals what I see as the fundamentally conservative core of the series. For all of the debate over the complexity of Walter White, a good man gone terribly wrong, for most viewers, the narrative is sewn together by a single thread—methamphetamine. That is, for the viewer, Walt's transformation and the complexity of his character hinge on the subjective assessment of all the horrible things he did, how he did them, and for what reasons. Why did a milquetoast chemistry teacher lie, steal, and murder? Why did he destroy what he loved most? As we have seen, on the one hand, there is the rational "for the family" answer and, on the other, the more sinister "for me" self-gratifying rationale. Meth is the bridge of both, whether a rational reaction to irrational circumstances or affective indulgence.[38] And so we inevitably return to either the horrible things Walt did with methamphetamine or the horrible things he did because of methamphetamine. The question that should be asked and one that is quite evident yet never sufficiently addressed by the series is not why he made the choices he made but, rather, why he was asked to make them at all.

Recall the precariousness of the Whites' life. Walt works two jobs, and Skyler does what she can to help make ends meet and eventually has to go back to work; juggling credit-card bills, they are trapped in a monthly cycle, robbing Peter to pay Paul. Then comes the cancer, and meth is a means to an ends. Despite all the pains taken by the show's writers to help viewers identify with the Whites' middle-class predicament, *Breaking Bad* buries a fundamental question. Why was this stunningly average American family in such a situation to begin with? Why when Walt suddenly faces death must he choose between cooking meth to provide for his family and leaving them in the poor house after he is gone? That is not much of a choice.

In the series pilot, as the opening credits still roll across the screen, the first words uttered by Walt Jr. are sour complaints about his cold morning shower. In a scene weighed down with the drudgeries of everyday life, a quick breakfast before beginning another workday, talk of low-cholesterol "veggie bacon" and Echinacea, a failing water heater shines through. As we follow Walt's daily routine, at school and his second job, we learn more of the indignities he suffers. As a teacher, Walt is bored and alienated by disrespectful, disinterested students who do not share his passion for chemistry. Working his second job at A1 Car Wash, Walt is bullied by its owner, Bogdan Wolynetz, who routinely forces him from his work as a cashier to perform manual labor, wiping down cars at the front of the business. With Walt on his hands and knees scrubbing the wheels and tires of a brand-new sports car, its owner, one of Walt's students, chides, "Hey, Mr. White, make those tires shine," and then snaps a picture with his cell phone, documenting Walt's humiliation. Driving home, Walt removes the handicapped-parking permit from his rearview mirror, perhaps as a minor act of defiance to the indignities suffered throughout the day, but a broken glove box that refuses to close reminds him otherwise. As Walt arrives home to a party thrown for his fiftieth birthday, Skyler whispers, "You are so late," instead of greeting him lovingly. At the party, Hank obnoxiously upstages Walt, forcing him to handle his pistol and loudly offering to take Walt on a ride-along with the DEA to "knock down a meth lab" in hopes of getting some "excitement" in his life. In bed after the party, the couple sketch out the mundane details and chores of the coming weekend, as Skyler gives the "birthday boy" his present, awkwardly masturbating him with one hand, as she works her computer with her other hand, monitoring the online auction of one of her garage-sale finds. In the opening minutes of the series, *Breaking Bad* delivers all the old clichés of the working-class sitcom: alienating work, a nagging wife, obnoxious relatives, an unsatisfying sex life, all set against the backdrop of looming poverty.

The next day back at the car wash, as Walt struggles with a large barrel and gawps at a beautiful woman, he collapses. Waking up in an ambulance on the way to a hospital, he begs the paramedic to drop him off at a corner somewhere, pleading that he just did not have "the greatest insurance." At the hospital, learning of his inoperable lung cancer, he ignores the diagnosis, concerned only with a bright yellow mustard stain on his doctor's lapel. Returning home to Skyler arguing over the phone with creditors and questioning Walt about a fifteen-dollar credit-card purchase, he keeps the cancer to himself. Another day at A1, coughing and clearly weakened, Walt stares off blankly. Snapping to attention as he is ordered off the cash register yet again, he explodes, "Fuck you, Bogdan! Fuck you and your eyebrows!" Slapping air fresheners off their hangers as he storms out, Walt turns and screams defiantly, "Fuck you!" grabbing his crotch and adding, "Wipe down this!" Later, as Walt sits by the pool behind his house, striking matches one by one and watching them burn before flicking them into the water, he calls Hank and takes him up on the ride-along. Here is the rupture, twenty-two minutes into five seasons and sixty-two episodes: Walter White breaks bad.

The Whites' class position is painfully obvious. Just the points that I have outlined return again, reaffirming the family's material conditions. In fact, through the lens of the first half of the pilot, we might say that the key to Walt's transformation into Heisenberg—Mr. Chips to Scarface—was not his cancer diagnosis, the ride-along, the chance meeting with Jesse Pinkman, or even the original batch of meth they cook in the Winnebago but, rather, telling Bogdan, "Fuck you! Wipe down this!" Telling off the boss, to "take this job and shove it," that supreme gesture of all working-class fantasies, not entering some murky criminal underworld, is the true rupture and the point where Walter White breaks bad.

Hints of this continue. In the season 2 episode "Over," which details Walt's first attempts to leave the meth business, what is one of the first things that he does with his ill-gotten gains? He fixes the water heater. A minor repair that cost Walt just a few hundred dollars is positioned as a problem, a profoundly working-class problem, solved by the meth business. Walt acts out other familiar working-class fantasies, basically giving his old car away to the mechanic whom he had just paid for repairing it. He buys a sports car and promptly destroys it in a parking lot. Later he buys himself a luxury sedan and, despite Skyler's protests, a sports car for Walt Jr.

Of course, Walt returns to A1 to settle scores with Bogdan. The pivotal season 4 episode "Cornered," in which Walt famously declares that he "is the danger," he is "the one who knocks," contains another important detail. A fake inspection engineered by Walt's attorney, Saul Goodman, causes Bogdan to fear an audit of his business practices and costly repairs, thereby coercing him into selling A1 to Skyler and for far less than he asked initially. But when Walt returns to A1 to pick up the keys, he is reminded of the humiliation he suffered at Bogdan's hands:

BOGDAN: Here we are. Just like you left it. And where is your pretty wife?

WALT: She has other business to attend to.

BOGDAN: Well, like I say to her, place sells as is, understand?

WALT: Yes, I understand.

BOGDAN: Good, good. I don't want her coming back with more demands. She gave me hard time when we settled on price.

WALT: We're all on the same page, Bogdan.

BOGDAN: So here's everything you need. I keep very good files. So you are the boss now, huh? You think you're ready?

WALT: Yes, I . . . I think so.

BOGDAN: Being boss is tough. I know you think I was hard on you, but you'll learn, being in charge is not easy. It takes hard work.

WALT: You've seen me work hard, Bogdan.

BOGDAN: Yeah? I don't know. Not so much, maybe. Maybe when you are the boss, you will just keep your feet up and relax. The real important thing, and not everyone knows this, is to be tough. Boss has to be tough. Has to say no to people. Has to make cashiers wipe down cars, even if they don't want to. I'm sure you can handle. And if not, you can always call your wife, huh?

Even though Walt has claimed A1 in a hostile takeover of sorts, he is clearly still intimidated by his old boss's attacks on his masculinity. But before they part ways, Walt musters the courage for a final "fuck you!" As Bogdan laments his many years at A1, he reaches to take his framed "first dollar" from the wall where it hangs but is stopped by Walt, who calmly reminds him that the sale is "as is." As Bogdan turns to walk out, Walt cracks open the frame and uses the prized dollar to buy a soda from a vending machine. In an episode in which Walt's declaration that he is "the danger" brings Heisenberg into full view, a final bit of revenge on the boss who bullied him for years is a clear, however subordinate, narrative.

But *Breaking Bad* is no working-class revenge fantasy. Ask anyone, rabid fans or those who have not even seen an episode, and they will most certainly tell you that *Breaking Bad* is *about methamphetamine*. Though it is staring at us right in the face, methamphetamine allows Walt and by extension the viewer to ignore his cancer, lack of insurance, material suffering, and humiliating class predicament. Methamphetamine is the fetish that negates more difficult questions. Why was a family that seemed to live well within its means stretched so thin? Why did Walt's teacher's salary not go further? Why did a modest and dedicated public servant not simply have adequate health care and life insurance? These are questions working people confront daily, and the answers are the crushing realities of life in a society of growing inequality. Employment is uncertain, housing insecure, and health care illusory. There is no safety net and *no cure for cancer*. Dissatisfied, alienated, bored, and bullied much like Walter White, the American public goes all in, vindictively committing to the drug war over and over again, one (drug) fetish after another, if only in hopes of carrying on, acting as if it does not know. In this way, we can understand the drug war as the death of our own design, engineered again and again, displacing, if only for a moment, the unavoidable inequalities of life under late capitalism and the certainties of human mortality. *The drug war is a death wish.*

To elaborate this point, it is useful to recall the transformative power that illicit drugs are thought to possess. Exaggerated notions of purity and potency help transform a particular drug, which may in fact have accepted medical uses, into a "new" and exceptional threat. Again, this works by invoking a linear causality, whereby purity/potency creates demand, demand leads to use, use leads to addiction, and addiction transforms casual users into subhuman monstrosities. Methamphetamine transformed Wendy, Spooge, and Skank into degraded zombies, and it turned Walter White into Heisenberg, a ruthless killer and "monster reincarnation of Horatio Alger." We might say, then, that it is not only the power of transformation but also the power of monstrosity that animates the methamphetamine and drug-war imaginaries. Again, this is not simply the work of an imaginative television series. In a House of Representatives subcommittee hearing on the methamphetamine problem titled *Fighting Methamphetamine in the Heartland*, a sheriff from a small Kansas county read the following remarks, inscribing the monstrous power of methamphetamine onto the congressional record:

The drug itself knows no social, ethnic or gender boundaries. It victimizes all people, regardless of age, regardless of their address, regardless of their marital status. It does not care if you have children or dependents. With one or two encounters with the *monster called methamphetamine*, it will own you. It will control you. It will make decisions for you. It will beckon you to steal, to abandon loved ones, to neglect your children, and to disregard your responsibilities such as work and family. It will cause you to seek medical attention. It will force your family to turn to social support systems for assistance.[39]

For this officer, methamphetamine is the monster. Like demonic possession, it claims souls quickly and entirely. Regardless of pedigree or promise, those who are "owned and controlled" by the monster soon lie, cheat, and steal. And as the possessed abandon their children, families, and jobs, disorder spreads beyond users to the already-overburdened medical and social welfare programs paid for by the taxes of hardworking people. Another bit of testimony from an Indiana prosecutor in the same House of Representatives subcommittee hearing elaborates the monstrosity of methamphetamine further: "Philosophically, I recognize that education and treatment programs that work are vital to decreasing the phenomenal demand that fuels the *methamphetamine monster*. However, interdiction combined with swift and effective law enforcement is the best hope for destroying the organized networks that pump these poisons through our communities."[40] While the prosecutor pays lip service to the philosophy of education and treatment, he is also clear to endorse "swift and effective law enforcement" as necessary to interrupt the direct causal line leading from demand to monstrosity. On both accounts, the deputy and prosecutor position themselves, and hence the police power, as the only solution to the methamphetamine problem. This is not surprising, because, after all, police are in the business of fighting monsters.

Egon Bittner, who contributed much to the early sociological studies of American police, likened the relationship between the monster and police to that between the dragon and the dragon slayer:

For in modern folklore, too, he is a character who is ambivalently feared and admired, and no amount of public relations work can entirely abolish the sense that there is something of the dragon in the dragon-slayer. Because they are posted on the perimeters of order and justice in the hope that their presence will deter the forces of darkness and chaos, because they are meant to spare the rest of the people direct confrontations with the dreadful, perverse, lurid, and dangerous, police officers are perceived to have powers and secrets no one else shares. Their interest in and competence to deal with the untoward surrounds their activities with mystery and distrust. One needs only to consider the thoughts that come to mind at the sight of policemen moving into action: here they go to do something the rest of us have no stomach for![41]

The idea that police mark the boundaries of order and chaos, sheltering the public from the "dreadful, perverse, lurid, and dangerous," is the fundamental myth of the police power and one that the methamphetamine imaginary invokes and helps to reproduce. This is to say that the monsters of *Breaking Bad*, Tuco, Krazy-8, No Doze, Wendy, Spooge, Skank, Gustavo, Jack and his racist henchmen, and of course Walter White, these monsters of modern folklore, are the monsters that the police fight. By granting life to the monsters of the methamphetamine imaginary, *Breaking Bad* reaffirms the legitimacy and necessity of the police power. And so we find that we cannot properly come to terms with monstrosity or the police without also confronting the intimate and abiding connection between the two, as the theorist Mark Neocleous has argued.[42] As he details in his revisiting of Thomas Hobbes's two biblical monsters, Behemoth[43] and Leviathan,[44] the security offered by the sovereign (Leviathan) is of course security from the chaos and disorder of the monster/beast (Behemoth). Yet in order to find refuge and security from the monster, political subjects must ignore the violent monstrosity of the sovereign—the state and its police. The security offered by the police power, as Neocleous puts it, displaces its own monstrosity.

Here we should recall Bittner's understanding of the police power. The willingness of the police, as Bittner suggests, "to deal with the untoward surrounds their activities with mystery and distrust." There is, as he says, a "distrust" surrounding those who so willingly face the monstrous. What Bittner overlooks is that distrust in the police stems not so much from the fact that they do what "we have no stomach for" but from the monstrosity of the state itself and from the recognition that the police too are monsters. As Nietzsche famously wrote, "Whoever chases

Figure 1.1. Cherokee County Kansas Sheriff insignia depicting methamphetamine as "the dragon" and, hence, a monster.

monsters should see to it that in the process he does not become a monster himself."[45] We might say that whoever chases monsters is always already a monster—there is always a dragon *within* the dragon slayer. It is, then, perhaps no coincidence that police in Cherokee County, Kansas, chose the dragon-slayer motif for patches signifying their commitment to "methamphetamine enforcement."

And so, too, we might say that the monsters brought into being by the cultural work of *Breaking Bad*—the monsters of the methamphetamine imaginary—bring into being the monstrosity of the drug war and the police power that wages it. Continuing these themes, chapter 2 confronts the ways the visual politics of antimeth programs reproduce the disparate and monstrous cultural logics of "white trash" as a livable part of contemporary life.

2

This Is Your Race on Meth

Certain assemblages of power require the production of a
face, others do not.
—Gilles Deleuze and Félix Guattari, *A Thousand Plateaus*

In late 2013, an Oklahoma woman, Anita Tate, brought her fourteen-
month-old daughter to an emergency room after the child developed
an unusual rash around her nose and mouth. Tests later showed that the
girl was positive for methamphetamine. Arrested and charged with child
endangerment, Tate admitted to smoking meth in the bathroom of her
home while the child slept in the living room. When the ABC affiliate in
Oklahoma City reported on the case, it went like this:

> ANCHOR 1: Brand new at ten, a case of child endangerment that will
> just make you sick.
> ANCHOR 2: A mother is in jail after police found meth in her child's
> system. Let me show you Anita Tate's mug shot. Investigators say that
> she took her fourteen-month-old daughter to the hospital because
> she kept crying and her nose was red; her mouth was red as well.
> Turns out the toddler tested positive for meth. Tate admitted that she
> uses the drug saying, quote, "I smoke it; I know I'm white trash" and
> "Even though I'm a dope head, I love my child." Tate's daughter was
> taken into protective custody.[1]

Cases like this one play out countless times a year on news stations
across the country. While the Oklahoma City story is just one of many
meant to provoke the public's punitive and voyeuristic sensibilities, the
forty-second spot also usefully details the ways in which the visualities[2]
of the methamphetamine imaginary are implicated in the production
of distinct social hierarchies and subject positions. In this case, news
producers fashioned the woman's arrest, her mug shot, and her pitiable

ARREST AFFIDAVIT

"I smoke it, I know I'm white trash."

ANITA TATE

Figure 2.1. Local news reporting on one woman's methamphetamine-related child-endangerment charges and her admission of being "white trash."

admission to smoking meth and being white trash into a moralistic report that in their words was meant to make viewers "sick." Lost amid the rush to use Tate and her child's misfortune as news fodder, however, is the sad irony that "child-endangerment" charges followed only after Tate brought her daughter to the hospital for medical care. Her plea that even though she is a "dope head," she still loves her child—as if drug users are incapable of loving their children—elaborates this contradiction in heartbreaking detail. Aired on the evening news and circulated on social media, Tate's mug shot and confession can now easily be found by entering the key words "white + trash + meth" into an internet search engine. For anyone curious enough to plug the words into Google, Tate's face is a cultural referent for a peculiar and virulent identity.

Not only does Tate serve as a reference point for what a meth user is (white trash) and what a meth user does (abuses children), but the identity is apparently so inescapable that she dejectedly applies it to herself. Here in a mundane format, Tate is reduced to essential categories and virtually expelled from conventional social life. Through a critical reading of two well-known antimeth crime-control projects—Faces of Meth and the Meth Project's "Not Even Once" campaign—this chapter details how crime control and visual representation converge, helping to reproduce the distinct figure of the "white trash meth head."

Making Meth, Making Race

In 2011, the American sociologist Eduardo Bonilla-Silva gave the Ethnic and Racial Studies Annual Lecture at the group's meeting in London.[3] The aim of Bonilla-Silva's talk was to encourage his audience to think about the ways in which racial domination is accomplished through a quotidian yet insidious racial grammar. For Bonilla-Silva, *grammar* does not end with language composition but encompasses the deep structure, logic, and rules of social interaction, which are negotiated and reproduced through and as practice. It is this racial grammar that helps structure how race is seen, understood, felt, and lived in everyday life. To illustrate his points, Bonilla-Silva asked his audience to consider a few simple but powerful examples. For instance, take the term *historically black college and university* (HBCU), which at first glance is a rather innocuous way of linguistically designating institutions that have traditionally focused on the needs of black students and the black community. Yet, as Bonilla-Silva rightly points out, the character and difference of HBCUs are always already encoded in their very name, obscuring the question of where the historically *white* colleges and universities are. The answer is, of course, everywhere. It is this normalized, "invisible weight" of whiteness that provides meaning for the difference and crafted inferiority of the other. As Bonilla-Silva adeptly argues, this sort of racial grammar is at work all around us, quietly but dramatically structuring dominant notions of beauty, art, and violence. True as Bonilla-Silva's points are, they are not revelations. However, his thought experiment does raise an interesting question. That is, what should we make of methamphetamine, encoded through the practice of racial grammar as a "white" drug?[4] Thinking through this lens, to christen methamphetamine a "white" drug is to suggest that all other drugs are in fact "black." That is, meth is unusual only because it ensnares whites in the supposed crime, violence, degradation, and indecency of "black" drug use. This logic goes further, as it is not just whites but also more specifically a derelict white trash who are given form and shape by the racial grammar of methamphetamine. For instance, in an impromptu interview with reporters following a local conference on the "methamphetamine epidemic," Oklahoma governor Frank Keating gave his own, particularly candid version of this sort of racial grammar: "It's a white trash drug—methamphetamines largely are consumed by the lower socio-economic element of white people and I think we need to shame it. Just like crack cocaine was a black trash drug and is a black trash drug."[5] It is not heroin, marijuana, or moonshine that the governor sets out as a white-trash drug but methamphetamine. Through a false equivalence to already-racialized understandings of crack cocaine, Keating puts the methamphetamine imaginary to work reinforcing a distinct social hierarchy and disparate social relations. By assigning white trash certain characteristics, the normality of approved or hegemonic forms of whiteness and associated privileges all but disappear. And so, through the methamphetamine and drug-war imaginaries, included whites, non-whites, and white trash reproduce the cultural logics of whiteness and white social position.

But what of white trash apart from methamphetamine? Commonly, *white trash* is a catchall insult used by members of the middle and upper classes to objectify and stigmatize uncouth and uncivilized poor white people, who often live on the "wrong side of the tracks" or the untraveled rural parts of the country. Though I grew up in the stunningly white surroundings of a small Kansas farm town, race was still very much a fundamental force of everyday life. This plays out in a particularly virulent and powerful racial grammar, which Barbara and Karen Fields call "racecraft."[6] An example of racecraft that I encountered numerous times in my formative years usually began with the familiar disclaimer, "I am not a racist." And with that, the local philosopher would set out schooling me on the particulars of intrarace distinction: "You see, there are good black people, and then there are niggers, just like there are good white people, and then there is white trash." This is how racecraft draws on class to fabricate the material realties of race in the United States. To be white is to be an accepted member of the community. Here whiteness is achieved in innumerable ways. Come from a "good family." Do not receive state assistance. Do work a full-time job or appear to. Keep your yard tidy. Drive a nice or at least clean car. Do not chain smoke, have tattoos, or have children out of wedlock. Do have all of your teeth. In short, to be white, do not be white trash. Respectable blackness is accomplished in many of the same ways. In 1996, the comedian Chris Rock stirred considerable controversy when he drew on and advanced this sort of thinking. In his HBO special *Bring the Pain*, which *Variety* called one of the most remarkable hours of comedy to ever air on television,[7] Rock joked,

> There's like a civil war going on with black people. And there's two sides: there's black people, and there's niggas. And the niggas have got to go. Every time black people want to have a good time, ignorant niggas fuck it up! Can't keep a disco open more than three weeks—grand opening, grand closing. Can't go to a movie the first week it comes out 'cause niggas are shooting at the screen. . . . Now they got some shit: they're trying to get rid of welfare. Every time you see welfare on the news, they show black people. Black people don't give a shit about welfare; niggas are shaking in their boots. . . . But it ain't only black people on welfare; white people are on welfare too. . . . The rest of the country is full of broke-ass white people, living in a trailer home, eating mayonnaise sandwiches, fucking their sisters, listening to John Cougar Mellencamp records.[8]

In this particular bit, Rock too draws on particularly class-based understandings of race, using welfare to separate disreputable blacks and whites from the balance of conventional society. So it may be that, in some perverse way, to invoke the distinctions between "whites and white trash" and "black people and niggas" is not racist in the strictest sense, because these categories rely on durable class signifiers to justify social exclusion. In the process, however, the apparent failures and misgivings of the poor help to craft distinct racial categories out of thin air. Along these lines, the sociologist Matt Wray offers a particularly accessible and useful description: "*White trash*. For many, the name evokes images of trailer parks, *meth labs*, beat-up Camaros on cinder blocks, and poor rural folks with too many kids and not enough government cheese. It's a put-down, the name given to those whites who don't make it, either because they're too lazy or too stupid. Or maybe it's because something's wrong with their inbred genes. Whatever the reason, it's their own damn fault they live like that."[9] Wray's description is a veritable shopping list of sins sure to earn the dishonor of the label. The *poverty* and *insecurity* of a cheap mobile home. The *flawed consumption* of an impractical, defective car. The *immorality* of families too large to manage. The *drugs*, the *dependence*—the proof is in the pudding: they get what they deserve.[10]

But white trash did not simply emerge organically from trailer parks and backwoods hovels overnight. As Wray and his collaborator Annalee Newitz have written elsewhere, the term's divergent lineage traces back nearly 200 years, to 1830s Baltimore. Here, the pair suggests, it was not whites but black slaves who first coined the term to describe the poor white servants who worked alongside them.[11] The *Oxford English Dictionary* seems to agree, finding an early American use of the term in the personal journal of F. A. Kemble, who in 1833 from a plantation in Georgia wrote, "the slaves themselves entertain the very highest contempt for white servants who they designate as 'poor white trash.'"[12] This confirms what we already know, *white trash*, like all racial projects, is also mired in class oppression. In this case, an already-dispossessed group sought to maintain social boundaries and create distance from another dispossessed group. While it may be that free blacks and black slaves coined the term, it is important to be clear from the outset that it is highly unlikely that *white trash* would exist in its current form if not for the cultural work of wealthy, upper-class whites and the political economy that separated them from poor whites and black slaves.

In the expansive and influential book *The Invention of the White Race*, Theodore W. Allen makes important distinctions, at least for our purposes here, between forms of national and racial oppression.[13] While Allen's concept of national oppression, synonymous with colonial oppression, has obvious racial dimensions, the distinction lies in the groups that enforce national and colonial rule. So, for instance, "territorial acquisitions" in India by Britain and in the Philippines by the United States reveal stark racial lines between the mostly white colonizers and the nonwhite colonized. Yet in both instances, colonizers incorporated particular members of elite classes of the subject populations into the new bourgeois class and state apparatus, enlisting them in the production and maintenance of colonial order. Though this is clearly a racialized project, Allen argues that it is more accurate to consider it a broader project of national or colonial oppression. Under a system of pure racial oppression, Allen argues, the working classes of the dominant group are the primary agents in the production and maintenance of racial order: "The assault upon the tribal affinities, customs, laws and institutions of the Africans, the American Indians and the Irish by English/British and Anglo-American colonialism reduced all members of the oppressed group to one undifferentiated social status, a status beneath that of any member of any social class within the colonizing population. *This is the hallmark of racial oppression* in its colonial origins, and as it has persisted in subsequent historical contexts."[14] In our case, *white trash* as a method to distinguish between classes and police ethnic and racial boundaries emerged most prominently in the early 1800s competition between Irish Catholic and Scotch-Irish Protestant immigrants.[15] Between 1815 and the early 1850s, nearly one million displaced Irish immigrated to the United States.[16] Arriving as a distinct race bearing the stigma of centuries of caste oppression and landlordism, poor Irish peasants assumed a social position comparable to that of free blacks in the North.[17] The historian Noel Ignatiev writes, "As they came to the cities, they were crowded into districts that became centers of crime, vice, and disease. There they commonly found themselves thrown together with free Negroes. Irish and Afro-Americans fought each other and the police, socialized and occasionally intermarried, and developed a common culture of the lowly. They also both suffered the scorn of those better situated."[18]

It was in short order and by no small accident that the 1850 Census was the first to include the new racial designation "mulattoe."[19] While Ignatiev is careful to point out that these so-called mulattoes were mostly the children of slaveholders who had escaped the Deep South, this racial construction no doubt served as convenient justification for the utter banishment of poor blacks, Irish, and mulattoes to the lowest and most reviled strata of social life. Horrible slurs, such as "niggers turned inside out" for the Irish and the literal stain of the label "smoked Irish" for blacks, details the fluidity between these groups.[20] As famine pushed more and more Irish across the Atlantic, Protestant Scotch-Irish began to claim a distinct ethnoracial heritage in order to differentiate themselves from the waves of destitute Catholic Irish. Again, *white trash* created division among similarly situated and marginalized people. While the competition and precariousness of a rapidly industrializing economy was clearly the impetus to distinguish whites from white trash, the veneer of racial, rather than class, animus continued to adorn the term. Yet as the historian Anthony Harkins suggests, it was a widely held belief among southern bourgeois whites at the turn of the century that the eradication of the antebellum slave economy had given rise to these "poor white trash"—too little capitalism, the logic goes, not too much. Just as conservative commentators even today wonder aloud if blacks were "better off" under the violent repression of chattel slavery,[21] Harkins points to social critics such as H. L. Mencken who "bemoaned the loss of the antebellum southern aristocracy during the Civil War and the subsequent emergence of a society dominated by the 'poor white trash' in whose veins flowed 'some of the worst blood of western Europe.'"[22]

It was around this time that many of the "hillbillies" who had settled the southern Appalachian states and the "Okies" and "sod-busters" of the rural Midwest became the subjects of a nascent scientific field— eugenics. Extending pseudoscientific logics that undergirded the distinct phenotype "mulattoe," eugenicists began to look for and of course find the causes of all manner of social misery in the "bad blood" of poor rural people. As the criminologist Nicole Rafter has shown, contemporary understandings of white trash continue on through the early eugenics and sociobiological "family studies" undertaken to trace the origins of alcoholism, idleness, and biological impairments. As she has effectively shown, visual representation also played an important role in helping to establish early positivist criminology and criminal anthropology. Cesare Lombroso, of course, relied heavily on the visual, filling his books with examples of the characteristics of "born criminals."[23] This continued on from Lombroso, to projects bent on diagnosing the "feeble-mindedness" of poor rural people.[24] Perhaps the most well known of the pseudoscientific eugenics studies focusing on the rural poor is H. H. Goddard's *The Kallikak Family: A Study in the Heredity of Feeblemindedness.* Published in 1912, Goddard's study was loaded with nearly forty images purporting to visually document generations of feeblemindedness that had descended to a young woman, Deborah, who had been "saved from depravity" by institutionalization.[25] Yet as we know from Stephen Jay Gould's important book *The Mismeasure of Man*, Goddard's photographic representations of the Kallikaks were not only disingenuous but also in fact a doctored work of "conscious skullduggery."[26]

While the popularity of eugenics fell far out of favor in the years leading up to and after the Second World War, the racial grammar of white trash, entwined with thinly veiled eugenic pseudoscience, continues. For instance, in 1993, not long after the newly formed Office of

National Drug Control Policy predicted that meth would be the drug plague of the '90s,[27] the archconservative political scientist Charles Murray penned an essay in the *Wall Street Journal* in which he warned of the "coming white underclass."[28] A short time later, Murray and his collaborator Richard Herrnstein published their fiercely contested *The Bell Curve*, a book scorned as "the work of disreputable race theorists and eccentric eugenicists."[29] Interestingly, while in the thick of defending *The Bell Curve*'s assertions of black intellectual inferiority, Murray dismissed "the black story" as "old news," pointing instead to rising levels of "white illegitimacy" and a loathsome "white trash" underclass. In the *Wall Street Journal* article, Murray writes,

> Instead, whites have had "white trash" concentrated in a few streets on the outskirts of town, sometimes a Skid Row of unattached white men in the large cities. But these scatterings have seldom been large enough to make up a neighborhood. . . . Look for certain schools in white neighborhoods to get a reputation as being unteachable, with large numbers of disruptive students and indifferent parents. Talk to the police; listen for stories about white neighborhoods where the incidence of domestic disputes and casual violence has been shooting up. Look for white neighborhoods with high concentrations of drug activity and large numbers of men who have dropped out of the labor force. Some readers will recall reading the occasional news story about such places already.[30]

Warning of "unteachable" schools in "white neighborhoods" wrought by "domestic disputes," "causal violence," and "drug activity," Murray invokes and elaborates a binary logic separating bourgeois whites from this supposed "coming" "white trash" underclass. Of course, time has proven Murray's base demographic calculus inaccurate and misguided as those that were employed, just two years later, by another conservative social scientist, John DiIulio, to herald the "coming of the [young black] super predators."[31] Perhaps haunted by charges of racism stemming from *The Bell Curve*, Murray has continued his fervent attack on marginalized whites under the supposed "color-blind" and "race-neutral" critiques of the disintegrating values of "White America." In his most recent book, *Coming Apart: The State of White America, 1960–2010*, Murray scolds, "America is coming apart at the seams—not the seams of race or ethnicity, but of class," as if to suggest that "White America" is devoid of racial and political meanings.[32] And as he did his 1993 essay, Murray's newest offering provides bourgeois whites the logic—what to "look for"—to diagnose the "unraveling" of "White America." This diagnostic logic is, of course, embedded within a particular aesthetic/epistemic position that uses "morality," consumption, style, and representation as a proxy for class position and hence worthiness.

For instance, Keith Hayward and Majid Yar's thoughtful analysis of the despised youth subculture "chavs" in the UK elaborates the importance of consumption and style in the constitution of race and class identities.[33] Famously satirized by the comedian Sasha Baron Cohen's character Ali G, *chav* is pejorative slang for (mostly) white English youth who follow American hip-hop fashion and wear expensive branded clothing, tracksuits, baseball hats, and ostentatious jewelry. Likely first drawn from the Romani word for child, *chavi*, the term attached to impoverished immigrants whose style did not seem to fit their skin color. Soon a host of vernacular definitions emerged—"council housed and violent" or "council housed vermin"—betraying virulent classed textures. As with white trash in the US, Hayward and Yar suggest that the animosity directed at chavs and other marginalized white identities results not only from poverty or the lack of material consumption but also from flawed consumption or, in their words, "excessive participation in forms of market-oriented consumption which are deemed *aesthetically* impoverished."[34] Marking stylistically repugnant consumerism and unproductive labor "chav style," much like Wray's "beat-up Camaro on cinder blocks," is a powerful aesthetic of class distinction. It follows, then, that the hostility toward "trash" is largely due to the appearance of a rejection or departure from the privileged and respected space of middle-class white cultural sensibilities.

There is more. Take for instance the 2002 film *8 Mile*, which depicts the struggles of B-Rabbit, a young, white rapper, as he tries to break into Detroit's underground hip-hop scene. Loosely based on the rapper Eminem's well-documented rise from poverty, the film sets a stark racial dichotomy between B-Rabbit and the (mostly) black rappers who control the Detroit scene.[35] In the film's final scene, in which B-Rabbit beats the champion Poppa-Doc in a battle rap (much like Rocky Balboa finally beating Apollo Creed), "white trash" takes center stage. As

B-Rabbit shouts, "I am white. I am a fucking bum. I do live in a trailer with my mom" and "Fuck y'all if you doubt me. I'm a piece of fucking white trash. I say it proudly," his whiteness becomes an offensive weapon that symbolically positions him—in terms of race and class— below his opponent, thereby cementing his underdog appeal. When used this way, even by everyday people, *white trash* becomes protest, a transgressive badge of honor meant to flip a symbolic middle finger up the class pile at those who look down with contempt. *8 Mile* reveals another interesting facet of the contemporary understandings of white trash. While, as we have seen, the social history of whiteness and white trash is firmly rooted in agricultural economies and rural geographies, Eminem makes known the urban character of the identity. The anthropologist John Hartigan's ethnographic work in the same neighborhoods that were the setting for *8 Mile* reveals not only the urban character of white trash but the heterogeneity of whiteness as well. Hartigan shows how different forms of whiteness, in his case "hillbilly," "gentrifiers," and "racists," are everyday intraclass distinctions formed along local neighborhood lines and most importantly *within* whiteness as much as *against* blackness.[36] While the outline of white trash might be apparent in the case of B-Rabbit (white) and Poppa Doc (black), differences within marginalized white identities and urban/rural white trash may be more difficult to see. Comparing Eminem to Philip John Clapp, better known as Johnny Knoxville, draws these subtleties out further. Whereas hip-hop and Detroit shapes Eminem's particular white-trash aesthetic along decidedly urban lines, Clapp's character is chock full of references to rural and southern culture. From the moniker that he chose to honor his hometown to his personal take on 1950s rockabilly style, Knoxville pays homage to the "out of style, the tasteless, the rejects of mainstream American society" and draws obvious influence from the king of southern white trash culture, Elvis Presley.[37] As Gael Sweeney has described, as an icon of white-trash culture, Elvis is "a figure of terror and the grotesque to the urban, most Northern, arbiters of 'good taste' and a spectacle of excess and release for his Southern white fans."[38] Like chavs in the UK, white-trash sins against "good taste" are proof enough for the social sanctions levied from above at those down the class pile, while from below, white trash endures as protest—a way to lay claim to an authentic sort of material deprivation.

Yet we should be cautious of blindly consuming white trash as transgression. Consider, for instance, the stand-up-comedy character "Etta May," billed as the "Queen of Southern Sass" and "Minnie Pearl with a migraine." Created and played by a theater professor from the University of Kentucky, Etta May takes the stage in "trailer-trash chic" 1950s cat's-eye glasses, brightly colored stretch pants, and "Aunt Jemima"–style do-rag, tackling unemployment, domestic violence, teen pregnancy, and other subjects commonly associated with the rural poor. However, without some nod to historical and material conditions that have made "white trash" a recognizable trope to satirize, Etta May is actually more *productive* of the dominant social order than transgressive.[39] This is particularly evident in Etta May's distinction between "rednecks" and white trash: "About rednecks, here's the thing. I'm white trash, and it's different from being a redneck. You Yankees don't understand the difference. Rednecks have jobs and a truck. White trash have food stamps, a bus fare, and chain smoke. Believe me, I'm below Larry the Cable Guy."[40] As she claims, "Believe me, I'm below Larry the Cable Guy," the Etta May caricature actually accesses and reaffirms the old, familiar logics distinguishing white trash from other marginalized white identities. The logic goes that even though "redneck," "hillbilly," and "cracker" are largely deplorable social categories, to be white trash is to have distinct moral failings.[41] As such, if we connect white trash to the particular historical and material conditions that produced it and understand it first as a method to produce disparate race/class relations, then its transgressive subtexts and its possibilities for emancipatory critique largely dissolve. Rejecting the notion that the pop singer Beyoncé is a source of feminist transgression, the feminist theorist bell hooks similarly argues that the singer's image is in fact antifeminist and even a form of "terrorism" committed against young black girls. Hooks argues that "it's fantasy that we can recoup the violating image and use it."[42] Which is to say that no matter the context, to adopt a style or image born of oppression is to unavoidably condone it. Perhaps recognizing the noxiousness of the caricature, Etta May's anonymous creator stated, "I like to keep my real name out of it because people are crazy."[43] Just as Eminem's, Johnny Knoxville's, and Etta May's particular takes on the white-trash aesthetic and ethic help to reproduce its particular cultural form, so too does the work of state and nonstate crime control. The remainder of this chapter confronts two well-known antimeth projects—Faces of Meth and the Meth Project—to describe how crime control helps to produce distinct subject positions and race and class hierarchies.

This Is Your Face on Meth

In 2004, Multnomah County, Oregon, deputy Brian King released a series of photos of suspected meth users that he had booked into the county jail. King believed the mug shots were so powerful that they could teach viewers, especially school-aged children, why they should not use methamphetamine. Dubbing the project Faces of Meth, King arranged two mug shots in simple causal order to provide powerful visual evidence of meth's devastating effects.

The program gained widespread popularity as the centerpiece of Unnecessary Epidemic—an award-winning five-part series on meth published by the *Oregonian*, a Portland newspaper. As the image in figure 2.2 shows, from the inception of the program, it drew from the already-existing reservoir of preunderstanding about meth users and, of course, the meth zombie trope. Later, the project launched a website to allow the public to freely download the images and purchase intervention materials. Proving the sheer popularity and mass circulation of the images, one YouTube montage, provocatively titled "Drugs Make You Ugly," has been viewed an astounding 8.1 million times and elicited more than 22,000 viewer comments. Perpetually made and remade, interpreted and reinterpreted, or as Keith Hayward describes, "uploaded and downloaded, Flickr-ed, Facebook-ed and PhotoShop-ed," these visceral images of human suffering are borderless and boundless—*liquid*.[44]

Beyond the project's opportunistic use of booking photos, there are a number of technical problems with the logics that undergird it. First and most obviously, it is clear that King cherry-picked images that would provide the most dramatic effects. Selecting the most shocking images no doubt exaggerates meth's effects, with the implication that all users eventually appear as these faces do. As certain as the images represent the suffering of some users, other cases certainly exist among them that contradict the zombie trope. It is also rather dishonest to christen these images Faces of Meth or the face of any other drug for that matter, as it is highly unlikely the people featured by the program use meth

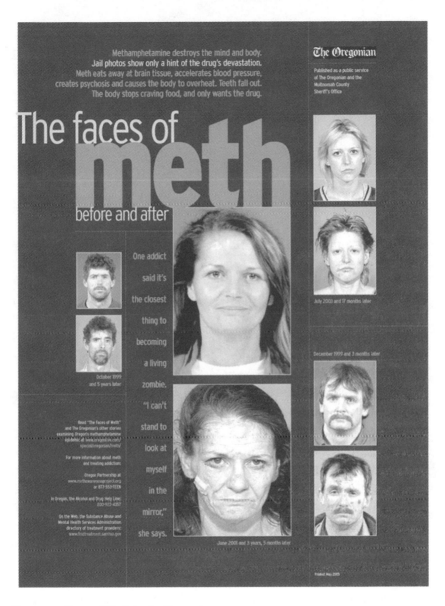

Figure 2.2. Faces of Meth in the *Oregonian*.

exclusively or that changes observed between the two images can be attributed only to drug use. Finally, each of the mug-shot pairs features what appears to be a white person. While we should not presume to know how these people would identify themselves, when linked to a drug already known as "white man's crack" and "Okie coke,"[45] Faces of Meth helps reproduce a distinct sort of racialized subjectivity. While illicit-drug use is a complicated issue that rarely breaks on clean demographic lines, the power of the image as employed here can make it seem as if it does. Indeed, as the Sentencing Project's Marc Mauer put it, "you don't *see* any pictures of young black men and women described as the face of meth."[46] To be sure, the program does nothing to challenge or complicate the widely held cultural belief that meth use is a distinctly white-trash phenomenon. Given the project's routinization of worst cases, its hasty assumptions about drug use, and its uniquely racialized frame, we should therefore be skeptical of Faces of Meth's claim to objective photographic realism.

Not unlike youth boot camps and "scared straight" jail tours, Faces of Meth and the "Not Even Once" program (discussed later) are premised on shock tactics, fear appeals, and a misplaced emphasis on militaristic paternalism. Yet these tactics are not meant to help those who are already mired in the pains of drug abuse. Rather, the projects intend to capture the imagination of the more general public, thereby making it part of a broader cultural terrain that defines everyday life in penal terms—described by Michelle Brown as a *culture of punishment*.[47] Brown usefully draws attention to the importance of visual culture and the ways in which the visual allows citizens distanced from the material experiences of crime and punishment to participate in punitive spectacles and engage in moral judgment from afar.[48] Take, for instance, Maricopa County, Arizona, sheriff Joe Arpaio's "Jail Cam" project, which broadcast real-time footage of the inside of local jails. Creating gritty "reality" television from the everyday drudgeries of imprisonment, Jail Cam recast the pains of imprisonment into an entertainment commodity meant to address anonymous spectators outside jail walls.[49] In programs such as these, fear, pain, and humiliation are the tools used to deter voyeuristic spectators from being caught in a similar position.

Of course, Faces of Meth is shot through with this sort of thinking, as it advances a distorted yet tidy causality: "See what will happen if you use meth?" Without regard for personal biography or lived experi-ence, the program transforms the pain and humiliation of drug use and imprisonment into titillating commodities and markets a penalty of crude instruction. As Deputy King describes on the Faces of Meth web-site (www.facesofmeth.us), "I thank the men and women who, through their stories and photos, can share their experience with methamphet-amine so you never have to try it yourself to know what it can do. I have seen and interviewed each of these people in jail. I hope that in seeing this you will make choices to not use methamphetamine and that I will never see you come inside my jail." Here we can see the faith that King places in the power and promise of the visual as a crime-control project. As part of the program's brand, its website offers numerous testimoni-als speaking to the affective shock and grotesque "reality" of the photo-graphic "evidence." For example, the following two quotes, attributed to students, articulate the disgust engendered:

> One thing that I learned was how disgusting meth, and all other illegal drugs can make your mouth and teeth, and how they hurt your body, inside and out. I really liked how you brought examples of real life cases about people who have destroyed their lives and the lives of others. I think that having this sort of thing really makes people see it and go "ee-www, how nasty" and taking them away from the thought of even think-ing about trying it.

> Really looking at the people's faces after months of taking meth showed me so much more then [sic] some lecture would have. . . . I loved your way of explaining things, instead of lecturing you showed specific ex-amples and gave precise facts.

The students' mentioning that they know someone who has abused meth illustrates the interplay of image and experience, while still privi-leging the power of the images themselves. That is, these particular testimonies make the claim that the mug shots are in a way more power-ful, instructive, and hence "real" than their own experiences with friends and family who have used the drug. As another student offered, "I know people who have been on meth and those mug shots hit hard. I am never going to do Meth. It is a pressure I have been faced with but now I am even more educated." Another student offered an even more personal reflection, stating, "It's crazy how much those people reminded me of my dad and I just found out he was an addict. . . . It controlled his life and ruined our family. I never want to be like him and thanks to you now I never will." With the program legitimized by commonsense testimonials such as these and a coalition of educators, politicians, and drug-control agents, Faces of Meth's claims of effectiveness and opportunistic display of others' pain is seldom challenged. In fact, as one educator remarked, the program simply "let[s] the evidence speak for itself."

Yet, as we know, photographs, particularly booking photos or mug shots, never simply speak for themselves. In this instance, Faces of Meth and the methamphetamine imaginary more generally speak on behalf of the police and state power. Appearing on countless websites, in newspapers and documentary films, the images no doubt speak on behalf of capital as well. This does not assume an inescapable, top-down relationship, however—spectators are not simply passive consumers but are active agents complicit in the triptych of criminal transgression, punishment, and the visual. Judith Butler makes this point particularly well in her discussion of the visual evidence used during the trials of the LAPD officers acquitted of beating Rodney King:

> For if the jurors came to see in Rodney King's body a danger to the law, then this "seeing" requires to be read as that which was culled, cultivated, regulated—indeed, policed—in the course of the trial. This is not a simple act of seeing, an act of direct perception, but of the racial production of the visible, the workings of racial constraints on what it means to "see." Indeed, the trial calls to be read not only as instruction in racist modes of seeing but as a repeated and ritualistic production of blackness. . . . This is a seeing which is a reading, that is, a *contestable* construal, but one which nevertheless passes itself off as "seeing," a reading which became for that white community, and for countless others, the same thing as seeing.[50]

As Butler rightly points out, reading images like those in the trial is an active and contested process that is very much contingent on a historically determined horizon of preunderstanding, which is nested within and bound to the broader social and cultural imaginary. In this case, jurors failed to see King as a victim because their ways of seeing and hence knowing were predetermined and constrained by historical entwinements of the police power and white supremacy. In a sense, then, the evidence may very well "speak for itself," but it does so within the context of a visual field that is actively produced by broader histories of power. The visual culture theorist Nicholas Mirzoeff describes this sort of visual predetermination and preconceit as "visuality"—the ways in which we see, how we are able, allowed, or made to see—the hegemony of the visual field.[51]

Though Faces of Meth cannot represent an objective reality of meth use outside certain cultural and political contexts, at its core remains an unwavering faith in the camera, photograph, and mug shot to report the objective truths and facts about crime and drug use. Developing in tandem with the nascent fields of criminology and criminal justice, photographic portraiture, like fingerprinting, quickly became an important tool for police and a scientific proxy for legal "proof" inscribing criminality, guilt, and shame on the bodies of the accused. In these mug shots reimagined as Faces of Meth, spectators are provided the "facts" of methamphetamine—which is to say the power of methamphetamine to *transform* users (normal people) into monstrous *white trash*. In the series *Portraits of Black Americans 1987–1990*, the famed photographer Baldwin Lee had this to say about the politics and visuality of the mug shot:

> In form, each of my new pictures was virtually identical to a mug shot: a head surrounded by a tight frame. The camera's proximity to the subjects had the effect of cropping away not just their surroundings, but also the context in which they existed. Only after the fact did I see that this cropping eliminated social, political, and cultural issues that had been integral to the content of my earlier pictures. These headshots focused on their subjects' psychological and emotional character instead. Making them was different from work I had done previously. Freed from the task of asserting or defending political and social viewpoint, I found that taking pictures was less difficult.[52]

Important here is Lee's assertion that framing subjects in mug-shot fashion draws out the "psychological and emotional character" of the subject. This is certainly the case with Faces of Meth, as the deterrent "shock" it intends to provoke is reliant on the viscerality of bodies in pain. Structured by the project's frame,[53] the images make invisible the structural and spatial contexts in which these state captured and photographed bodies are positioned. Like Lee's series, the project crops away "not just their surroundings, but also the context in which they existed." While the project clearly draws on the "psychological and emotional character" of its subjects, I am not certain that this method frees the photographer from "the task of asserting or defending political and social viewpoint" as all mug shots are inherently political projects, awash in cultural tensions that cannot be simply "cropped away." The pain and suffering of arrest, the transformative power of methamphetamine, and the authority of state power are always at work within Faces of Meth.

Providing photographic evidence of what meth users look like, the project also operates as a late-modern physiognomic archive—approximating the face for intellect, social standing, and moral character. Like the physiognomy of old that equated facial beauty with virtue, the project displays the "ugliness" supposedly brought on by meth use, as vice. Instructing viewers to read the outside for the inside, the project employs a criminological aesthetics whereby binary terms—clean/unclean, rational/irrational—structure a system of value making proper whiteness invisible and white trash *unavoidable*.[54] As the journalist Jack Shafer has remarked, "If you were to reduce the current moral panic to a single image, it would be a photo of a meth user whose gums are pus-streaked and whose rotting teeth—what teeth he still has—are blackened and broken."[55] The project cements the literal "face" of a certain type of crime and criminal, imagined and reduced to a crude foundation, in the methamphetamine and drug-war imaginaries, exercising the power not simply to represent but to order social life.

Reducing the complexities of sociality and lived experiences to simple before-and-after frames, the project elaborates movement and transformation, crossing boundaries and borders from conventionality into what Julia Kristeva calls *abjection*.[56] Described by Kristeva as not simply unhealthy or unclean, the abject is that which is "thrown out," that which troubles identity, systems, and order, "that which does not respect borders, positions or rules."[57] For Kristeva, any crime is abject because it exposes the fragility of law and conjures the figure of immorality that transgresses established borders between the acceptable and unacceptable, the normal and abnormal—pure and polluted. Like Walter White's transformation to Heisenberg, these mug-shot pairs document a white body's descent into white-trash abjection. Importantly, not only does the causal arrangement "before" and "after" signify breached boundaries, but by beginning with a mug shot, the project documents the decent of already-abject criminal bodies deeper into zombified monstrosity. Abjection detailed by the bloody decay of users' bodies imbues the faces of meth with a Gothic monstrosity, setting apart meth zombies from the parade of folk devils who seem to retreat from view as quickly as they appear. Documenting transformation of abject bodies from pure to polluted, clean to unclean, the campaign focuses the power of the image and the power to punish on marginalized, subordinate, and stained white trash, positioning them outside community, law, and bourgeois conventionality. Viewing meth as the white-trash referent to crack cocaine also helps imagine bodies and faces along an aesthetic and physiognomic continuum of whiteness. As such, these faces marked by decaying flesh provide penal spectators very specific photographic evidence of the criminality lurking in their "community"—threatening its stability. Just as constructed anxieties surrounding "black" criminality render whiteness largely invisible, notions of "white trash" criminality advanced by projects like Faces of Meth reaffirm and obscure the boundaries of white privilege—carving a raced and classed hierarchy from relative homogeneity.

For instance, on the "Drugs Make You Ugly" YouTube video, an anonymous spectator commented, "it appears that doing meth turns you into mullet-headed trailer trash."[58] The idea that meth turns you into trash, marked not only by facial sores and lesions but a repugnant hairstyle and trailer home, is important because it only really makes sense in relation to a privileged yet largely invisible understanding of whiteness. Respectable whites do not have mullets, live in trailers, or use meth. Clearly, then, the abjection and monstrosity built into the methamphetamine imaginary results not simply from transgression of juridical boundaries but also from the class-based sins of improper consumption and polluting one's own body. The social and cultural sanctions attached to white-trash meth heads are thus in response to the sins committed against white bodies as proxy for the dominant racial order.

Indeed, evidenced by the program's popularity and wide circulation, the images are clearly dynamic and performative, recasting everyday actors as penal spectators who negotiate and ascribe value to the lives of others. As if the complexity of sociality and lived experience is reducible to straightforward costs and benefits analysis, the project unavoidably returns to the troubling problematic "Why would someone do that to themselves?" and reinforces the individual rationality of criminal transgression in at least two ways. First, "before" and "after" arrangements situate crime's etiology invariably within the individual, wholly dependent on the personality, rational decision making, IQ, or "born criminality" of the user. Second, if "choice" is indeed the sole "cause" of bloody disfigurement and meth-induced criminality, the faces of meth document the existence of the irrational—the not always seen yet ever present specter that rejects juridical and moral convention. Even discourses that might frame the images in more nuanced sociological terms, such as those bound up in class-based notions of white trash, often fall back on a certain adherence to and normalization of the figure of the rational individual through a cultural tautology claiming that meth "turns you into mullet-headed trailer trash" and that the drug is inherent to the culture—simply something white trash "do."

The project's representation of the meth-driven journey into abjection also bears important similarities to another antidrug public-service announcement that made cultural icons of an egg scorching in a pan and the adjoining catch phrase, "This is your brain on drugs. Any questions?" Through the crude instructions undergirding the frying egg and pained Faces of Meth, the state defines and polices boundaries between legitimate and illegitimate, normal and deviant, self and other. Yet between the two projects, the images and what they symbolize differ markedly. Whereas the "brain on drugs" campaign metaphorically presents an uncracked egg as the "normal" brain and a cracked frying egg as the "abnormal," drug-addled brain, Faces of Meth uses the flesh of the human face for affect and effect. Movement from the figurative (egg) and biologically internal (brain) to the literal (face) and external (flesh) further exposes Faces of Meth's physiognomic core. Exhibiting a Lombrosian fixation on physical abnormalities, Faces of Meth shows an anxious public what meth users look like once marked by the stigmata of their crimes. These stigmata do not simply identify a Lombrosian criminal man but quietly bear something more sinister. As Claire Valier writes, the horror "is located precisely at the boundary between psyche and flesh, and reveals emotional expressions to be embodied practices."[59] As we can see, especially in comparison to the "brain on drugs" advertisement, the project details how meth users cross boundaries from psyche (egg) to flesh (face)—*fantasy to the real*. As such, these borderless and boundless images of meth use—these faces of meth— should be understood as a movement away from the figurative to an embodied emotionality of the Gothic horrors of criminal transgression, derived from and intimately entwined with class-based understandings of white identities.

As Wendy, Spooge, and Skank from *Breaking Bad* also usefully illustrate, a fundamental part of the methamphetamine imaginary is the transgression of racial and corporeal norms, harnessing the power of legitimate pronouncement and cultural narrative, so that on the street, lesions, rotting teeth, and even a thin frame evoke the specter of white-trash criminality. Here the faces of the dispossessed mark the boundaries between rationality and irrationality, good and bad, alive and dead. On the one hand, the images appeal to the spectator's reason to weigh the pains and pleasures of methamphetamine use—"do not do meth, or you will look like this." On the other hand, the images beg the question "why would someone do this to themselves?"

This simple calculus of rational individualism arouses a vindictive cognitive dissonance aimed toward those who seem to shirk the everyday drudgeries shouldered by "respectable citizens" and reinforces the logics separating self from the monstrous other. Again, as a few anonymous comments confirm, these are not simply criminals but something more disgusting: "All of them are straight fuckin scumbags of earth & are a waste of air and space!!!!"; "Haha, what a bunch of losers! . . . I don't feel sorry for anyone who loses their life or goes to prison for doing meth or any kind of drug like that. it does nothing for a person but make them slums [*sic*] of the earth." Emphasizing only the irrational criminality of users, the project's punitive display is at the expense of any consideration of historical, social, economic, and political context. Indeed, as another anonymous comment, "haha there [*sic*] own fucking fault," reveals, these images reinforce a view of drug users as products of unhindered free will and rational choice.[60]

The Proof Is in the Picture: They Did It to Themselves, They Get What They Deserve

The notion of getting what one deserves emerges from and supports a worldview in which drug users are utterly disposable and ungrievable human waste.[61] In this sense, the images do the work of state power by fabricating and reinforcing the conventional understandings of drug users, severed from the culture and history from which they emerge and circulate. Here, the real and the represented are intimately intertwined, refashioning the forms of life and affective sensibilities of a particularly exclusive and punitive social system.

While the Faces of Meth project clearly displays the cultural logics of binary representation—clean/unclean, rational/irrational—it is important also to consider a third category, the spectrality of these things. As Slavoj Žižek suggests, the specter is born from encounters with freedom. Like Walter White, a man who rejected his family and respectable middle-class life for his self-indulgent dream of empire, Faces of Meth perhaps represent the anxious fears and contradictory desires generated by those who seem to pursue the freedoms and hedonistic pleasures of illicit-drug use and to escape the stasis of bourgeois conventionality. As Jock Young writes in his book *The Vertigo of Late Modernity*, "It cannot be an accident that the stereotype of the underclass with its idleness, dependency, hedonism and institutionalized irresponsibility, with its drug use, teenage pregnancies and fecklessness, represents all the traits which the respectable citizen has to suppress in order to maintain his or her lifestyle."[62]

Much of the collective impulse to view and punish these faces springs from the longing for the "sacred suspension of ordinary rules" and a secret admiration of the transgressive—the enduring human fascination with forbidden people, places, and things.[63] For Katherine Biber, the specter is that which returns from a place of repression, a haunting past, which portends a terrifying future.[64] Imagining meth users as spectral figures haunting the boundaries of conventionality is, like zombies, a recurrent device in journalistic accounts of the drug. For instance, the journalist Scott Anderson warns in his book *Shadow People: How Meth-Driven Crime Is Eating at the Heart of Rural America* of an illusory, spectral other, inhabiting the dark recesses of everyday life:

[Shadow people] refers to hallucinogenic figures glimpsed by methamphetamine addicts after days without sleep. But in reality it's the addicts themselves who are living in a shadow, growing in numbers, becoming an alarming subculture on the periphery of rural America, engaging in crimes that are having devastating impact on places where traditional life is valued most. It touches the California Gold Country, even as families venture through summer fairs, walking in drifts of barbecue smoke, carnival lights and the strangely intoxicating fragrance of cheap beer over steer manure. Meth touches the fields of Iowa and Nebraska and the lives of men hauling chisel plows through slow erupting soil, until the sun fires clouds like shining wheat, until high school gymnasiums fill with screaming parents, until pickup trucks sail under water towers basked in the gorgeous light of a dying afternoon. It touches the rows of apartments and mobile homes in northern Georgia, from the seam of the Chattahoochee National Forest to Calhoun, the city where the hardware store leaves its items out overnight without chains, where the Sunday morning sound of church bells can be heard around every brick corner, where "Support our Troops" signs jut proudly up from chic, southern gardens. Meth touches countless shades of the rural dream. Those who live on the original outlands and search for inspiration in the country's past feel its Kaiser blade through felonies, through ongoing acts that continue to eviscerate their communities, cutting them apart, one piece at a time.[65]

Instead of meth-induced hallucinations, Anderson's shadow people are a nascent criminal class, plaguing (meth) lands where "traditional life" is supposedly valued most. Haunting idyllic visions of the rural dream, these spectral others help disavow long-standing concerns for outmigration, job loss, and crushing poverty, reminding yet again of the frail and precarious social and economic position of whiteness and of threatened rural geographies. Today, in times of pronounced social discord and material competition, fissures in the cultural construction race emerge or become more apparent, as they once did in competition between various groups of marginalized labor. Indeed, as the criminologist Colin Webster argues, it is here, in extremis, that the hegemonic force of white ethnicity pushes back to reaffirm its particular shape, profile, and presence.[66] The carefully selected images of the Faces of Meth are not simply representations of an external reality of the largely hidden world of methamphetamine use but rather are an active product that helps produce what is lived, felt, and understood about the present social order. They are both product and producer of the cultural and political dynamics of the methamphetamine and drug-war imaginaries and of unequal social relations. As Phil Carney reminds us, it matters less what a producer intended an image to mean, symbolize, or represent and more what the image does in the real and everyday:

> Not reducible to a representation, the photograph is part of the very stuff of our social life: it presents more than it represents, produces more than it reproduces and performs more than it signifies. In this way, the photographic spectacle cannot be reduced to code, symbol, illustration, wallpaper, scenographic backdrop, distraction, illusion, hallucination or simulation. It is not primarily a semiotic spectacle. It is not a static picture, but a dynamic power. As a social force, the photograph performs in a field where the material realities of cultural practices in the field of power and desire are at stake.[67]

Carney's point is not simply that a particular reality lies somewhere outside an image but that reality and representation blur to the point where reality is image and image is reality. The dynamic force of the image is particularly apparent with mug shots that literally perform the capture of a suspect and articulate the state's power to punish simultaneously. The mug shot is no mere positivistic instrument of identification, then, but a social force with the capacity to affix stigma, shame, and criminality on the body of the accused and the specific identity that the individual is thought to represent.

Just as Faces of Meth fits within the long-standing constellation of antidrug discourses, the project is also part of a much-broader politics of security. That is, the shock and fear generated by projects like Faces of Meth are characteristic of social anxieties and the perpetual disturbance of all social conditions undergirding the securitization of everyday life in liberal, capitalist democracies. Perhaps because of this, the pain of meth use lives on as an object of voyeuristic consumption. Following the success of Faces of Meth, its creators expanded the program to include before-and-after mug shots of heroin and cocaine users, rebranding the project From Drugs to Mugs. Further capitalizing on lurid binary imaginaries of meth-fueled corporeal decay, a California-based design company partnered with law enforcement to develop Face2Face, a computer-aided pedagogical policing program. Excitedly advertising a new system now with "Meth Mouth! (Sale Price: $2,995)," the company claims that the computer-generated simulations "showing the shocking visual changes meth causes are a necessary and powerful tool in the fight against the 'methamphetamine epidemic.'"[68] Certainly these images are painful and disturbing, having the capacity to shock and disrupt the comforting pace and routine of everyday life. Given this, we should ask how these "faces" might force spectators to confront issues they would rather avoid. In *Missing Bodies: The Politics of Visibility*, the sociologists Monica Casper and Lisa Jean Moore argue for an "ocular ethic" that refuses to "assign political value to some bodies at the expense of others, one that treats 'human subjects' in the fullness of their lived, embodied experiences."[69] Instead of seeing these faces as a simple object of punitive voyeurism, might we reimagine, reframe, and refashion them into a counternarrative to the dominant "individual rational" logic of drug use and better attend to the sufferings of inequality and the complexities of personal biography and lived experience? Reading these images differently, then, the very arrangement "before" and "after" poses a subtle challenge to the so-called rehabilitative successes of an ever-expanding retributive and punitive criminal justice system.

By displaying abject carceral subjects getting "worse" and not "better," we might choose to see the images as tangible evidence of the state's brutal indifference toward the most socially vulnerable. As the "face" of the meth epidemic, the program also gives a very human face to the many failures of the drug war. From this vantage, Faces of Meth is a viable and visible site to challenge the dominant governmental and criminal justice discourses claiming an interest in reducing crime and alleviating human suffering. In other words, rather than simply focusing on the poor choices and individual pathologies of a few pained drug users, fleshed out by a crude causal logic, a more empathetic view might concern itself with the structural inequalities that have produced these "faces" in terms of both representation and material lived experience. Ultimately, then, I argue that these images speak less to the specific effects of methamphetamine and more to the ways in which the systematic violence of the current social system is policed through both the physical capture of a body in a jail cell and the subsequent display and circulation of the photographic capture. Yet in these images is the opportunity to infuse contemporary penal spectatorship with an ocular ethic that might more justly recognize the lived experiences of those who are deemed abject and unproductive. For within crime's image lies not only the power to punish but the possibility, dare I say the choice, to see and imagine all that has been cropped away by the classed and racialized visualities of the police power.

As we will soon see, employing elite Hollywood talent, the hotly discussed "Not Even Once" campaign of the Meth Project takes fear appeals to their predictable ends, producing highly visible graphic ads imagining teen meth users, further demonstrating how the methamphetamine imaginary is reproduced, commodified, and consumed.[70]

Methamphetamine: Not Even Once

Late in 2011, a public-service advertisement (PSA) meant to warn young adults of the dangers of binge drinking stirred considerable public contempt. Produced by the state of Pennsylvania's Liquor Control Board, the advertisement featured an image of a young woman's tangled legs on a bathroom floor, underwear around her ankles, and the caption, "she didn't want to do it, but she couldn't say no."[71] Critics claimed that the underlying warning—drink too much and fall victim to rape—placed the onus of sexual assault on victims, rather than the social conditions encouraging binge drinking and violence. Even though the Liquor Control Board defended the PSA and its broader antidrinking campaign, it eventually relented to public pressure and removed the ad from circulation. Reaching at least as far back as the ill-famed 1930s film *Reefer Madness*, "fear appeals" like Pennsylvania's are in no way new. Though well worn, the distinct ideological and technological logics employed by the campaigns offer insight to the shape and direction of contemporary crime control and the constitution of victim, offender, and other. Employing a tactic I describe as *pedagogical policing*, projects such as this intend to deter, in fact scare, spectators into adopting prosocial behaviors. Built on fear, sophisticated advertising techniques, and free-market rationalities, campaigns like Pennsylvania's mark an important intersection of late-modern consumer culture and crime control.[72]

Figure 2.3. The Meth Project's "15 bucks" public-service advertisement.

While some people might see the disparate images featured in the campaign as perpetuating broad social inequalities, others view attempts to shame particular behaviors and stigmatize certain identities as perfectly sound and commonsense acts of deterrence. Despite ongoing contention and a rather large body of contradictory evidence,[73] fear-appeals programs like Faces of Meth remain popular among policy makers and the public alike, particularly in political climates favoring inexpensive, privatized public services.[74] Oddly, however, advocates of these sorts of projects claim to reduce crime and champion the vulnerable, by imagining, producing, and circulating markedly disparate images of crime and victimization. In the case of Pennsylvania's antidrinking campaign, the advertisement seemed to promote victim blaming and in many ways make light of brutal sexual violence.

Like Pennsylvania's campaign, the Montana Meth Project (MMP) and its later iteration the Meth Project (TMP) achieved notoriety because of the shocking tactics used to deter teen meth use. Characterizing itself as a "research-based marketing campaign that realistically and graphically communicates the risks of methamphetamine," TMP expands the fear-driven logics of *Reefer Madness* with graphic images of teen meth users as pimps and prostitutes, who prey on family, friends, and strangers. By paring shocking images with indifferent warnings, like "15 bucks for sex isn't normal. But on meth it is," the project, like Faces of Meth, advances a crude "see what happens if you use meth" causality.

Fear appeals like those employed by Faces of Meth and the Meth Project are problematic not only because they prove only marginally effective but also because they support disparate social imaginaries of crime and victimization. Harnessing the power of the visual, the Meth Project's

public-service announcements help to reproduce a particularly disparate visuality that agitates white middle-class social anxieties through a
meth epidemic unfairly imagined as uniquely white and rural. As such,
the projects battle an epidemic they help imagine, create, and sustain.
Reinforcing self-justifying and ideological penal policies and practices,
what Pat Carlen and her colleagues call *imaginary penalities*, programs
such as these obscure alternatives for harm reduction and meaningful
social change.[75] To begin to contest the ways in which the methamphetamine imaginary is put to work in public policy and crime control, it
is important to take inventory of claims made by groups like the Meth
Project concerning methamphetamine and its alleged social and corporeal corrosiveness. So, for instance, the project defines "Meth in the U.S."
with a number of dubious claims on its website:

> According to the U.S. Department of Justice, methamphetamine is one of
> the greatest drug threats to the nation. In 2011, the agency reported Meth
> is at its highest levels of availability, purity, and lowest cost since 2005
> due to increased supply from Mexico and growing rates of small-scale
> domestic production.
>
> Methamphetamine's effects cost the U.S. between $16.2 and $48.3 bil-
> lion per year. Meth is one of the most addictive substances known and its
> use imposes a significant disproportionate burden on individuals and
> society in money spent on treatment, healthcare, and foster care services,
> as well as the costs of crime and lost productivity.[76]

Though meth appears in the Department of Justice's "drug threat assessment," the TMP's ambiguous problem statement offers little context
as to what actually constitutes "one of the greatest drug threats to the
nation." Similarly, TMP claims the drug has not been more available,
pure, or cheap since 2005, a familiar warning made of other drugs such
as marijuana. Because no citation is provided, we can only assume the
statement is referring to a DEA program called STRIDE (System to
Retrieve Information from Drug Evidence), which is the only program
that collects this sort of data. While STRIDE might support this claim,
TMP fails to include the important disclaimer that the estimates are
"not a representative sample of drugs available in the United States."[77]
Omission of this important caveat bolsters the project's assertions and

helps guide the methamphetamine imaginary along the path of emergency and epidemic. The statement also makes the offhand claim that meth is "one of the most addictive substances known," but as we have seen, independent research and the state's own data offer a different, if not altogether contradictory, picture. Lastly, the problem statement cites a RAND study estimating the "economic costs of meth use in the US."[78] Gathering data from seven separate domains, the study—actually "sponsored" by the Meth Project and the National Institute on Drug Abuse—arrives at wide-ranging estimates, from $16.2 billion per year on the low end to $48.3 billion per year on the high end. Indeed, for journalists and many uncritical readers, fantastic, however imprecise, estimates of "billions" of dollars lost to meth use may be reason enough to support authoritarian drug-control practices. The Meth Project imagines its own reality of the methamphetamine problem and attendant remedies or *imaginary penalities*, thereby obscuring alternatives to its fear-based—"not even once"—prohibitionist frame.

From inception, "Not Even Once," like Faces of Meth, has been championed by conservative firebrands like former "drug czar" John Walters, who called it an "extraordinary example of the results we can achieve when we combine the power of advertising with the dedication and expertise of the leaders of this community."[79] However, like other scare and fear-appeal campaigns, independent empirical evaluations have directly challenged the program's claims of effectiveness.[80] In fact, at least one study found evidence that the advertisements may actually increase the acceptability of meth use and decrease the perceived dangers of using drugs among teens.[81] The stubborn faith in the campaign, despite mounting contradictory evidence, reminds of the much-maligned Drug Abuse Resistance and Education (DARE) program, founded by the equally maligned LAPD chief Daryl Gates. Now in its fourth decade, DARE carries on in stubborn indifference to considerable evidence to its ineffectual and perhaps harmful outcomes.[82] Like DARE, the Meth Project's entire raison d'être rests on a collection of imprecise assumptions about meth use and a misplaced faith in pedagogical policing. Yet I am not so much concerned with refuting the project's claims of effectiveness but instead with how the images themselves may perpetuate or exacerbate long-standing social inequalities. With graphic fear appeals as the centerpiece, the organization advances a very narrow and imaginary view of the causes and consequences of meth use. Despite all this, TMP's national profile grows, with at least eight states having established their own "Meth Projects."

Jeff Ferrell once remarked, "our whole damn world is awash in images, and images of images, and more so every day."[83] Circulating in the cultural ether, images like those under discussion here help structure and are in fact inseparable from the "real" circumstances of crime and punishment. Likewise, as Desmond Manderson puts it, "The 'war against drugs' is a civil war, fought out on the level of image and symbol. At stake is the social meaning to be attributed to images as tangible as the needle, as incorporeal as consciousness and as all-consuming as sex."[84] Indeed, the Meth Project's "gritty" advertisements help fashion a visceral emotionality "as tangible as the needle," standing in for the all the dangers of methamphetamine, real or imagined. The image is not simply a staid representation of a particular point in time and space, and its social force is a product of the viewer's subjectivity and broader ideological structures of the culture from which it emerged. Therefore, rather than viewing these public-service announcements and their particular aesthetic as an approximation or artistic interpretation of social life, the aim is to view them as dynamic, forceful social productions, so that we might better attend to what they do in the real and everyday.

Shortly after the MMP's launch, the editorial "With Scenes of Blood and Pain, Ads Battle Methamphetamine in Montana" appeared in the *New York Times*.[85] Describing how MMP had blanketed radio, television, newspapers, and billboards with advertisements to become the biggest advertiser in the state, the article also quoted the project's founder, Thomas Siebel, touting that "state officials" wanted to make the program a national template to tackle the methamphetamine problem:

Kalispell, Mont., Feb. 18—The camera follows the teenager as she showers for her night out and looks down to discover the drain swirling with blood. She turns and sees her methamphetamine-addicted self cowering below, oozing from scabs she has picked all over her body because the drug made her think there were bugs crawling beneath her skin, and she lets out a scream worthy of "Psycho."

Turn on prime time television here, and chances are this or another commercial like it will interrupt. The spots are part of the Montana Meth

Project, a saturation campaign paid for by Thomas M. Siebel, a software billionaire and part-time resident who fell in love with Montana's vast skies and soaring mountains as a ranch hand in college and now wants to shock the state away from a drug that has ravaged it.

Since it began in September, the project has become the biggest advertiser in the state, blanketing radio, television, newspapers and billboards with advertisements so raw that officials quickly asked that they be removed from television before 7 p.m. Now, with other states expressing interest in the campaign, Mr. Siebel and state officials say they want to make it a national template for halting a problem that has cursed many largely poor, rural states.[86]

In addition to reproducing meth's "largely poor and rural" trope, the piece highlighted the "blood and pain" that would soon make the Montana Meth Project famous. As one of the teens interviewed for the piece described, the advertisements are "like a car wreck, you can't take your eyes off it. . . . It's totally gross, totally graphic, you know it's going to be bad, but all you can do is watch it go down."[87] This observation is crucial, as it captures the project's foundational logic—to shock, scare, and disgust young viewers. To be sure, these "totally gross, totally graphic" images of meth-fueled crime and victimization are no accident. From the project's earliest days, prominent directors and cinematographers responsible for the acclaimed films *American History X*, *Black Swan*, *21 Grams*, and *The Dark Knight* trilogy have taken lead roles in the project.[88] These artists, like their associated films, deliver a dark, "hard hitting," "gritty," "unflinching," however imaginary, aesthetic, that according to Siebel is intended to "stigmatize use, making meth use socially unacceptable."[89] Like Pennsylvania's antidrinking advertisement, to "stigmatize use," TMP has imbued familiar *Reefer Madness* fear appeals with a grotesque and often sexually sadistic aesthetic. Of course, the advertisements could take any form, but by taking this one, they fashion a particular visuality, ordering "how we see, how we are able, allowed, or made to see" the "realities" of meth use.[90]

While clearly crafting the disparate visualities of the methamphetamine imaginary, to resonate with public consciousness beyond knee-jerk visceral response, the advertisements count on a public eager to engage with scenes of crime, victimization, and punishment from a distance—as spectator.

Whether prison tour or public-service advertisement campaign, penal spectatorship allows the public to witness and consume the pain of others, without direct participation in the visceral realities of crime, victimization, and punishment. This is an important consideration, because like Faces of Meth, the project's images forcefully impose the underlying pedagogical mantra "see what you happens if you do meth," in all of its bloody and horrifying detail. Accessing, contemplating, and judging the lives of others through highly stylized advertisements, the project harnesses the "peculiar energy" bound up in the enduring human fixation on the traumatic and grotesque. As Michelle Brown puts it, "much like passing the scene of an accident," the project's advertisements—featuring brutal scenes of victimization, violence, and corporeal decay—rely on the "remarkable amount of collective enthusiasm and energy in this looking, an inability in fact to turn away."[91] Again, as one teen described, "like a car wreck, you can't take your eyes off"; shocking images of "blood and pain" are a defining feature of penal spectatorship and the Meth Project's advertisements.

Admittedly, the project hopes to increase its effectiveness with overtly "disgusting" images of corporeal decay and sexual victimization, what we might call *visualities of disgust*. For TMP, this means coupling graphic warnings of the drug's supposed somatic effects with scenes of drug-fueled crime and victimization. Arguing that "fear" and "disgust" together is a more powerful deterrent than fear alone, marketing researchers recently attempted to quantify and thus legitimize the logics of disgust.[92] Not unlike the RAND study discussed earlier, TMP published the research findings to legitimize its work:

> A new study published in the Journal of Marketing Research has cited the Meth Project's advertising as effective in deterring substance abuse. The new study, by researchers at the W. P. Carey School of Business at Arizona State University, compared different types of advertisements—ads that used only fear tactics to convey their message, ads like the Meth Project's that added an additional element on top of the fear that would disgust target audiences, and ads that were emotionally neutral. The researchers tested the effectiveness of several advertisements—including the Meth Project's—with a group of college students and found that ads that relied on fear alone to convey their message did not lead to immediate changes in attitudes or behavior.

However, according to the study, the Meth Project ads and others that incorporated an element of "disgust," such as rotting teeth, skin sores or infections, did compel viewers to "undertake distancing behaviors," such as deciding not to use illegal drugs.[93]

Clearly meant to provoke the rational self-interest of penal spectators with the reminder "see what happens if you use meth," the project is not a major departure from projects intending to shock and shame onlookers. However, the particular criminological aesthetics and visualities developed and employed provoke social insecurities along very specific race, class, and gender lines. Products of the imaginations of elite film-industry creatives, advertising executives, and the project's billionaire founder, the project's overstated warnings give an imagined "face" to the supposed "white" and "rural" geographies of the United States.

The crude pedagogy undergirding the project exaggerates already starkly gendered distinctions in criminal offending, victimization, and the drug's effects on bodies and families. For instance, many of the advertisements seem to excite a punitive fascination with women and girls who transgress mainstream social conventions. Like the "15 bucks" ad described earlier, many warn that meth users will become victims of sexual crime or be forced into sex work. Importantly, almost all feature young women, as if to suggest that meth use does not lead young men to sex work or sexual victimization. The project imagines a brutal subjectivity, built firmly on seedy sexual vulnerabilities, in which young women exist only by virtue of things being done to them. However, the few ads that do play on the sexual vulnerabilities and insecurities of young men do so from a different vantage altogether. For instance, the ad "Hook-up," featuring a sickly young man and the text "actually, doing meth won't make it easier to hook up," suggests that his sexual virility, not safety, will suffer. Even advertisements that do not feature a character powerfully manipulate sexual insecurities. One such advertisement, "Bathroom," showing a filthy public restroom and the text "No one thinks they'll lose their virginity here. Meth will change that," imagines a horrible turn in adolescent development in which meth use begets sex work or rape in public space.

Another piece, titled "Girlfriend," features both a young man and woman, with the caption, "my girlfriend would do anything for me, so

I made her sell her body." This advertisement clearly advances notions of subordination of women and girls to their meth-using male counterparts. Turned out by opportunistic boyfriends, as the logic goes, young women are invariably transformed by the drug into dispossessed sex workers. Reproduction of these normative practices contributes to highly gendered binary logics of representation, where women are simply victims and men are virulent predators—one visible, the other invisible. In this way, the advertisements follow the logic of gender dualism, in which long-standing discourses of white womanhood offer the privilege and protection of whiteness while simultaneously structuring dependency and subservience to criminal men. Thus, the project's underlying logic, "see what happens if you use meth," reinforces a dualistic logic warning young women that their transgressive behavior begets further abuse by and subordination to the men in their lives.

Importantly, TMP's gendered imaginaries seem to complement a growing collection of meth-specific policies that promise to befall women more harshly than men. States such as Kansas have imposed meth-specific "child-endangerment" laws to punish those who expose children to meth or meth-making materials. While "aggravated child endangerment," a felony, carries an underlying prison sentence and untold collateral consequences, "child endangerment" involving all other drugs such as crack and heroin are treated as misdemeanors and as substantially less serious by definition. Even though the statute is not sex specific, it is not a huge conceptual leap to assume the law will punish women more harshly than men. In fact, there is some evidence to suggest that similar measures have contributed to the noticeable increase in the number of women incarcerated in federal prisons for drug crimes.[94] Imagining a vision of meth use and social life in which women and girls are subordinate to meth-fueled "mad men," the criminological aesthetics of the Meth Project's intervention materials hardly challenge broader binary systems of value.

Playing on corporeal insecurities, the advertisements again follow disparate, particularly gendered cultural logics. For instance, the advertisement "Lipstick," displaying a close-up image of a young girl's disfigured mouth, replete with sores, horribly rotten teeth, and the caption, "You'll never worry about lipstick on your teeth again," powerfully links meth's physical decay to the decay of conventional feminine beauty. Unsurprisingly, advertisements of this sort featuring young men are un-related to beauty and rather describe users digging at skin or chasing illusory "meth bugs" or warn of overdose or death.[95]

It is important to recall that the campaign does not direct its warnings of "meth bugs" and "meth mouth" at the bodies of an anonymous popu-lation but specifically at the bodies of young white users. Given meth's construction as a "white trash" drug, the project effectively and forcefully warns of the decay of white privilege and the precariousness of white so-cial position. While whites are often viewed as raceless or in race-neutral terms, the scars, marks, and sores, inseparable from popular of notions of methamphetamine abuse buttressed by the project, imagine and define a stained, polluted form of whiteness. A powerful racializing practice, the images captivate the voyeuristic middle-class self to further entwine and encode notions of "white trash" into the methamphetamine and drug-war imaginaries. The project's prominent use of the "meth mouth" trope is an-other way it reinforces disparate class distinctions. Recalling Jack Shafer's remarks on meth mouth, the meth zombie and its blackened and bro-ken teeth operate as a master signifier of meth-driven corporeal decay. Importantly, Naomi Murakawa draws critical attention to the intellectual dishonesty of failing to consider other conditions, such as poor nutrition, limited access to health care, and the other drugs that might also contrib-ute to meth mouth.[96] Despite these obvious contradictions, meth mouth endures as a unique diagnosis, a cultural pejorative, and a forceful racial-izing practice. In this way, claims made by the project police gender, race, and class lines simultaneously, marking and naming subjects who have dishonored and transgressed middle-class white sensibilities.

Several advertisements reflect the campaign's recent direction to in-clude family in its warnings rather than only users. As Siebel explains, "Our first campaign focused on the impact Meth has on the individual—the user. . . . For this next phase, we listened closely to our target audience—the teenagers in the state most affected by this epidemic—and used their input to drive our strategy. They wanted us to show the collateral damage that occurs to users' families and friends."[97] So, for instance, an advertisement featuring a young girl's graduation picture with the caption, "Before meth I had a sister, now I have a RUNAWAY," instructs children, parents, family, and friends of the emotional anguish entwined with the drug.

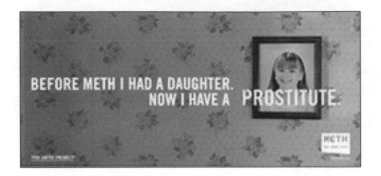

Figure 2.4. The Meth Project's "Prostitute" public-service advertisement.

Given meth's association with white users and rural geographies, the new focus seems intended to agitate concerns for the American "heartland" and "traditional" family. In other words, a "white" drug that leads sons and daughters down the road to violent criminality, prostitution, and rape strikes the heart of the American dream itself—however mythical. Take for example the recent case of Jody Ockert, who, from her small Kansas town, drew the attention of the US media, under headlines like "Grandmother Accused of Selling Meth While Babysitting."[98] Ockert, thirty-six, allegedly sold meth to undercover narcotics officers in her home, while also caring for her two-year-old granddaughter. Of course, the woman's apparent indifference toward her innocent granddaughter is easy for the public to revile. However, it is perhaps Ockert's age that begs spectators to ponder meth's effects on families. The narrative, cobbled together by the stained sexuality of a child-neglecting, meth-dealing, thirty-six-year-old grandmother, characterizes meth's assault on the American family and traditional morality, provoking visceral passions of the most punitive imaginaries.

As in the "Prostitute" advertisement, which somehow evokes a middle-class aesthetic with modest wallpaper and a simple school photo, the Meth Project cautions of an "epidemic" that reaches into the living rooms of working-class families and drags their children off to horrible ends.

Featuring conspicuous violence, the project also draws on and reinforces the specter of volatile and menacing "tweakers" like Tuco Salamanca. For example, the advertisement "Beating," showing two boys rifling through the pockets of a man lying on a dirty floor and with the caption, "Beating an old man for money isn't normal, but on meth it is," warns yet again that the drug makes unpredictable violence a certainty. Perhaps more importantly and unsurprisingly, none of these advertisements includes a woman or girl under the drug's violent spell. It seems that in the project's punitive imagination, only men are capable of violence, thereby relegating women and girls to relational difficulties, wrecked beauty, and sexual victimization. Lastly, each advances the logic of instant addiction, characterized by the trademarked motto "Meth: not even once." Remarkably similar to Nancy Reagan's famous slogan "Just Say No," "not even once" imparts with clarity that meth's ruin ensues after just the first use. Thus, with allusions to the crack epidemic, the Meth Project instructs an anxious public of the emergency it confronts. With warnings of the fragile sexualities of young women and the violent potentials of young men, TMP's crude instructions agitate broader social and cultural anxieties about the state of traditional American family life and the precariousness of white social position, serving only to widen existing social fissures and intraclass contempt.

As with Faces of Meth's humble origins, what began as a privately funded project in one sparsely populated US state is now a nationally visible campaign, with an annual budget of more than $30 million.[99] Despite volumes of research critical of the effectiveness of fear appeals, the Meth Project still proudly advertises its supposed role in significant declines in teen meth use in several states. Indifferent to or perhaps unable to challenge broader social structures that foster drug abuse, violence, and social exclusion, the Meth Project's punitive imaginaries do make useful political fodder. The project's "disgusting" visualities, which can be understood as part Hollywood drama and part marketing campaign, powerfully reveal the entwinements of penal spectatorship and nonstate crime control. Purely a project of the imaginary, the actual deterrent effects of the program are secondary to its ability to capture the attention and gaze of the voyeuristic public. And so to accomplish its goals, the project need not meaningfully reduce meth use; it just has to appear to—or claim to.

***

Images can be powerful, haunting things. Indeed the punitive and market-based image-centered techniques harnessed by Faces of Meth and the Meth Project have power to move us to feel and act in sometimes uncomfortable and surprising ways. My concern is not so much that these projects fail to accomplish the mission of eradicating methamphetamine use or even that they bolster claims of effectiveness in order to legitimize their efforts—indeed criminal justice is littered with such programs. Rather, I take issue with the disparate binary social relations that the projects reproduce and the myth of a runaway "meth epidemic" that they presuppose.

I have argued that the two projects—fusing the police power with the power of the image—are productive of punitive ways of seeing and knowing, whereby the figure of purity, or hegemonic whiteness, is visibly defaced into white trash. In this sense, both projects must be seen as not only cultural (mis)representations but also inherently political projects. Emerging from and influencing the ways in which people imagine their relationship to others and indeed their own existence, projects such as these do little to improve existing social arrangements and, in fact, make things appreciably worse. Built on panicked warnings of the monstrous other, both external and from within—whites versus white trash—Faces of Meth and "Not Even Once" harness the power of the image to police social boundaries and intensify divisive competition in the economic and social realms.[100] That the class interests of the projects' founders (police officer, billionaire real estate magnate) are in keeping with the broader authoritarian and neoliberal doctrines is not lost on me—nor is it coincidence. As such, the projects must be positioned within a broader system of order that expands the deliberate political strategy of endless (drug) war to new spaces and cultural territories and at the interpersonal level instructs citizens of the boundaries of acceptable moral and legal behavior. By developing a critical ocular ethic or *countervisuality*, we open up space for different ways of seeing, knowing, and imaging the pains of meth use and very real human suffering.[101] After all, the American carceral state, with millions behind bars and millions more under the thumb of its vast correctional fields, does "blood and pain" quite well; it has, however, failed to master a comparable degree of restraint and compassion.

As this chapter has looked at two well-known antimeth crime-control projects as important sites of cultural production, where visual cultural helps reproduce disparate racial hierarchies, chapter 3 continues many of these themes, detailing the ways in which the methamphetamine imaginary is implicated in a variety of governing rationalities.

3

Governing through Meth

I predict in the near future that right-wingers will use drug
hysteria as a pretext to set up an international police apparatus.
—William S. Burroughs, in *Drugstore Cowboy*

Writing for the *Washington Post* in late 2014, the columnist Radley Balko
reported on how the state of Nebraska was getting a "lesson that other
states have already learned." Balko drew from an *Omaha World Herald*
article alleging that laws imposed in 2005 to control the methamphetamine precursor pseudoephedrine had effectively erased domestic
"mom-and-pop" methamphetamine production. The lesson as Balko
would have it was that because of the lack of supply, Mexican drug
cartels had set up shop in towns across Nebraska and elsewhere in the
Midwest to accommodate the always-present demand for methamphetamine. The original *World-Herald* report said,

> One of Mexico's most powerful drug cartels is now the main distributor
> of methamphetamine in Nebraska, federal law enforcement officials say.
> The Sinaloa Cartel has built a sophisticated drug-trafficking operation in
> Omaha over the past five to eight years, according to the FBI. Cartels in-
> creased their presence in Nebraska about the same time state officials ef-
> fectively shut down local meth labs through laws limiting the sale of cold
> medicines, U.S. Attorney Deborah Gilg said. Several top Nebraska law en-
> forcement officials say methamphetamine trafficking from Mexico is the
> most serious drug threat to the state, and the problem is slowly growing.[1]

Balko cut his teeth at the Cato Institute, a libertarian think tank co-
founded and funded by the billionaire archconservative Charles Koch,
and he has been a vocal critic of police militarization, which he sees as
a consequence of the drug war. In this particular editorial, he wastes
no time pointing out the unintended consequences of yet another bad

drug-war policy. Not only had precursor restrictions failed to significantly curb the meth trade; they opened up an illicit market for pseudoephedrine, gave rise to "smurfs"[2] and "pill brokers," and paved the way for Mexican cartels into middle America, the same cartels decapitating people south of the boarder—out of the frying pan, into the fire. The only solution as Balko sees it is outright legalization: "Here's one idea that makes too much sense for anyone to seriously consider: Legalize amphetamines for adults. Divert some of the money currently spent on enforcement toward the treatment of addicts. Save the rest. Watch the black markets dry up, and with them the itinerant crime, toxicity and smuggling. Cold and allergy sufferers get relief. Cops can concentrate on other crimes. Pharmacists can go back to being health-care workers, instead of deputized drug cops."[3]

One might wonder why a Koch-funded journalist would advocate such a radical departure from core conservative values. The answer perhaps is that underlying the seemingly progressive gloss of legalization is the mother of all conservative values—making money. Early projections are that marijuana legalization is a boon for state and local economies, with one report suggesting a floor of $30 billion a year if marijuana were legalized nationwide.[4] Of course, any such economic development promises to be unevenly distributed. As Michelle Alexander questioned shortly after Colorado's legalization, "After 40 years of impoverished black kids getting prison time for selling weed, and their families and futures destroyed. Now, white men are planning to get rich doing precisely the same thing?"[5]

Legalization of methamphetamine in the United States would immediately open various markets to private capital and create new markets altogether, as it has with marijuana. Koch Industries, maker and worldwide distributors of chemicals, plastics, and fertilizers, among other things, seems uniquely placed to compete in the "legal meth" market, if such an improbable thing ever materialized. So while it may be that Balko's particular legalization/decriminalization position is sincere, it also promises to dramatically benefit his longtime employer's bottom line and the politics of free-market ideology. All this speculation aside, what Balko's commentary does effectively detail is that methamphetamine and all illicit drugs, for that matter, are useful instruments to introduce other topics and work toward other, sometimes-insidious goals. As the historian Suzanna Reiss has convincingly argued,

The United States government has never waged a war on drugs. On the contrary, drugs in general—and so-called "narcotic" drugs such as cocaine in particular—constitute part of a powerful arsenal that the government flexibly deploys to wage war and to demonstrate its capacity to bring health, peace, and economic prosperity. *Drugs historically have not been targets but rather tools*; the ability to supply, withhold, stockpile and police drugs, and to influence the public conversation about drugs, has been central to projections of US imperial power since the middle of the twentieth century.[6]

While I wholeheartedly agree with Reiss's point here, we should take care not to let nonstate actors and private capital completely off the hook. As a regular contributor to the *Washington Post* and a number of other high-profile media outlets, Balko has the ability to both engage and shape the methamphetamine and drug-war imaginaries. Here he problematizes the methamphetamine imaginary to elaborate how government intervention not only failed to improve the situation but actually made it worse. His solution, legalization, is one that people on both the right and the left share. But for Balko, legalization actually means privatization. And as the proposed legalization would cause "black markets to dry up," methamphetamine and its ingredients would no doubt be traded in private "free markets" already dominated by the Koch brothers and their ilk. In this light, Balko's meth talk is a useful example of the ways in which actors of all kinds engage the cultural force of the methamphetamine imaginary to do political work and effectively *govern through meth*.

The phrase *governing through meth* is a nod to Jonathan Simon's influential *Governing through Crime*.[7] As is Simon's, my concern in this chapter is not necessarily how methamphetamine is policed and controlled but rather how it operates as a conduit of the police and state power. As the epigraph from William S. Burroughs's appearance in the 1989 film *Drugstore Cowboy* suggests, drugs have indeed enabled the police power to extend far beyond the field of crime control. However, an addendum to Burroughs's declaration should be included, as it is not just "right wingers" who have used the methamphetamine and drug-war imaginaries to embolden the police power. In service of state power and private capital, the drug war has always been a bipartisan project.[8]

The practice of governing through meth is less concerned with apprehending, prosecuting, or even punishing lawbreakers and more concerned with representing methamphetamine in order to access and engender fear and insecurity. As this chapter details, meth talkers rhetorically and discursively link it to a broad array of social insecurities ranging from natural disaster and environmental hazards to terrorism. As part of a broader politics of security, antimeth security projects call for increasingly intrusive legislation and coercive policing practices to rein in the "meth heads" thought to plague local communities. These projects draw together a collection of diverse agencies and expert meth talkers who have ideological and material interests in meth control. But in order for antimeth security projects to remain viable both as a vocation and as an object of consumption, insecurities must be continually reimagined, refashioned, and repackaged. As such, the methamphetamine and drug-war imaginaries are constantly revolutionized. As Mark Neocleous writes, "It is through this politics of security that the constant revolutionizing of production and uninterrupted disturbance of capitalist order are fabricated, structured and administered."[9] The continual state of insecurity, over which the politics of security are enacted, is the engine of state power and bedrock on which the state rests.[10]

This chapter takes a detailed look at how the methamphetamine imaginary is at once produced by and at work within the governing practices of state and local governments and the work of nonstate meth talkers. Focusing on 2005, the year that precursor restrictions were established en masse, the chapter details how local politicians and police—by overstating realities of use, politicizing official statistics, and reframing key events—used methamphetamine to accomplish broader political goals, fused methamphetamine with the terror war, and situated it within a broader politics of security.

In 1994, William I. Koch, the brother of Charles and David Koch, founded the Koch Crime Commission in Wichita, Kansas. Koch said that he was moved to begin the project after he and his young son witnessed "gang violence" at a public Fourth of July celebration the previous year. Endorsed by Kansas governor Joan Finney in 1994 and later by her successor Bill Graves in 1995, the commission's stated charge was to understand the causes of crime, particularly youth crime, in Kansas. The issues initially taken up by the commission, youth boot camps, gangs, and private prisons, became hot-button topics in the coming decades. Likewise, the consultants hired by the commission, James Q. Wilson and Charles Murray, were influential conservative figures in American public policy throughout the '80s and '90s. Under a new moniker, the Koch Crime Institute took up methamphetamine as one of its main concerns and launched its "Anti-Meth Site" in 1999, one of the first online resources of its kind. Around that time, the Kansas Department of Health and Environment (KDHE) and the Kansas Bureau of Investigation (KBI) began the innovative Meth Watch program. According to the program's website,

> KDHE and KBI felt an urgent need to curtail drug lab activity by making the theft or purchase of the main precursor, ephedrine and pseudo-ephedrine containing products, more difficult. The Kansas Meth Watch Program was designed by KDHE, KBI, and a team of Kansas retailers to limit the accessibility of these precursors, as well as raise the general awareness of the meth lab problem in Kansas. Kansas retailers selling the ingredients or equipment are encouraged to participate in this important initiative.
>
> If you've noticed the increase in theft or large quantity purchases of ephedrine or pseudoephedrine or other precursor products, your store is likely, and involuntarily, contributing to the deadly meth problem in Kansas. Participating in Meth Watch will decrease theft and the likelihood of "meth cookers" viewing your store as a supplier in their drug production.
>
> The Meth Watch Program has grown in scope from retailers to include farm suppliers, veterinarians, community organizers, drug use prevention organizations, and law enforcement.[11]

Starting in Kansas and since adopted by numerous states and Canada, Meth Watch mimics the rationalities and techniques of Neighborhood Watch by marshaling a coalition of retailers, police, and citizens trained to spot indicators of methamphetamine use and production. Premised on vigilant suspicion, Meth Watch exemplifies neoliberal security strategies by shifting responsibilities and costs to the community and nonstate groups taking up antimeth work as a vocation. Outside of cursory training programs and videos, Meth Watch primarily entails visual products and

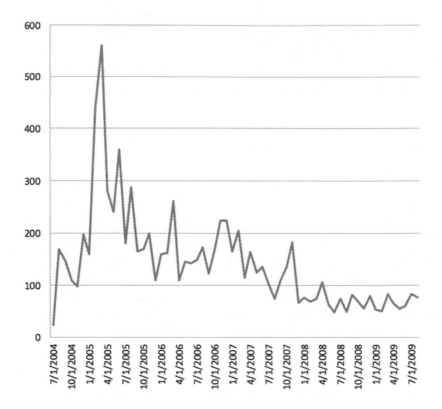

Figure 3.1. The increase in the number of newspaper articles concerning methamphetamine, 2004–2009.

signage—stickers, posters, street signs—warning the public to be on the lookout for suspicious activities that might relate to methamphetamine. That state agencies engineered such a program, enlisting not only police but also merchants, farmers, and citizens of all kinds, reveals the unique profile of the drug's threats, the cultural geographies to which it maps, and the politics it engages. To my knowledge, there are no, nor have there ever been, "crack watch" or "weed watch" programs similarly employed.

By 2003, KCI's antimeth work had morphed into a stand-alone project, the Kansas Methamphetamine Prevention Project (KMPP), which worked closely with and was eventually housed at KBI headquarters in Topeka. This is an important point as it allows us to keep the material and ideological foundations of antimeth work in mind and consider its influence on state agencies such as KBI. That year, KMPP contracted with a private provider to collect and document each mention of methamphetamine made in Kansas newspapers.[12] According to a KMPP administrator, this was done in order to gain a better understanding of the public sentiment around methamphetamine than what could be gathered from basic internet searches. This unique collection of articles provided by the KMPP documents a rather dramatic increase in methamphetamine-related news beginning late 2004.[13]

Newspaper Politics of Methamphetamine

January 2005: Sparking the increased attention on methamphetamine were talks of legislation to restrict pseudoephedrine, a crucial ingredient for mom-and-pop-style meth production. Introducing the preferred technology of control, news reports urged Kansans to follow the lead of neighboring Oklahoma, which passed pseudoephedrine restrictions the year before. Many newspaper articles quoted government officials who warned that failure to pass similar legislation would bring a torrent of meth crimes to Kansas as "meth heads" moved north. Front-page articles with fantastic headlines such as "Meth Makers Flock Here" conjured images of throngs of meth-addled Oklahomans amassed along the state's southern border, linking once-mundane cold medicines to meth heads laying siege on local communities.

This particularly dire warning from Larry Welch, then director of KBI, appeared in many of the articles: "We've tried about everything to fight this plague, from education, prevention, and prison to prayer. I'm pleased with the apparent success those efforts have shown. But in the last few months there have been alarming increases of the reports of Oklahomans coming to Kansas to obtain the precursor chemicals and make methamphetamine here."[14] Descriptions of a "plague" resistant to interventions "from prison to prayer" figure prominently here, sounding the alarm of emergency. Other reports quipped, "It didn't take a genius to anticipate the druggies would move operations into a more friendly state."[15] Again, everyday discourse imagining meth users as invading "druggies" crossing the permeable boundaries of a neighboring state fashions a radical alterity of those who were once friends and neighbors.

Figure 3.2. Police and politicians warn of potential
consequences if the "meth crackdown" bill is not passed.

Not long after these debates began, Kansas governor Kathleen Sebelius delivered the annual State of the State address. Outlining her public-
safety agenda for the coming year, Sebelius named crime, by way of the
"illicit methamphetamine industry," natural disaster, and terrorism as
the principal threats to the health, safety, and security of Kansas:

> Kansas cannot be a truly healthy state unless it is both safe and secure.
> All our citizens must feel safe from crime and secure from the threat of
> terrorism, and feel protected from the natural disasters that have demon-
> strated their power, both here and around the world, over the past year.

Effective protection from terrorism and natural disasters requires the best possible communication among a wide range of government agencies. Using Homeland Security funds, we are well on our way to making sure that first responders—police, fire, and other emergency personnel—can talk directly with each other and can coordinate early warnings, searches, rescues, and relief efforts.

As for crimes that affect all Kansans, nothing is more important than stopping the illicit methamphetamine industry in its tracks. Working with the Kansas Bureau of Investigation, the Kansas Highway Patrol, and the Attorney General, I have charged a task force with developing legislation, and I am pleased that some lawmakers have already embraced this idea by pre-filing a bill on the subject. We simply must make it more difficult for meth producers to obtain the chemicals that they use to concoct their deadly drugs. Oklahoma has already enacted a law that does just this, and I feel confident that we will have strong, effective laws in place by mid-year.[16]

What Governor Sebelius failed to mention was that the "illicit methamphetamine industry," as indicated even by the erroneous seized-labs measure, had declined each year from its peak of 425 in 2001 to 191 in 2004, placing Kansas far behind neighboring Missouri (1,115), Iowa (478), and Oklahoma (427).[17] Nevertheless, Sebelius named meth her criminal justice priority, ahead of sex offenders, criminal street gangs, and other familiar folk devils. Even more important, however, is Sebelius's odd triptych of meth, terrorism, and natural disaster. To be sure, the "illicit meth industry" is first and foremost an issue for police. However, meth's geographies and production methods make it more mutable than other drugs typically within the remit of the police power. For instance, around this time, Kansas state senator Jerry Moran introduced the Clean, Learn, Educate, Abolish, Neutralize and Undermine Production Act (CLEAN-UP) to target meth's environmental risks. Here we can see that along with the usual projects of criminalization and control, meth draws in special teams to clean up labs, medical and child-welfare specialists, and even realtors to deal with homes where labs are found.

Similarly, by placing the "illicit methamphetamine industry" on equal footing with natural disasters such as Hurricane Katrina and the horrors of September 11, 2001, Sebelius maps a singular logic—threat. *Drug control merges with disaster preparedness and antiterror projects.* Or perhaps more to the point, these seemingly disparate projects are shown to be structured by the same logics and animated by the same power. Like these other two security fields, meth-control efforts, particularly those focusing on controlling "precursors," employ precrime, risk-reduction, and securitization strategies aiming to eliminate meth crimes before they occur. With this, Sebelius alludes to an assemblage of local "police, fire, and other emergency personnel," all funded by "Homeland Security" and charged with "early warnings, searches, rescues, and relief efforts." Homeland *security* indeed. Immediately following the governor's public-safety plans were her remarks on military personnel and related legislation:

> In large part, we in Kansas are secure because of the immense sacrifices of our military. Sixteen Kansans have made the ultimate sacrifice in Iraq and Afghanistan. . . . I join with all Kansans in expressing our grief over these most profound losses, as well as those suffered by the families of the 42 Fort Riley soldiers who have lost their lives. . . .
>
> But wishing our Kansas soldiers "God speed" is not enough. We need to comfort, care for, and protect their families. And we should ease the financial burdens that these families often face. That is why later this month I will propose a Military Bill of Rights for Kansans who serve. This important legislation will offer financial assistance to state employees called to duty, address broader financial issues for all Kansans who serve, and create a relief fund for military families. Those who serve abroad honor us at home by defending the very democratic values that have made this state and this nation great.[18]

In Sebelius's remarks on military personnel, we can see the economic dimension of her security project. Ironically, the proposed legislation aims to ensure financial security for military personnel and their families to honor the "immense sacrifices" made in the "war on terror," sacrifices made for security. Of course, the provision of economic security presupposes some degree of insecurity. But it is important to be clear that in this relationship, security is not simply the binary opposite of insecurity but rather a governing practice that markets new security mechanisms and broadens state power. For instance, Neocleous traces the roots of national security to Franklin Delano Roosevelt's New Deal programs, which helped "cultivate the idea of 'economic security' and popularize the new means by which such security could be achieved: through social, political and cultural reconstruction engineered by the state."[19] The New Deal programs were not simply state benevolence but part of a broader strategy to engineer and structure capital markets and to pacify unruly and potentially explosive populations. Not only does Sebelius's proposed legislation follow the particular logics of economic and social security; it suggests not only that honoring the sacrifices of military personnel is proper but that failure to do so may in fact weaken homeland security.

The legislation that Sebelius hoped would "stop the illicit methamphetamine industry in its tracks" was introduced in early January by Kansas senate majority leader Derek Schmidt. Although precursor restrictions had proven only marginally effective in other states, Kansas's leaders put their antimeth eggs in one basket: Senate Bill 27, or the "meth crackdown" bill.[20]

In a newspaper article with the headline "Schmidt Proposes Anti-Methamphetamine Bill," Schmidt described how he and others had "worked very closely with law enforcement agencies across Kansas to identify a bottleneck in the meth production process" and were "working to choke it off."[21] Early on, however, news media reported that the legislation stalled, with Schmidt scolding, "these folks need to have the courage to say that the convenience of a chain pharmacy outweighs the safety of Kansans."[22] Employing all-too-familiar "with us or against us" rhetoric, Schmidt belittled opposition to the bill as a matter of simple convenience, preferred over the "safety of Kansans," strengthening the link between precursor restrictions and questions of safety and security. Kyle Smith of KBI also weighed in, stating, "the sooner we can get the Oklahoma approach in place the sooner we can we can cut down on the problem and the safer Kansas will be."[23]

January 19, 2005: Despite the relative complexity of the issues, debates over the bill proved short-lived following the murder of Greenwood County sheriff Matt Samuels. Initial coverage stated that "Samuels was shot around 10 a.m. Wednesday while he was serving a search warrant at a home and an arrest warrant for a man wanted on burglary and theft charges and for violating parole."[24] This is correct. Samuels was attempting to serve arrest warrants for twenty-three-year-old Scott

Cheever, who was wanted by local police for stealing his parents' vehicle and violating probation. By accounts, Samuels went into the home alone and without his bulletproof vest to try to convince Cheever to surrender. Cheever then shot Samuels, killing him at the scene. Though it was later learned that Cheever planned to cook and was in fact under the influence of methamphetamine, it is very important to acknowledge that police did not seek Cheever or anyone else at the scene for crimes related to methamphetamine.

Just a short time later, the media consensus was that Samuels "was shot to death while serving warrants at a suspected methamphetamine lab in a rural home near Virgil."[25] Though police later found meth-making materials in the home, it is a linguistic sleight of hand and in fact quite dishonest to describe the circumstances of Samuels's death in this way. To be sure, had the home been "a suspected methamphetamine lab" at the time, police would have secured additional warrants, and when entering the home, Samuels would have most certainly had backup and worn additional protective equipment.

Of course, the murder of a respected sheriff at the hands of a meth user immediately untangled the complexities of the precursor-restriction debate. Newspapers across the state ran stories with headlines like "Sheriff Gunned Down," echoing the lawlessness of the Old West frontier. And though just two weeks earlier politicians of both parties voiced serious reservations about the proposed "meth crackdown" bill, the discussion ceased and turned toward victims like Samuels who powerfully signified the violent realities of the "meth epidemic." With the realization among rural Kansans that criminals in their towns murder police as well, Samuels's death brought the depravity of big-city crime to them too. Here, in this unique context, methamphetamine becomes emblematic of the state's inability to protect its citizens from the violence and insecurity of late-capitalist life. Which is to say, if police are unable to protect themselves, then they are perhaps even less likely to protect the public. The murder of a police officer, that great reminder of the state's mortality and impotence, sets the stage for the continued expansion and fortification of the police power. Later, speaking at Samuels's funeral, Sebelius articulated what Jonathan Simon calls the broad grammar for recognizing and rewarding the victims of violent crime.[26] Echoing her position on the Military Bill of Rights, Sebelius

Figure 3.3. Communities respond to the murder of
Sheriff Samuels.

pleaded, "We owe them a debt that cannot be repaid, but one of the best
ways to keep Samuels's memory alive is to recognize daily the sacrifices
made by the men and women of the law enforcement community. We
must support them and their families. We do that by giving them good
training and good salaries and by passing laws that give them the tools
to do their job."[27] For Sebelius, honoring Samuels and other fallen police

officers is again infused with the logics of security. In this instance, she aims to secure more training, more money, more authority, and more equipment—in other words, criminal justice expansion en masse. Lost in this sort of plea is any critical reflection of how aggressive drug-war tactics may have contributed to this and countless other deaths. Without critical reflection, such honoring begs the bureaucratic machinery that contributed to Samuels's murder, the same machinery that will deliver Cheever's punishment, to carry on uncontested. Writing about road-side shrines erected in honor of by-standers killed in high-speed police chases, Jeff Ferrell makes a similar critique of the unflinching willingness to incur any cost in blind furtherance of the drug war. In these instances, as Ferrell aptly puts it, *speed kills*.[28] As history now shows, Kansas's meth war was in fact just getting up to speed.

February 2005: Following Samuels's funeral, local media reported with some dismay that for the first time in a decade, Kansas had dropped from the "top 10 list" of seized meth labs. These reports met immediate ridicule from Special Agent Kyle Smith of the Kansas Bureau of Investigation, who cited poor record keeping as explanation for the drop.[29] "We have to get better stats," he said, warning that the KBI "didn't want to lean on them [small departments] unless it begins to hurt funding."[30] It is important to emphasize that the KBI offered only faulty record keeping as an explanation for the drop, not actual changes in meth production or consumption. Shortly thereafter, under the headline "Shame on Us!," local writers offered a retraction explaining that they ran reports of the drop as the "lead story on page 1, because it was a very slow news week."[31] The anonymous retraction neatly illustrates how the predictability of the yearly "lab data" and meth's more general newsworthiness make a useful placeholder for local journalists, especially during a "very slow news week." The retraction also usefully reveals the sway local police agencies hold over small-town reporters, as the lack of accurate record keeping was quickly adopted as the reason for the decline in the number of labs discovered.

Less than a month after the murder of Sheriff Samuels, representatives of the people of Kansas unanimously passed the "meth crackdown" bill. Again following the lead of Oklahoma, which named its law after fallen officers, Kansas renamed its bill the "Matt Samuels Chemical Control Act." The law required that all medications containing pseudo-ephedrine be sold by licensed pharmacists, limited how much a single person could purchase, and required customers to be at least eighteen years old and to provide valid identification and a signature in order to discourage smurfing. As the excerpt from an *Emporia Gazette* article describes, Samuels's death made the bill "impossible to vote against": "A few weeks ago the bill was limping along now it's zooming along, what happened? Unfortunately the death of Matt Samuels is what happened and it's the last straw for many people in Kansas who have watched the growth of the meth trade with fear and despair."[32] Acknowledging the significance of Samuels's murder, the author attributes passage of the act to the "fear and despair" of the "meth trade." The comment again illustrates the force and effect of the methamphetamine imaginary and the expediency of governing through meth. Whether methamphetamine was the cause of Samuels's death matters little because for the people of Kansas, a *meth war rages*. As the official record of the vote shows, Schmidt did little to add nuance to the debate or assuage public fears:

Mr. Vice President: I vote aye on SB 27. This measure will choke off easy access to ephedrine and pseudoephedrine tablets. It is a necessary step to combat methamphetamine production—with all of its enormous social, health, and economic costs. This measure also acknowledges that the meth problem evolves over time, and it puts in place an ongoing process to monitor trends in meth production, to identify opportunities to stem those trends, and to recommend specific steps future legislatures may take to seize those opportunities. The Senate also saw fit in this bill to rename the Chemical Control Act as the Sheriff Matt Samuels Chemical Control Act. This step honors the memory of the late Greenwood County Sheriff who was murdered while serving an arrest warrant at a suspected methamphetamine laboratory. That crime took place just before 10 a.m. on January 19, 2005—the same time the Senate Judiciary Committee was beginning deliberations on SB 27. My hope is that when historians someday record the story of the methamphetamine scourge Kansas faced during the early years of the 21st century, they will credit passage of the Samuels Act with helping consign that story to history.[33]

More fantastically heroic than true, Schmidt's account emboldens the narrative of a monstrous "scourge" consigned to history through the diligence of politicians and police. Etching the distorted account on the official record of the Kansas legislature, the statement nurtured Schmidt's drug-warrior bona fides as avenger of innocent victims and fallen heroes. However resolute he seemed at the time, just after the signing, Schmidt was apparently less certain, warning, "This isn't a magic bullet that will make meth go away, but it should put a major dent in meth production in Kansas." The push-and-pull narrative Schmidt offers, one of marginal successes amid rising dangers, keeps rhetorical doors open for continued battles and perpetual war. Applied layer after layer, these discursive gestures, however subtle and understated, fashion the methamphetamine imaginary and lived realities of the drug war in new social contexts. Running statewide as the session ended was coverage of legislative accomplishments—sex predators, health care, abortion, death penalty, gun rights, and child pornography—which read like a laundry list of culture-war wedge issues. Yet despite their perennial newsworthiness, Schmidt named his antimeth legislation "one of the great accomplishments of this legislative session."[34]

Implemented July 1, the Matt Samuels Act was already being declared a success by police and politicians by early September. According to Smith of the KBI, "We are seeing a distinct drop as the law goes into effect. . . . Before you could go down to your smoke shop or truck stop and buy it by the case. There was no restriction on it."[35] Of course, it is highly problematic to claim success of any measure such as this less than two months after implementation. Nevertheless, speaking on behalf of the KBI, Smith claimed "drops [of] 64 percent since new law took effect" as evidence of the law's effectiveness, despite nearly four years of precipitous decline in the number of seized labs.[36] Here it is also important to recall that just a few months prior, Smith and others with the KBI disputed a decline in meth labs, citing the inherent flaws in these very data. Now, despite their previous and very public objections, Smith and others pointed to declining lab seizures as evidence of the legislation's success and the legitimacy of their work.

Throughout the year, coverage of Cheever's prosecution described him as both a meth-fueled killer and a victim of the drug. Headlines like "Accused Sheriff Killer Has Checkered Past" and "Meth Addiction Plagued Accused Killer" reflect this odd duality. Drawing on his biography, Cheever's mother pleaded, "Scott didn't do this, Meth did, he's not a murderer, if it wasn't for Meth I know he wouldn't have done it."[37]

Figure 3.4. Murderer and murdered entwined.

Echoing the assertions of Cheever's mother, local news media published numerous articles telling of a typical small-town boy, involved in sports and his community, until he became tangled up with the monster methamphetamine. A local paper described, "He took a job working on oil-rigs, . . . and he became hooked on crystal meth. He even actually owed so much money to a dealer, that he tried to rob the Johnson's General Store in Eureka on May 24, 2000."[38]

Still, the family hoped that Cheever's time in prison would "shake him up enough," and though his mother pleaded with him to avoid his old friends and the "drug culture" after his release, Scott bragged that "he had learned seven different ways to make crank" in prison.[39] From a lean working-class childhood to "using drugs, disobeying, lying and stealing" and then to prison, Cheever's story reaches a sad yet familiar conclusion. The underside of Cheever's monstrous representation is of course Samuels. That these two very different lives—trusted family man, troubled delinquent—met the same fate reminds that none are safe from the monster methamphetamine. As the claim "Scott didn't do this, meth did" suggests, the drug is cause and effect, beginning and end.

As the year came to a close, Kansas news media began to report that crack cocaine had replaced methamphetamine as the "drug of choice" in the state. As one police officer quoted in the coverage reasoned, "We were spending so much time on meth, we didn't have as much time to devote to other cases. Now we're beginning to devote more resources to crack."[40] Growing from a single article, the idea of "crack replacing meth" ran in newspapers statewide, recast under headlines like "Crack More Prominent in Kansas" and "Crack Outpacing Meth in Kansas," mapping dubious assertions onto the entire state. Another officer's comments, "We're just lucky we don't have the heroin cycle in there, like some larger areas do," perfectly illustrate the cyclical nature of social insecurity. Because of the overemphasis on methamphetamine, an escalating crack-cocaine epidemic fills the void. From the vantage of an uncritical public, the drug war is a game of Whac-A-Mole, in which police barely keep pace with new threats as they emerge.

Finally, late in 2005, part of the Patriot Act, fittingly named the Combat Methamphetamine Epidemic Act, imposed pseudoephedrine restrictions as federal law. This is not to say that meth-control efforts in the state ceased or even receded from view. On the contrary, the issues surrounding the drug were taken up effortlessly by subsequent administrations. In 2007, a new state attorney general reinvigorated meth's specter with Janus-faced warnings of the raging battle. Speaking of the continued decline of meth labs, Paul Morrison urged, "Despite this great accomplishment, there is still much work to be done to stop the importation and manufacturing of meth and the damage it does to our communities. We cracked down on one source of meth, but we can't ignore the other sources. For the sake of Kansas families and children, we must put a stop to the production, importation and addiction of meth."[41] While sure to claim credit for keeping Kansans safe, Morrison is also certain to remind his constituents that the drug war rages. As he sees it, if any opportunity exists for families or children to ever use meth, then more material and ideological "work" should be done. Here is where the crisis maintains.

In 2010, as a candidate for attorney general, Derek Schmidt had opportunity to cash in on the drug-warrior bona fides he had built as the public face of the "meth crackdown" and the Matt Samuels Chemical Control Act. As his campaign website claimed, "In the Senate, Schmidt led the charge against meth labs, child pornography, human trafficking and Medicaid fraud. He also was the lead Senate sponsor of Jessica's Law, which puts violent child molesters in prison for life."[42] Proving meth's political expediency, Schmidt featured his supposed "charge against meth labs" throughout his successful bid for attorney general. And since assuming office, Schmidt has continued the charge, evidenced by his plans for a "new electronic weapon in the war on meth": "Keeping pseudoephedrine out of the hands of meth producers is one of the most effective ways to stop meth production. . . . This new electronic system strengthens our ability to do that on an instant basis, and will serve as a valuable tool in finding and shutting down meth labs."[43]

Schmidt has also mandated that the prosecution of all major meth-related cases in the state go through his office. So rather than prosecuting offenders locally, Smith's office claims jurisdiction and assigns special prosecutors to each meth case. Upon conviction, his office issues a press release announcing the punishment, and at the end of each year, he revisits the number of people his office has sent to prison. Through press-release bulletins announcing "Independence man sentenced to 6 years for manufacturing meth" and "AG's Office sends 35 to prison for meth in 2012," Schmidt nurtures the methamphetamine imaginary, his drug-warrior credentials, and the power of his office.[44]

In 2005, methamphetamine also delivered on promises of funding, as Kansas was one of just a handful of states awarded a grant from the Rural Law Enforcement Meth Initiative (RLEMI) of the economic stimulus. As part of the RLEMI, leaders developed a strategic plan with several goals to reduce meth use and production. Of the goals, which included improving access and accuracy of data, securing funding for police and treatment providers, increasing access to drug-abuse treatment, promoting policies to reduce methamphetamine production, and increasing capacity to serve drug-endangered children, goal number 5, "Increase public awareness and professional knowledge about methamphetamine," is particularly important here:

Over the last five years Kansas has experienced a dramatic reduction in meth lab seizures. However, law enforcement continues to be assailed by problems related to meth importation and drug trafficking networks. The decrease in lab activity has led some community members and policy makers to conclude that the problems caused by meth in Kansas have also dwindled. *If the public perceives the meth problem in Kansas to be "solved," it will be difficult to solicit necessary support for funding requests, increased treatment resources, and prevention strategies.*

Ongoing awareness efforts are necessary to ensure that the public perception of the meth problem in Kansas is accurate. As new and dangerous meth manufacturing methods, such as the "one-pot method," become increasingly prevalent in rural areas of the state, community members and professionals must be informed of these emerging trends. Educational opportunities for professionals must be readily available. Law enforcement efforts to address meth, especially in rural communities, are strengthened when retailers report sales of suspicious items, social service providers identify families affected by meth, and prosecutors effectively prosecute meth cases.[45]

In very clear language, the plan's authors reveal their vested interest in the methamphetamine imaginary—money and funding. "Ongoing awareness efforts" take the shape of "Office of National Drug Control Policy meth public service announcements" to be broadcast "in multiple media markets across the state," implementation of the proprietary "Meth 360 curriculum" in several rural communities, and funding "educational opportunities" for intervention workers. As will be described later, these antimeth projects, which began in the late 1990s and received a considerable boost in 2005, laid the groundwork for subsequent iterations of antimeth and drug-control security projects, which continue today.

Despite meth being among the least common illicit street drugs in the United States, the reimaging and revolution of antimeth projects continues. For instance, after federal legislation effectively ended arguments over precursor restrictions, Oregon and Mississippi upped the ante, becoming the first states to make pseudoephedrine available only through prescription. In 2011, the small city of Parsons, Kansas, followed suit, making it a criminal offense to possess pseudoephedrine without a prescription. Insisting the measure's necessity to combat the "local meth epidemic," the local police chief remarked, "we know this ordinance won't cure the problem, however it will send the message to smurfers and meth heads that they are not welcome in Parsons."[46] Though the penalties were equal to those for marijuana possession, the city's attorney downplayed the law, speculating that violators would "probably be fined anywhere from $125 to $200 and be given a 30 day suspended jail sentence with unsupervised probation."[47] In the case of a security measure with limited legal and geographic scope, the "the message" to which the police chief refers is meant for the community rather than the "pill smurfers" and "meth heads" it supposedly targets. The law's impotence, acknowledged by both police and prosecutor, shows antimeth projects such as this to be patently ideological gestures, not sincere attempts to ameliorate suffering. Kansas also revised its child-endangerment laws to address meth specifically. However, the new "aggravated endangerment of a child" statute left "endangerment" from all other drugs including heroin and crack misdemeanors and substantively less serious by definition.[48] Crimes against children like this one exclude the convicted from certain jobs and require compliance with child-abuse registries. Echoing long after the sentence expires, this sort of measure exposes impassioned desires to distinguish and separate meth users from the community and even from other types of drug users. Along these lines, the state also added "violent" and "drug" offenders to its compulsory sex-offender website. Predictably, only those who are convicted of manufacturing drugs and those who are found in violation of pseudoephedrine-control laws are required to register as drug offenders.[49] Set aside for special punishments, meth users are positioned by these security projects further outside the law and bourgeois social convention. Yet there are powerful emotions bound up in the projects, reflecting an interest not only to be secure from the threats of methamphetamine but to punish those who are deemed responsible. This notion is forcefully detailed in an editorial published June 9, 2005, by the *Madison News*, a small-town Kansas paper:

> Editorial: Thursday was an Aha! Moment for those of us on the Greenwood County Citizens Drug Task Force. County Attorney Ross McIlvain was present at the meeting to shed light on a rather dim subject: Kansas Sentencing Guidelines.
>
> At the meeting at Hamilton Elementary School, McIlvain brought copies of the guidelines and explained the penalties for not only drug

offenders but other felons. Things suddenly became perfectly clear for all of us: Being arrested on methamphetamine charges in Kansas is a slap on the wrist! Criminals know it. Law enforcement officers know it. Attorneys know it. Prosecutors know it! And guess what? Law makers know it because they approved it!

The guidelines are mapped out in a grid of boxes and every crime has to fit in a little box. That box determines the number of months that the criminal will serve in jail or on probation. We were horrified to learn that thanks to the loose sentencing guidelines our state has adopted, it is practically impossible to send drug offenders to jail because they are not violent criminals. Tell that to the Samuels family. Not only have we learned firsthand that meth users are indeed violent, they drain the system with the plethora of criminal activity that ruins in their wake. Burglary, theft, domestic violence and child abuse only to name a few.

These guidelines have made it absolutely pointless for the Greenwood County Sheriff's department to snag the drug users and meth makers in this county because once the jailer slams the cell door, he's pulling out the key to unlock it again. As one local farmer put it: "It's like spending the day bailing hay and putting it in the barn. Then getting up the next morning, cutting the wire, spreading out the hay in the field and doing it all over again the next day."

There is absolutely no incentive for the deadbeat to stop what he or she is doing because the penalty never gets any worse. Over the past few months we have had reason to question how our methamphetamine problem has gotten so far out of control in this county. We've heard the rantings all over the county. "Why wasn't Scott Cheever in jail?!" The blame has been shifted from law enforcement, to prosecution, to the judge, to the defense attorney, etc. The reason that Scott Cheever and all the other drug users are not in jail is because they didn't fit into the right "little box" on the sentencing grid.

Technically, Cheever didn't use a gun when he robbed the convenience store in Eureka several years ago, which was his big offense. Therefore categorizing him as a non-violent criminal. Despite the fact that the man who was injured in the robbery said that he feared for his life, the judge couldn't be any more harsh during sentencing than he could be with any other common robber. Judges now are bound to that sentencing grid. Sentencing used to be up to the discretion of the judge. Not anymore.

So where did these sentencing guidelines come from? The senate bill that approved the use of the sentencing grid was the brainchild of Sen. David Adkins and was passed in 1999. Rep. Peggy Mast was present at the task force meeting on Thursday night and she expressed how she was adamantly opposed to this bill and its approval. She has promised the citizens of Greenwood County that law enforcement is priority to her and she will make this her top priority in the new legislative year.

If you would like more information about how the sentencing grid works, you can contact the Kansas Sentencing Commission at Jayhawk Tower, 700 SW Jackson Street, Suite 501, Topeka, Ks. 66603, 785–296–0923. This newspaper and members of the task force would like to thank Ross for attending our meeting and clarifying where some problems are and how we can work to change them. We won't stop until things change.[50]

Borrowing a local farmer's metaphor, the author fixes a uniquely rural veneer to the old revolving-door trope of American criminal justice. As one can imagine, residents of Greenwood County were angry and out-raged at a system that appeared to have failed to deal with Scott Cheever before he could murder Sheriff Samuels. And while the author's view of the criminal justice system as dysfunctional and lenient is not unique to Kansas or this particular point in history, the editorial does provide an opportunity to talk through how punishment plays out in the meth-amphetamine imaginary, for indeed, many of the assertions made here are based not so much on fact but on fantasy. On the basis of the 2005 Kansas sentencing guidelines, a person arrested for simple possession of less than a gram of methamphetamine would face anywhere from ten to twelve months in prison, provided this person had no more than one previous misdemeanor conviction. In such a case, it is quite likely that a judge would have granted a suspended sentence and an assignment to intensive probation for eighteen months or more. With a single personal felony, the person would forgo probation and instead face incarcera-tion for a term ranging from twenty-three to twenty-six months. So, in the context of the actual 2005 sentencing guidelines, I suppose the idea that being convicted of methamphetamine charges in Kansas was nothing but a "slap on the wrist" really depends on just what that means. Working as an intensive probation officer in Kansas at this time as I did and knowing the practices of the criminal justice system as I do, I see an underlying prison sentence of no less than ten months for a first-offense simple possession equal to half the weight of a common sugar packet as anything but a slap on the wrist. To be sure, the incessant meetings, drug tests, and surprise employment and home visits of a typical probation sentence are no treat, say nothing of the constant threat of imprisonment if one fails to comply. Whatever the case may be, it is not now, nor was it then, as the editorial suggests, "practically impossible" to send meth offenders to prison. This becomes all the more apparent when considering the sentences that Kansas assigned for manufacturing the drug. In 2005, a person convicted of such a crime, even if he or she had never been arrested before, would face a prison sentence ranging from 138 to 154 months. Put another way, regardless of the scale of the operation—small batches or industrial "super labs"—once convicted, a person would face confinement of no less than a decade, regardless of his or her prior behavior.

In 2014, nearly a decade after Samuels's murder, not much had changed. Though like other states, Kansas struggled with prison overcrowding, it had actually increased punishments for meth users, dealers, and producers from its 2005 standards. For first-time offenders, not only had underlying prison sentences increased by four months, but judges were also encouraged to sentence probationers to a new rehabilitation program that integrated detoxification, drug education, outpatient and inpatient treatment, and relapse-prevention programs within existing community corrections programs. While these measures were initially framed and received as a progressive step toward decarceration of nonviolent, first-time drug offenders, three years after implementation, evaluators concluded the program; SB123 had not only failed to meet its goal of decarceration but had actually pushed more low-level drug offenders from lesser forms of community supervision to intensive probation and community corrections programs.[51] Similar to critiques of drug courts, evaluators found that SB123 effectively "net-widened" the Kansas criminal justice system, enhancing punishments for low-level drug offenders under the guise of treatment and decarceration.[52] Compared to manufacture and distribution of all drugs, methamphetamine remained more serious in the eyes of the state. In 2014, manufacture of meth still carried a sentencing range of 138 to 154 months for first-time offenders, while the penalties for cocaine were set at 92 to 103 months. While the cutoff for simple possession of methamphetamine remained one gram or less, the standards for simple possession of cocaine and marijuana were three and a half grams and twenty-five grams, respectively. On the more serious end of the scale, a first-time offender convicted of possession with intent to distribute a kilogram or more of cocaine would face a prison sentence of 138 to 154 months, while just one hundred grams of methamphetamine would garner the same sentence. On the basis of the state's standards for distribution, one can reasonably conclude that Kansas sees methamphetamine as ten times more serious than its counterpart cocaine. And in no small irony, it seems as though the state has fabricated its own version of the notorious "100 to 1" powder-to-crack-cocaine sentencing disparity of the federal sentencing guidelines.

The small swath of the history of one midwestern state detailed here maps an important period in the methamphetamine imaginary and the local politics of the drug war, but it would be a mistake to confine these politics to the local. Because methamphetamine has been imagined as a distinctly white and rural problem, these antimeth projects animate manifold criminalizations and securitizations in new social and cultural spaces. However, security from "meth heads" is in many ways the same as security from "global jihadists"; it is only the context that changes. Important to consider is how small-town meth users and producers fit within what Simon Hallsworth and John Lea have called an entire enemy population or what the Department of Homeland Security imagines as its "universal adversary."[53]

Powerfully illustrating the ubiquity and universality of the drug-war/terror-war enemy Other is George W. Bush's signing statement attached to the Combat Methamphetamine Epidemic Act, which was passed as part of the reauthorization of the USA Patriot Act. Here Bush argues that the controversial and invasive legislation is needed for the ongoing battle fought against "international terrorists" and "local drug dealers" alike:

> This is a really important piece of legislation. It is a piece of legislation that's vital to win the war on terror and to protect the American people. The law allows our intelligence and law enforcement officials to continue to share information. It allows them to continue to use tools against terrorists that they use against drug dealers and other criminals. It will im-

prove our nation's security while we safeguard the civil liberties of our people. The legislation strengthens the Justice Department so it can better detect and disrupt terrorist threats. And the bill gives law enforcement new tools to combat threats to our citizens, from *international terrorists to local drug dealers.*

As we wage the war on terror overseas, we're also going after the terrorists here at home. And one of the most important tools we have used to protect the American people is the Patriot Act. The Patriot Act closed dangerous gaps in America's law enforcement and intelligence capabilities, gaps the terrorists exploited when they attacked us on September 11th. The Patriot Act was passed with overwhelming bipartisan support. It strengthened our national security in two important ways.

First, it authorized law enforcement and intelligence officers to share vital information.

Before the Patriot Act, criminal investigators were often separated from intelligence officers by a legal and bureaucratic wall. The Patriot Act tore down the wall. And as a result, law enforcement and intelligence officers are sharing information, working together and bringing terrorists to justice.

Secondly, the Patriot Act has allowed agents to pursue terrorists with the same tools they use against other criminals. Before the Patriot Act, it was easier to track the phone contacts of a drug dealer than the phone contacts of an enemy operative. Before the Patriot Act, it was easier to get the credit card receipts of a tax cheater than trace the financial support of an Al Qaida fundraiser.

The Patriot Act corrected these double standards and the United States is safer as a result.

Over the past four years, America's law enforcement and intelligence personnel have proved that the Patriot Act works. Federal, state and local law enforcement have used the Patriot Act to break up terror cells in Ohio, New York, Oregon and Virginia. We've prosecuted terrorist operatives and supporters in California and Texas, New Jersey, Illinois, Washington and North Carolina. The Patriot Act has accomplished exactly what it was designed to do. It has helped us detect terror cells, disrupt terrorist plots and save American lives.

The bill I sign today extends these vital provisions. It also gives our nation new protections and added defenses. This legislation creates a new position of assistant attorney general for national security. This will allow the Justice Department to bring together its national security, counterterrorism, counterintelligence and foreign intelligence surveillance operations under a single authority.

This reorganization fulfills one of the critical recommendations of the WMD commission. It will help our brave men and women in law enforcement connect the dots before the terrorists strike.

This bill also will help protect Americans from the growing threat of methamphetamine. Meth is easy to make, it is highly addictive, it is ruining too many lives across our country. The bill introduces common sense safeguards that would make many of the ingredients used in manufacturing meth harder to obtain in bulk and easier for law enforcement to track. For example, the bill places limits on large-scale purchases of over-the-counter drugs that are used to manufacture meth. It requires stores to keep these ingredients behind the counter or in locked display cases. The bill also increases penalties for smuggling and selling of meth. Our nation is committed to protecting our citizens and our young people from the scourge of methamphetamine.

The Patriot Act has served America well, yet we cannot let the fact that America has not been attacked since September the 11th lull us into the illusion that the terrorist threat has disappeared. We still face dangerous enemies. The terrorists haven't lost the will or the ability to kill innocent folks.

Our military, law enforcement, homeland security and intelligence professionals are working day and night to protect us from this threat. We're safer for their efforts. We will continue to give them the tools to get the job done. And now, it's my honor to sign the USA Patriot Improvement and Reauthorization Act of 2005.
—George W. Bush, March 9, 2006[54]

For Bush, what is clear from the outset is that the first iteration of the Patriot Act served its purpose: it averted attacks and kept America safe. But as did Kansas authorities, Bush warns that the public should guard against a false sense of security, as the danger is still very real and "the terrorists haven't lost the will or the ability to kill innocent folks." For the Bush administration, the events of September 11, 2001, irrevocably blurred the once-clean lines between self and other, police and military, foreign and domestic. The world is different. More is needed. The war on terror now enlists a range of "military, law enforcement, homeland security and intelligence professionals" in a borderless struggle against an illusory enemy. As "foreign terrorists" blur with "local drug dealers," the "brave men and women in law enforcement" are now on the front lines of this global war, working to "connect the dots before the terrorists strike." As did Kansas lawmakers with the "meth crackdown," Bush frames the Patriot Act / Combat Methamphetamine Act as a common-sense measure to protect the public from terrorists and the "growing threat" of the "scourge of methamphetamine." This sort of logic helps to normalize increasingly coercive governance and opens up new possibilities for state and nonstate functionaries to market security projects for consumption.[55] A return to the newspaper coverage gathered by the KMPP details this convergence further. An article reporting on a "Terror Spotting" seminar held in Kansas quotes a "counter-terror" specialist instructing citizens to use the same techniques to "terror spot" that are used to locate "the meth house or the drug dealer." The terror spotter / meth talker warns,

> Who's going to notice these indicators out in the community? Law enforcement? They can't be everywhere all the time. They can't be expected to be. That's just unrealistic. That's why classes are being created for the public to learn what to watch for. . . . It's not unlike recognizing the signs of other threats—such as the meth house or the drug dealer. What you'll see with meth labs is a funny smell, cellophane over the windows, traffic going in and out. Learning to recognize tip-offs of terrorist activity is the same idea as that.[56]

Here we see both the conflation of the drug and terror wars and the expansion at the local level and the wide application of commodified security wares as instruction and expert knowledge. As securitization imperceptibly expands, a growing cadre of meth-talking/terror-talking "experts" like this one summon citizen hypervigilance, responsibilization, and a suspicious eye trained on vague community "indicators" and other "signs of threat." With the menacing reminder that police "can't be everywhere all the time," the training presses public participation in street-level antimeth and antiterror work. The idea that police cannot be everywhere all the time reveals the centrality of the methamphetamine imaginary and more broadly the ways in which the insecure imagination is put to work in the practices of governing.

In the 2013 documentary *The Unknown Known: The Life and Times of Donald Rumsfeld*, filmmaker Errol Morris asked the former secretary of defense to elaborate on previous descriptions of the circumstances that led to the Pearl Harbor attacks:

> RUMSFELD: We didn't know we didn't know that they could do what they did the way they did it. We had people working on breaking codes. We had people thinking through, what are the kinds of things they might do? And, lo and behold, the carriers were able to—on a Sunday morning—get very close to Hawaii, launch their planes, and impose enormous destruction.
>
> MORRIS: Was it failure of imagination or failure to look at the intelligence that was available?
>
> RUMSFELD: They had thought through a great many more obvious possibilities. People were chasing the wrong rabbit. That one possibility was not something that they had imagined was likely.

Chasing the wrong rabbit, as Rumsfeld describes it, not the complex history of American foreign policy, explains the events of that infamous day. If only those who were responsible had imagined, invented, and imposed the correct or simply more security measures, Pearl Harbor and, by implication, the September 11 attacks would have been averted. To think the unthinkable, predict the unpredictable, and imagine the unimaginable is the security state's dream. And since the police "can't be everywhere all the time," it falls to the public to actively engage and perpetually imagine all the threats and dangers that surround us. Of course, the film's title alludes to a famous line of Rumsfeldian thinking. At a press conference in February 2002, responding to questions about Iraq's involvement in the September 11 attacks and if it did indeed possess "weapons of mass destruction," Rumsfeld brought into being his matrix of "knowns and unknowns": "Reports that say that something hasn't happened are always interesting to me, because as we know, there are known knowns; there are things we know we know. We also know there are known unknowns; that is to say we know there are some things we do not know. But there are also unknown unknowns—the ones we don't know we don't know. And if one looks throughout the history of our country and other free countries, it is the latter category that tend to be the difficult ones."[57]

And so it goes: to imagine the known, the unknown, what has or could happen, is to rationalize and justify nearly any precaution. This uncertainty-drenched logic is precisely what animates the methamphetamine and drug-war imaginaries and the contemporary politics of security. Through television programs, novels, and warning after relentless warning, we imagine the dangers that surround us—jihadists, school shooters, shoe bombs, global pandemics, drifting serial killers, and of course, drug epidemics.

The "Meth Watch" sign set against the backdrop of a small Kansas town—population 391—is characteristic of this sort of thinking and the ways in which the methamphetamine imaginary is sewn into a vast security project, which as Neocleous puts it, swirls from "inside to the outside and back again, folding the foreign and domestic, the international and the everyday, into one another."[58] It is here that the drug war is at once global and local. Despite an abundance of facts that may contradict or at least place in better context the perpetual warnings of epidemic and emergency, an already-existing template of preunderstanding grows local tendrils of a global drug war. As the following letter to the editor of a small Kansas paper shows, meth's terrifying imaginary hangs heavy in the air, begging all to turn inward and look on with suspicion: "Country rentals are prime locations. Meth labs are growing every day in Kansas. Little houses in rural areas, which can be rented, are prime locations for Meth makers to hide out in. We have lost one sheriff in Greenwood County, which points how dangerous these people can be. Screen your potential renters carefully. Stay safe."[59] And so the familiar security mantra "if you see something, say something" takes on a particular rural dimension. Be on the (meth) watch, imagine and prepare, stay safe.

Yet the insecure imaginary represented by Rumsfeld's ontological inventory, as Slavoj Žižek has pointed out, neglects an important fourth category—the unknown known—the Freudian unconscious, "the knowledge which doesn't know itself," those things we know but choose to deny.[60] In the context of the looming invasion of Iraq, the dangers

Figure 3.5. Look out! Be on the "Meth Watch"! Photo by David Westfall.

as Rumsfeld saw them were "unknown unknowns," the weapons, fortifications, and intentions that the Bush administration could not anticipate or imagine. Crucial here are those things hiding in plain sight, that which is disavowed, those things "I know, but I don't want to know that I know, so I don't know."[61] As Žižek argues, the horrors of war—torture, "collateral damage," murdered civilians—were always expected, assumed, and known but nonetheless denied by much of the American public. And as the torture at Abu Ghraib prison eventually proved, the unknown knowns are symptomatic of the most violent and obscene elements of society. In the context of the drug war, ignored and disavowed are the perpetual and mounting injustices of a punitive criminal justice system that fails to address the problems of drug use and, of course, the even more certain and unavoidable inequalities of life under late capitalism. Yet sometimes overlooked in studies of state power is how marginal functionaries produce and maintain coercive governance. Chapter 4 treats the everyday utterances and cultural work of police officers seriously, in order to reckon how the drug war is made livable in sparsely populated towns across the rural United States.

4

The War Out There

Well, it's war out there, and it's fought by poor white men,
from the plateau to the falls of the Cumberland.
—Old Crow Medicine Show, "Methamphetamine"

The past four drug-war decades, marked by an uninterrupted parade of cultural scapegoats—graffiti writers, youth gangs, homeless "squeegee men"—have seen police at the center of vibrant imaginaries of crime, identity, and urban life. Beyond city streets, however, the crime and insecurity entwined with policing changes, if not fades. To be sure, policing the rural US conjures visions of idyllic, slow-moving, safe places reminiscent of the beloved "Mayberry." As sheriff of the imaginary town, Andy Griffith and his bumbling sidekick, Barney Fife, patrolled the living rooms of postwar America for eight seasons. Andy, who famously never wore a gun, dealt with the quirks of small-town life, many of which involved the rock-throwing scoundrel Ernest T. Bass, with humor and kindness but never force. As a letter to the editor of a small-town Kansas newspaper suggests, the Mayberry[1] trope of rural policing is alive and well and interlaced with the methamphetamine and drug-war imaginaries. Under the headline "Barney Fife Need Not Apply," the author challenges the perceived triviality of rural police work and the bucolic tedium of rural life: "Our officers are asked to respond to emergent situations . . . and must keep up to date in the latest techniques of both the criminal and the police unit and work with other officers in the county and the state in tracking down meth labs, marijuana fields and other illegal activities. Barney Fife need not apply for a job out here in central Kansas. He would be eaten alive. And for that matter, so would Sheriff Taylor."[2] Like the Mayberry trope that subordinates rural policing to urban, the drug-war imaginary draws on images of inner-city ghettos, rather than wide-open spaces and small rural towns. Pointing to "meth labs and marijuana fields" as a new understanding of rural crime, the author elaborates the dire circumstances of life "out here in central Kansas" and thus the legitimacy of rural policing.

While similarities probably outnumber differences, we can see how the old *gemeinshaft/gesellschaft* dichotomy is still evident in everyday representations of small-town policing. On the one hand, limited resources and infrastructure force small-town police to take up animal control, code enforcement, and other duties, bolstering the view of rural policing as less important, if not less exciting, than policing the city. On the other hand, the increased visibility of small towns places a premium on personal relationships, making officers more mindful of their symbolic work.

Nevertheless, whether urban or rural, the core logic of the police power is security, which is produced and maintained through everyday interactions with the public and the physical presence of officers as they patrol streets and skies. In this way, police are a condensation symbol, tying various and oft-disparate cultural meanings into a single affective field, reminding of the potentialities of criminal victimization and a means of protection simultaneously. This is not to suggest that police are monolithic, representing only the specter of crime and the state's promise of protection. To be sure, in these times of protest and civil unrest, for some people, police are just as likely to represent the certainties of state violence as benevolence.[3] While state violence is often as unmistakable as a baton blow, the symbolic work of police, however banal, is no less destructive. Unable to govern through violent repression alone, the police power must also win the hearts and minds of the general public through softer ideological measures. The police power is thus produced, at least in part, by its "voice"—the assumed facts of crime and punishment—circulating as official state discourse and dramatized "crime stories" overrunning nightly news broadcasts. This "entitlement and capacity to speak about the world," as Ian Loader puts it, is seldom challenged.[4] As "legitimate namers" and authorities on all matters criminal, police begin in a winning position with the power to "diagnose, classify, authorize and represent both individuals and the world." Therefore, we must see police as important cultural agents "whose individual and collective utterances circulate meanings that contribute in potentially telling ways to the formation of opinion and belief."[5]

As Christopher Wilson has put it, police hold privileged standing in formal political debates, in that they are understood as the standard-bearers of broader cultural understandings of civility and respect.[6] With police thought to possess special insight into the human condition, their individual and collective utterances are often taken as fact or escape scrutiny altogether. In this sense, the cultural work of police, what Joe Sim calls "state talk," exaggerates the dangerousness of policing, obfuscates misconduct, and legitimizes state violence.[7] One of the ways that this is accomplished is through the habituated myth that policing is *war* between cops and criminals, a lasting cliché that attaches a violent materiality to the methamphetamine and drug-war imaginaries.[8] That the uniformed police are viewed by many people as frontline soldiers in the wars on drugs and crime or the "thin blue line" between order and chaos, despite sound evidence that only a fraction of police work actually involves crime, let alone violence and the use of force, should be viewed not simply as misrepresentation but as one of the ways in which police actively fabricate social order. As such, the cultural work of small-town police who draw on and produce the methamphetamine and drug-war imaginaries offers important insight into the shape and direction of late-modern crime control and everyday life beyond the familiar terrains of the city and its "ghetto."[9]

As William Chambliss has charged, "The police, prosecutors, and courts have an insatiable need for offenders in order to justify their existence, and poor minorities bear the brunt of that need, but poor minorities are not the only ones who suffer being processed and labeled deviant. Working-class white youths in the suburbs and small towns are the functional equivalent of the ghetto poor."[10] Of course, Chambliss does not equate the criminalization of working-class whites with the legacy of slavery and systematic violence shouldered by the "ghetto poor." Rather, Chambliss draws our attention to the symbiosis between state power and social insecurity. As such, to twist Voltaire's famous dictum "if God didn't exist, it would be necessary to invent him," perhaps we can say that for the state, if the criminal does not exist, it is necessary to invent him. Yet we must also be clear that this invention does not occur as the state pleases—as even state power is bound by already-existing circumstances given and transmitted from the past.[11]

Through this lens, meth's contrived rurality and racialization allows us to question the fabrication of the police power and the drug war in unique social contexts. For instance, in an article titled "Armored to

Fight Rural Meth Crimes," published shortly after the murder of Matt Samuels, the state's promise of lawful violence and vengeance emerges in stunning detail in small towns of the rural Midwest:

Kingman—Randy Hill has been a law enforcement officer in Kingman County for more than 20 years now, the past eight as sheriff. Over that time, he figures he has driven in just about every one of the 864 square miles of the county just west of Wichita. But methamphetamine has redefined the landscape so dramatically the past few years that Kingman County seems like a whole new land. "You have to look at everything differently," Hill said.

Including how you dress for work. Kingman County has just purchased seven sets of tactical gear—bulletproof vests and helmets—to wear in addition to the standard body armor. Rural sheriff's departments and small-town police departments across the state are doing the same to deal with the increasing threats brought on by meth. "Dangerous drugs make for dangerous people," Hill said.

Staying Vigilant
When Hill patrols Kingman County now, he has to wonder whether that 20-ounce pop bottle tossed into the ditch is just litter from a motorist—or the remnant of a rolling meth lab. A vacant farmhouse in a distant corner of the county may be nothing more than a monument to declining agriculture fortunes—or it could be a prime nest for crooks seeking an out-of-the-way place to cook meth. A Gott water jug may have fallen off a tractor as a farmer was heading to the field—or a meth cooker may have dumped it after using it to hold anhydrous ammonia. That babbling brook may be a great place for a private picnic—or a destination for meth-makers in need of a spot to cool the mixture they're cooking. Serving a warrant on someone you have known for years could explode into a life-or-death situation if meth is part of the equation. "You don't know what they're thinking, or if they're thinking at all, when you walk up on them," Hill said.

A reflection of what rural law enforcement offices are up against these days came Jan. 19, when Greenwood County Sheriff Matt Samuels was shot to death while attempting to serve warrants at a rural house where he didn't know meth was being made. The man Samuels was attempting to take into custody—Scott Cheever, who now faces a capital murder charge—is someone he had known for years. "It's a slap across the face—a kick in the stomach," said Winfield police officer Chad Gordon. "You can't hit home much more than that. . . . It can happen to any of us."

Looking at everything differently, as the sheriff puts it, schematizes a social system in which vacant farmhouses might harbor meth cooks, a pop bottle might be a meth lab, a jug might have held stolen anhydrous ammonia, and a routine arrest warrant might cost you your life. In other words, the optic developed, perhaps commanded, by the methamphetamine and drug-war imaginaries is one in which small-town police see the drug *everywhere*. As the article's subtitle reminds, "Dangerous drugs make for dangerous people"; this is war.

Though once perhaps relegated to routine patrol, small-town police who have been enlisted in the meth war claim new tactics, funding, and legitimacy.[12] Understanding or at least representing themselves as the frayed thread on which civilization and social order dangle, police imagine a constant state of emergency and thus operate as frontline soldiers, however clichéd, of a perpetual (drug) war. Yet we should not only concern ourselves with the gap between semblance and substance but also attend to what the "war" does in the everyday. Real or imagined, right or wrong, even in its most routine and perhaps inconsequential form, the drug war is crucial to the fabrication of a distinct social order. As Mark Neocleous writes, "The drugs war is a means by which the 'low intensity conflict' of pacification is brought back into the domestic frame, via a replication of one of the fundamental tropes of security discourse: the articulation of an 'emergency situation' with a 'clear and present danger' threatening the fundamental fabric of society."[13] Neocleous's point is particularly important for the rural US spaces and cultural landscapes that before the declaration of the "methamphetamine epidemic" had arguably not experienced the drug war in the ways the city had. With methamphetamine cooked up with household supplies by anyone and anywhere—backwoods labs, trunks of cars—its threats are at once everywhere and nowhere.

Perpetual states of emergency are schematized and made livable by the symbolic and cultural work of police—"armored to fight rural meth crimes"—who wage and bring the drug war to the supposedly idyllic

Figure 4.1. Front page of the *Wichita Eagle*, describing
how local police were "armored to fight rural meth."

landscapes of states like Kansas.[14] Rendering the implicit insecurities
of the drug war livable legitimizes the work and necessity of the police
power, thereby also working to pacify new territories and populations.
With this in mind, the remainder of this chapter draws on ethnographic
fieldwork and semistructured interviews to detail the ways in which the
cultural work of police makes the drug war livable in small towns in the
rural Midwest.

In 2010 and 2011, I interviewed nearly forty Kansas police officers
with the aim of understanding how their particular views on crime and

drug problems helped to reproduce the methamphetamine and drug-war imaginaries as a livable dimension of everyday life. In the field, I portrayed the study as one concerned with differences between urban and rural policing, the officers' assessments of local crime problems, and their particular policy recommendations. In hopes of encouraging honest discussions of local problems, I did not declare an interest in methamphetamine or any particular crime or illicit drug. The four communities that I visited—one large city and three small towns—were selected to approximate a continuum of rural and urban places. I selected the three small communities specifically because they had been designated as Midwest High Intensity Drug Trafficking Area "hotspots" and have had local drug task forces specifically concerned with methamphetamine.[15]

Taking place "on the road" in patrol cars or "back at the house" (stations), the interviews began with informal, open-ended discussions of everyday community life. Resoundingly, city police described quality of life through the lens of crime rates that improved from years past. In fact, many anchored their assessments against the well-documented violence of the late '80s and early '90s and the subsequent crime decline. As one officer from the urban community described, "I would say it's gotten a little bit better. I'm trying to think about the crime trends and things like that. I would say it's gotten a little bit better to about the same, and I'm judging based on the stories that I hear from officers that have been here before me, you know, on how things were even before I got here."

Police in the small rural communities, on the other hand, were uncertain and undeniably anxious, particularly regarding local economies. Many described changes in the local community going from a sort of *gemeinshaft* solidarity in which you "know everybody" to significant job loss, declining populations, and social insecurity. For instance, one officer explained how his small town had changed dramatically in recent years with the departure of key industries: "[Community 2] is a small town, approximately 6,400 people, approximately. We have lost one of the local factories to somebody in Mexico. You know how that goes. Just a small-town atmosphere. You know everybody, and everybody is friendly. They wave at people. During the day shift, they wave at you and stuff. Maybe not the night shift, but the day shift. I think the biggest notice will probably be in the fall when the school year takes over.

Then we'll know how many people we've actually lost." Important is the officer's description of a factory lost to "somebody in Mexico," which does not simply describe job loss but jobs lost to a very specific location and thus for a specific reason. Drawing attention to forces well beyond his control, his comment reflects the overarching sense of economic insecurity, identified by many of the rural police. Another rural officer, a twenty-six-year police veteran and the chief of his small department, offered a slightly different take:

> Sure. When I first came here twenty-six years ago, we [in community 3] had a population of about 2,000. Many of those folks were elderly folks that had generational ties to the community maybe clear back into the mid-1800s, when the town was first settled. A lot of them were business people, maybe children or grandchildren of early businesspeople here. There was a sense of prosperity. So many of those folks have died. Many of those businesses that were prominent business, prominent names in this community, also died. Then, as a result, a lot of the homes fell into disrepair, decay.

For this officer, the death of his community is no mere metaphor but a description of years of watching the elderly pass on, businesses close up, and buildings slowly rot and fall in on themselves. These broader structural changes are important as they both reflect and shape understandings of local social problems, the nature of everyday police work, and this officer's understanding of community. He continued,

> We have several folks who own a number of properties. They rent them out cheaply. They rent a house for $75, $150 a month. So that brought in a new element. We have people moving in from larger areas like maybe Kansas City, Topeka, Wichita, because rent is so cheap here and, if they're on any type of public assistance, their rent check will go further. Now, the big argument here is welfare is so easy here, and I always tell people, the standard for welfare is the same whether you live here or in Colby, Kansas. It's no different. The difference is this. We have people who are slumlords that offer housing for $75 to $150 a month. That same housing in a large city would probably be $400 or $500 a month. So those public-assistance dollars stretch further. They don't work. A lot of them

are on disability or public assistance. And when they come, they bring
their problems with them. Sometimes you'll have family members follow
them, friends follow them, and then it begins to grow.

Beginning again with idyllic notions of a town with long-standing gen-
erational ties, compared to a present marked by disrepair, decay, and
welfare recipients drawn by promises of cheap rent, this officer maps a
grim vision of the local community. Losing a factory to "somebody in
Mexico," however, does not focus the attention of local people on the
broader structural arrangements that make outsourcing production jobs
a commonsense business decision. Likewise, observations of "slum lords"
bringing people on "public assistance" and the "problems [they] bring
with them" fail to confront why it is so difficult for the poor and elderly to
get by in bigger cities, let alone to question ruthless profiteering and capital accumulation—whether "slumlords" or multinational corporations.

    While officers sometimes spoke at length about the real-world con-
sequences of deindustrialization and precarious local economies, when
it came time to explain those consequences, these facts were mostly
disavowed and their angst directed elsewhere. So, for instance, when
discussions turned to how local residents cope with change, most of the
officers linked economic uncertainty and dependency to drug use and
crime. As an officer from community 4 described, "There were several
places that employed people and the industrial park that went out of
business. So there was a lot of job loss here in this community. There
were people that just couldn't get out, and now they're on state assistance. I think a lot of them have turned to stealing and manufacturing
of drugs. I've seen this community go in the toilet, so to speak." Here, job
loss leads to "state assistance" and then to the "stealing and manufacturing of drugs" for "people that just couldn't get out." This is important as
it seems to suggest a familiar deterministic end, where the unemployed
have no recourse other than crime—rational decision or otherwise.
This theme was echoed by an officer from community 2, who described
changes in community safety in terms of the visibility and overt behavior of some of his "frequent fliers":

    Less safe, no. Different safe, yes. This is just society and mankind as a
    whole has changed. It used to be that things were done under the cloak

of night, if you will. Now it doesn't really matter. People will do whatever, whenever, any time of day. So the citizens are more aware of the crime, but I wouldn't say it's really changed a whole lot. I mean, fortunately we are a smaller community, so we don't have the excitement of other, of your large metropolitan areas. We just kind of—like I said, its not really any less safe, basically, for lack of a better term, and forgive my candor here, but they're called frequent fliers, people we deal with.

Whether describing outsiders attempting to stretch public-assistance dollars further, the brazen behavior of frequent fliers, or the criminogenics of the recession, the officers in the small rural communities invariably connected social change to the behavior of specific types of people. Here we can see how the officers' worldview flows from and reinforces a very individualistic understanding of social life.

Broad discussions of community turned naturally to the specifics of local crime problems, with the question "What crime(s) do you consider the greatest threat?" Urban officers were in near total agreement that thefts and burglaries were the most pressing crimes on their beats. Likewise, officers overwhelmingly reported that most, if not all, property crimes were drug related. As an officer from the state's largest city warned, "It all involves drugs. It involves drugs. It all surrounds—your burglaries, your robberies, a lot of this, the prostitution that's in the area—it all surrounds drugs, period. Whether that be meth, crack, cocaine, heroin." For this officer, the logic is quite clear: nearly all crime is drug driven.

Given this named link between drugs and crime, many officers stressed the importance of aggressive drug policing. Indeed, as another described, the effects of drug use ripple across social life, transforming workers into unproductive criminals unable to care for their families:

Because, you know, actually drugs in my opinion leads to so many things. And you know, you get somebody one day they have a job making a living for the family, and the next thing they're, you know, experimenting in whatever narcotic they're choosing to experiment in. And they get hooked on that. Now they lose their job, they lose their family. So now they're out here having to support their habit. So they're out here committing crimes. You get larcenies, you get burglaries, robberies, prostitution. It all stems, if you ask all these people and you check to see what their recreational—what they do for recreation, it's usually a drug. They usually, you know, involved in crack cocaine or meth.

Though the officer provides an uncomplicated, straightforward take on crack and meth use as recreation leading to a life of crime, other assessments were more explicit. For example, one officer powerfully described what he sees as a nexus of drugs, crime, and race: "It's all drug driven. My favorite kind of crime to target, and the one I personally believe affects families on a more quality-of-life level, is burglary. It invades their privacy. There's mostly rental homes that I deal with. A lot of folks don't have rental insurance, so that's something I educate them on all my calls. I love hunting burglars. Typically they are anywhere from middle-aged to high school students. They're typically black, and I'd say probably 40 percent of them are gang members." While it is unclear that all burglaries are "drug driven" or committed by young, black gang members, given the position of police as cultural producers, the idea of "hunting" burglars is nonetheless startling. One is indeed left wondering how claims like this one further embed a certain vision of crime, criminality, and community in the social and political imaginary.

While rural officers featured drugs in their assessments of local crime problems even more so than urban police did, they did not have the specter of young, black gang members to draw on. In terms of "greatest threat," many of the rural officers described a larger tangle of drugs and crime, including domestic violence and crimes against children. As a patrol officer from community 2 explained, "It's hard for me to separate maybe three of what I would call your primary criminal issues that we deal with a lot. One is the narcotics or the drug issue. Two is your domestic violence issue. And three is your child crimes issue. I mean, if I'm going to talk about broad, categorically speaking, I think those three are the primary ones that we deal with more so than anything."

Concerning drug types, I asked each officer, "Which drug presents the biggest problem for your community?" Of the twenty urban police I interviewed, ten named crack cocaine first, followed by meth (eight) and marijuana (two). Follow-up discussions gleaned important details in constructions of crack as urban and meth as rural artifacts. For instance, when discussing a part of the city known for prostitution, several officers described racial differences in drug consumption with certainty. An officer from the large city described, "When I started here, it was all—it was either cocaine or crack cocaine, and then it's eventually moved to meth amongst the white prostitutes. The black girls are still, yeah, they still smoke crack. I think a lot of them will use either one though, whatever is going to get them high." As this and the following excerpt illustrate, though officers held distinct beliefs about racialized drug use, none had a distinct understanding as to why. This is important, as it appears that police also rely on cultural scripts assigning crack to urban spaces and meth to the rural. An officer from the large city explained, "I don't know what their preference is for it or why, but it always seems like, since I've been here, it used to be crack cocaine was widespread amongst all your nationalities or whatever. And the last five to ten years, it seems like the white culture has moved more towards the methamphetamine, where the black culture seems like, the ones that use, they stay with crack cocaine." For this officer, differences between whites' and blacks' drug use are mostly cultural. And though officers described black, white, and Hispanic crack use, they also characterized crack as a "black drug" regardless of who used it. These logics appeared again and were reinforced by descriptions of meth as "white man's crack."

> Where I used to see crack primarily with blacks or African Americans—and, I mean, we see whites do it too, but primarily it seems like there's a big shift, as far as I can see, it's primarily whites that are using the meth. As far as things changed, I don't know if anything has really changed. I mean, all I know is they get addicted to the stuff, and they're willing to go out and do whatever it takes to get their fix. Just crack was the same way.
>
> I really don't know. I mean we used to catch people cooking crack, but now I don't know. I don't know why. . . . We used to kind of joke about it a little bit and say, you know, it's kind of the white man's crack, you know. Because it was basically what the white guys were using. But why it's primarily white, I don't know.

Though both crack and meth are relatively uncommon—used by about 0.2 percent of the population—drug use rarely happens in such simple white and black terms. There are after all about twice as many white crack users as black.[16] However, by naming crack a "black drug" and meth "white man's crack," police cast meth-using "white trash" in with an already-despised group of inner-city black crack users.

Like the urban officers, small-town police blamed drugs for the balance of the crime in their communities, with one key difference: every officer (seventeen) named methamphetamine as the greatest problem and the principal driver of local crime. For example, though a patrol supervisor from community 4 identifies poverty and domestic violence as everyday concerns, he again situates them within a tangle of other problems aggravated, perhaps driven, by methamphetamine:

> But I would say probably domestics. Even the domestics that we go to all the time, it's the same family, because the situation is already volatile. Both members are already mad. And in I'm not going to say most cases but in a lot of cases, neither one of them want you there. So neither one is your friend because neither one of you want your nose in their business, even though we were called there to potentially save someone from danger. And being that meth is a big problem here, domestics are a big problem here. I would say a lot of the really heated arguments are—this is really an impoverished part of the country I guess. There are a lot of people that live either at or below the poverty level here. So a lot of the arguments that we have are amongst people of that status that typically use the meth. Meth has a lot of side effects, I'm sure you've heard. Hallucinations, paranoia. So you're in a domestic where the situation is already volatile with a person that's on drugs and is paranoid anyway. So you go into a situation like that, and your officer safety has to be spurting out the top of your priority list because you really need to just focus on "this situation needs to be handled the safest way it can." I'd say that's probably the most dangerous.

While the officer describes complicated and volatile social relations, the assertion "being that meth is a big problem here, domestics are a big problem here" seems to suggest that methamphetamine use causes, rather than occurs alongside, interpersonal violence. As we have seen throughout the previous chapters, methamphetamine is used to explain or rather ignore more immutable community difficulties such as domestic violence and poverty.

It is important to note that while each officer was quick to name methamphetamine as the greatest drug problem locally, these assertions were not supported by their own arrest statistics, published by the Kansas Bureau of Investigation. For instance, in 2010, the first year of the interviews and fieldwork, police in the three small towns made 131 drug arrests—7 percent of all arrests they made that year.[17] That same year, arrests for all "synthetic drugs" accounted for 6 percent of all drug arrests nationally. Following this metric places arrests for all synthetic drugs around eight total arrests for all three Kansas communities. More cautiously, even if every single drug arrest was for meth, the drug still only accounted for 7 percent of all arrests that year. Admittedly, arrest statistics are not ideal indicators of community dysfunction and fail to capture subtle difficulties entwined with faltering local economies and widespread drug and alcohol abuse. It is for this reason that when seeking to grapple with the cultural life of social problems such as a "rural meth epidemic," we must pay close attention to the meth talk and pronouncements of police and local authorities.

Supporting the fuzzy logic of local meth problems was the lack of a coherent answer to the way the drugs reached the community. As far as one detective from community 4 was concerned, local mom-and-pop labs are the source of the meth in his the community: "As far as meth goes here, I would say the biggest majority of our supply comes from local production. We do have people that travel out and will go to other, larger metropolitan areas such as Kansas City or Tulsa and pick up and bring back. And we probably even have a little bit that's transported in. But a lot of ours is local usage, and they're just making enough for themselves to get by." While the detective pointed to local producers as the wellspring of the meth supply, other officers discussed clandestine labs as a problem of the past. In fact, police in communities 2 and 3 had not reported a seized meth lab in the three years prior, further putting the realities of local meth problems into question. Some officers, like one from community 4, credited the work of state and federal police in changing the shape of local meth markets: "Manufacturing of methamphetamine is the worst. It kind of slacked off there for a while because we were hitting it so hard, specifically the KBI task force, the HIDTA task force. Those were really pounding them, and it kind of backed off there for a while in this immediate area. But it has picked back up with—

they've discovered different precursors and methods, like the shake and bake. So we've seen kind of a spike in it here this last year. And, of course, marijuana is always big." Still, another officer from community 2 reported that while local meth labs may have dwindled, the majority of the meth in these communities is imported from Mexico, a reoccurring theme that I discuss in detail later: "I think a majority of it is coming from south of the border. And all that does is it makes the produce a little bit more expensive for the end user. If they want it, they're going to get it. So I think the labs that we're seeing around here now are people that are just—they're trying to make up their own products so they don't have to—and kind of boost their own economy just a little bit. I don't think that the usage has dropped off because I'm not seeing a decline in people that we're arresting for it."

Across communities, the officers provided competing and contradictory assessments of how their communities were supplied with methamphetamine. Again, it is important to note that all three communities are in close proximity and that the individual police departments routinely worked together and shared information across jurisdiction. Accordingly, it is unlikely that the meth market conditions were substantially different among the three locations. Rather, the incoherent responses regarding market specifics suggests incomplete knowledge of how much of the drug is in the community or even how it arrives. Despite this, the officers generally agreed that regardless of source and supply, demand and use remains high locally. Interestingly, outside of racialized intimations such as "south of the boarder," the officers did not access explicit notions of race when discussing how the drugs arrived in the community, whether trafficked in or produced locally. This is perhaps in part because of the racial homogeneity of the rural communities but also because of the racialization of meth as a white drug. That is, because of the overwhelming whiteness of the state and community and the hegemony of the methamphetamine imaginary, race was somewhat implicit. However, in the context of discussions of locals on welfare and living "below the poverty level," the officers' relative silence on race did in fact help to conjure the image of the white-trash meth head discussed at length earlier.

When I asked the officers, "Why do people start using meth?" most expressed faith in the gateway trajectory of drug use. As an officer from community 2 described, "It all starts out with marijuana. I think it just boils back down to—I can pretty well bet you 99.9 percent of them start off with marijuana. And they thought, 'Ah, marijuana didn't do nothing for me.' And then they'll have a friend of a friend who gets hooked onto it or started. I mean, some could probably even be drinking a drink, and they might put something in their drink or whatever, and they might like it and just keep going. So that's my belief. It starts out with marijuana." Many described a logical progression from marijuana to the drug that all named the greatest threat—meth. What is more, many, like one officer from the state's largest city, discussed the inevitability of meth's addictiveness in relation to crack cocaine: "Well, it's highly addictive. I mean, you talk to people, you know, that'll say, 'Yeah, hey, the first time I ever hit meth I knew I was screwed.' I had a guy tell me that. He goes, 'The first time I ever did meth,' he goes, 'I knew I was in trouble on the first hit.' He goes, 'I knew I was addicted right then.' And yeah, it's as addictive as crack, if anything." In this way, the pronouncements of police are one of the various sites that circulate and reinforce the "not even once" logics of methamphetamine addiction.

Of course, police do not exist in a vacuum separate from the broader culture. Perhaps speaking to the ideological power of the methamphetamine imaginary, however, nearly all officers in both urban and rural contexts supported the gateway hypothesis and reaffirmed the notion that meth is instantly addictive. Two officers, from communities 3 and 4, attested to meth's addictiveness:

I've had anywhere from thirty to fifty people that just said, "You know what, I've done marijuana. I've done pills. I've done this. I've done that. But you try one hit of meth, and it is like nothing you've ever experienced." And they just say one—it can 100 percent be true that one hit and they are hooked. It is just such a highly addictive drug and fairly easily accessible. So it's valid, I believe.

I'm not totally in disagreement. Obviously, methamphetamine keeps you up for hours on end, and when it is coming to that, you could work on it. I think a lot of that is improbable. They equate the first-time use to meth as 100 drops of dopamine. One drop, not even one drop of dopamine is equated to an orgasm. So if you imagine that hundreds of times, and then the stigma is dopamine is toxic to your brain. Once you've got that one drop, you're basically chasing the dragon, is what we've always called it. You're never going to get that same effect. And I think that's probably more geared towards the addiction. Maybe the first time they used it, that might have been it, but I don't believe any long-term use.

Because police are seldom-questioned street-level authorities, "gateway" and "not even once" logics persist as everyday narcopolitical rationalities and commonsense truisms of the methamphetamine and drug-war imaginaries.

Expanding on the centrality of choice, we discussed two reoccurring ideas connecting meth use to larger market and social forces. Concerned with meth's supposed blue-collar appeal, I asked, "Do people first try meth to work longer hours and make ends meet?" Most of the officers, like two from community 4, quickly dispelled the notion:

I have not seen that around here. I guess you could say that in the beginning or that could be an argument, but I've yet to see one of these people have a steady job at all or have anything of a decent life established and maintained. They have nothing going on for them at all. So I don't agree with that. I mean, that might be the excuse for someone on why they started it at first, but just kind of again trying to think about the people that we deal with around here with it, they never had anything going with them in the first place because they were choosing not to do anything with their life.

I think the ones that we deal with, they're unemployed. They're loners. I mean, they typically don't have like a steady residence. They just float around, stay with friends, stay here, stay there. They've got nothing. They don't have anything going on in their life, and we deal with them all the time. And irregardless [sic] if it's for meth—I just mean for a ton of other things, stealing or whatever, anything—it's those type of people. They don't have a job. They have nothing better to do. They don't have any bills. They don't have anything.

The idea that meth use is initiated to help cope with a life of wage labor in a precarious economy was widely dismissed. As these officers described, they viewed local users as ideal social derelicts—unemployed, homeless loners—with nothing "going on in their life." This sort of dismissal reappeared when I questioned whether "women use meth as a diet aid to fulfill societal expectations of beauty," described by the journalist Frank Owen in his book *No Speed Limit: The Highs and Lows of Meth* as the "Jenny Crank Diet."[18] As a couple officers from communities 2 and 3 explained,

> I've heard that. I don't see it. I try to—and I don't know if I may be one of the only ones that does it, and I don't know if it's really pushing the boundary or not—but if I hook up somebody that either I know is on it or that I suspect is on it, and I'll kind of ask a little bit more. Nothing to really condemn them criminally, but I'm curious. I ask quite a bit of people if they use it, why they use it. And they usually say it's just for the rush. I don't think I've ever heard anyone say, "Well, I needed to lose some weight."

> No. Because, I mean, do you want to lose weight and burn your teeth out? Or do you want to, you know—I mean, I think that's just an excuse to have an excuse.

While all of the officers were certainly aware that long hours, multiple jobs, and managing one's weight are issues that many people, particularly the poor and working class, confront, they did not endorse them as causes of meth use. Rather, most dismissed these as simply excuses and returned to the view that drug use and thus many crimes boil down to rational choice, hedonism, and free will. Whether for recreation or to escape miserable living conditions, drug use begins with individual choice, as an officer described:

> I think a lot of it is it's a stair step. I can't say that's for everybody, but you know, it's just like anything else. They try something. They go out and get drunk, they'll have a drink, they get drunk. They try a little weed when they're at a party or something. Somebody says, "Well, try some of this." "Well, why not? I've already smoked a little weed. Let me see what this is all about." They get in the wrong crowd, and I think it's just kind of a stair-step type of thing. It may not be for everybody, but I think people

do the lesser drug, and they just, "Oh, this ain't really doing it for me" or whatever. I don't know. Some people want an escape. The people that you see sometimes down here, they don't have much at all. I mean, they're living day to day in a motel room. It's got cockroaches and everything else. And I think it's their escape. "I can forget about things, feel good," whatever this crap does for them. They can forget about it for a while. It's all about life choices. People start off—there used to be a gal that was fairly attractive back when I first started, and she was a hooker. And I was like, you know, "You need to get out of this stuff." And I tried talking to her to get out of the stuff, and she kept using and kept using. Well, she ended up getting AIDS and everything else. And I've seen pictures of her when she was younger, and she was a very pretty girl. Well, if she's still alive now, I'd be surprised, but you just see the deterioration. These people make poor life choices. Be it they either drop out of school or whatever they're doing and then end up getting in a rut. And they get into this, and then it just all feeds on one another down here.

For this officer, the woman's pitiable transition from social acceptability to sex work, AIDS, and utter social exclusion simply boils down to "poor life choices."

In turn, the commitment to an individual rational conception of criminal behavior complements "get tough" law enforcement strategies and broader punitive sensibilities expressed by the officers. I found, as did William Garriott in his ethnography of policing methamphetamine in rural West Virginia, that officers were highly critical of state and local criminal justice practices that many described as the proverbial revolving door. A patrol officer from community 4 said, "Because ultimately we've seen the probation, we've seen the rehabilitation, and ultimately just, in my opinion, it doesn't work. I mean, just give them the prison time, give them the time—when they come out, they do it again. Give them a longer prison time, and get another conviction. It's just, you know, these people come out, and they just go straight back to it. We see it time and again." For this officer, the only respite from the revolving door of repeat offenders in his community is stiffer prison sentences. Thus, when asked, "What strategies would you pursue if given the flexibility to do so?" nearly all praised aggressive zero-tolerance practices, characterized by one officer as "busting heads":

That would be my—what my plan would be would increase our detective division and put some teeth in our detective division and let them go out and start working on this stuff, because if you get that, you could—it's just a food chain. If you start at the top and start knocking down the problem, the real source of the problem, then you're going to fix the property crimes. That's what I think my opinion is. If you're going to fix the problem within the community—and I'm saying [community 4] because I don't do anything outside the city—if I was going to try to do that within my community, I'd beef up my detective division and give them free rein to go out and address this. Aggressive, zero-tolerance, and start busting some heads and get these dopers off the street. That's what I would do.

For police whose position and ability to speak about matters of crime and punishment is rarely questioned, "busting heads" no doubt extends punitive worldviews beyond individual agencies to the broader community. Though not surprising, this language also demonstrates how the officers viewed some people not as fellow citizens or neighbors but as alien, different, and separate. Indeed, descriptions of users as "those type of people," "loners," "dopers," and "shitbags" reveal punitive sensibilities that animate policing as a stridently *them and us* endeavor—*a war*. This warlike, them-and-us sensibility was articulated powerfully by an officer who invoked the supposed permissiveness of supermaximum penitentiaries and American punishment more generally:

I've seen things, and it's been several years ago. It was a maximum-security prison they were showing, and it was somewhere in California. And you couldn't even be Jeffrey Dahmer and get sent to this place. I mean, you had to be basically the 1 percent of the badasses out there. You were sent to a prison because you killed somebody or something, and you went into the prison system. And you either killed a guard or somebody like that, then they sent you to this particular prison. Okay. Twenty-three hours a day you were in your single cell, and the only person you had contact with was the guard. You were out one hour a day to shower and eat, exercise, or something. And it really graded on me when they had these attorneys saying this was inhumane. Because I'm like, "Well, wait a minute. What did these people do to get here? What about the victims?"

I get frustrated about when I see everybody so worried about the criminal now that's in the penitentiary, boo-hoo. What about his victims? What about the child or the person that he took their life away from them, and the family that has to deal with this? And then you're worrying about this guy? I have a bit of a problem with that.

I'd just as soon stick a needle in his arm and say good-bye. I mean, I really don't have a problem with that because if you do that to somebody else, why are we paying to give you air-conditioning and working out with weights and everything else? Well, you're no use to me, no use to society.

Drawing on a punitive imaginary made of cable-television prison shows like *Locked Up*, the officer sees a crude binary of sanctified victims, on the one hand, and monstrous offenders who exploit the permissiveness of American criminal justice and the luxuries of its prisons, on the other. For him, some people are "no use to society," and the solution is quite clear: stick them with a needle and "say good-bye."

Though I observed some clear differences between urban and rural police, the interviews revealed several important consistencies. To be sure, all saw illicit drugs as the criminogenic center of community dysfunction. Likewise, all supported an individual and rational trajectory of use, beginning with marijuana and alcohol and leading to "harder" drugs. Likewise, officers at all sites saw themselves as crucial to social order and expressed steadfast faith in authoritarian policing practices. Finally and perhaps most importantly, while urban police named a variety of "drug threats," every rural officer named only meth. Together, these positions fashion a narrative with meth users and drug users more generally at the center of community decline and in the crosshairs of a criminal justice system that punishes with remarkable proficiency. Illustrating this were responses to the question that concluded all the interviews, "Imagine I am an important policy maker; what would you show me to illustrate meth's effects on your community?" One officer's response was particularly powerful:

I could show you houses. I could show you properties that are decaying and people living in them that probably shouldn't be living in them because they can't afford to live anywhere else, because whatever money they do have is going to support their habits. I could show you children in foster care due to drug use and the lifestyle that goes along with it. I could take you over to the jail and introduce you to some people that would—I could probably introduce you to some people that would say, "Yeah, I'm using, and I wish I'd never started." I mean, you get that type of thing, too. One thing about a small community is you get to know people, and so there is a lot of people out there that are using that will talk to you, because you know them. And so when you talk to them, what you find is—you sort of categorize them a little bit maybe, or I do—is you have those that are hooked that wish they'd never done it, but they've made that decision, and so they're suffering the consequences of that. And then you have those that are enjoying the ride, which they tend to be the more violent, sort of in-your-face type thing, people. But you know, I could show you that, and you could probably talk to some of those guys, and I'm sure they'd be willing to talk to you and tell you the story of their own life, and you could see.

The breadth of this response is stunning. For this small-town officer, meth infects nearly every corner of social life. Beginning with physical landscapes, the officer's imaginary tour reveals the decaying homes of rural towns and people trapped by addiction. Delivering children to foster care and parents to jail, the drug eviscerates communities one family at a time. He continued,

I would say on a numbers issue, when you begin to look at unemployment, you see a lot of small-town unemployment due to narcotics use, marijuana use, and alcohol use or abuse because it rolls over in their work ethics and ability to perform menial tasks in any kind of work environment. So, as far as how it impacts the community, it impacts your jobs, your growth opportunities, maintaining good employment. You could probably talk to a lot of your businesses, especially your factory work. It's difficult to maintain good employees because a lot of drug issues that go on with that.

Unlike those who grappled with structural causes of community decline, this officer sketched certain causality, describing problems of unemployment and stunted economic growth as consequences of drug and alcohol abuse. Thus, whether remorseful, "enjoying the ride," or violent and "in your face" without "work ethics," meth users are the root of nearly all economic and social misery.

***

When politicians speak of the heartland or police of high-crime hot spots, boundaries of difference, or what David Sibley calls geographies of exclusion, are drawn and maintained.[19] Yet warnings of the "rural meth epidemic" never exist in a vacuum or outside of context; they become meaningful only in relation to a drug war that is decades old. So when media reports tell of a small-town deputy killed during a raid on a meth lab or a "thirty-six-year-old grandmother" accused of selling meth while babysitting, familiar images of drug-related violence, derelict mothers, and dependent "crack babies" are reinvigorated and refashioned to new contexts. Importantly, then, we can see how the cultural work of police helps delimit social and spatial boundaries and locates the drug war firmly in new cultural space. It is here that working-class whites in small rural towns become, as Chambliss puts it, the "functional equivalent of the ghetto poor." While the cultural work of police draws on and reproduces the methamphetamine imaginary, the meth talk of police is also productive of broader ideological and social structures. For rural police who are less optimistic about the fate of their communities than are their urban counterparts, "factories lost to Mexico" and "slum lords" bringing "people on welfare" was the preferred grammar to discuss the uncertainty and disadvantage they negotiate as a course of duty. Individually, meth users are the very embodiment of the faulty morality and hedonism that "respectable citizens" must suppress in order to participate in the conventional capitalist economy. It is here, in the tensions between fear and desire, that policing engages the politics of backlash and produces vindictive logics of "busting heads." In this way, talk of meth-fueled criminality and degrading ruralities embedded within the imaginary should be understood as discourses invoking social insecurities and threats to the social order. As we have seen elsewhere, the methamphetamine imaginary activates a range of governing practices across myriad domains of social life. In this instance, rural drug users or even those fitting the "meth head" trope exist beyond conventional society, subject to increased surveillance and harsh punishment. Likewise, the broad community is encouraged to support cold-pill restrictions, neighborhood "Meth Watch" programs, and other security measures to which they themselves are possibly subject. It is therefore crucial to profane those sacred crime-control logics—crime waves and disintegrating traditions—that animate the methamphetamine imaginary. If police are important cultural and political producers and the issues that they prioritize are fundamental to state power and capitalist order building, then policing's project of "ordering the disorderly" and "mastering the masterless" must be a target of radical critique.[20] To be sure, the political and cultural economies of methamphetamine do considerable work in the name of order and security, but the drug war is first and foremost a project that perpetuates long-standing structures of violence and inequality.

The opening sentence of Truman Capote's famous true-crime novel *In Cold Blood* reads, "The village of Holcomb stands on the high wheat plains of western Kansas, a lonesome area that other Kansans call 'out there.'"[21] Capote and this chapter's epigraph imagine rural landscapes and a drug war fought by poor white men as somewhere "out there" in the cultural ether, beyond more familiar and knowable terrains. Chapter 5 extends these themes, detailing the ways in which the methamphetamine and drug-war imaginaries give shape to rural landscapes that have always existed somewhere out there and in binary relation to the urban imaginary.

5

Imagining Methland

For what is knowable is not only a function of objects—of
what is there to be known. It is also a function of subjects, of
observers—of what is desired and what needs to be known.
And what we have then throughout, in the country writing,
is not only the reality of the rural community; it is the ob-
server's position in and towards it; a position which is part of
the community being known.
—Raymond Williams, *The Country and the City*

In the earliest days of this project, in order to gain some conceptual
insight and grounding, I spent time with members of various criminal justice and social welfare agencies. Riding along with K-9 officers,
attending court hearings, and visiting with probation staff, social welfare
workers, and criminal-court judges proved invaluable, not so much for
technical information but for the personal philosophies about crime,
criminal justice, and human nature they invariably offered. In one such
conversation, an assistant county attorney responsible for prosecuting
all of the major drug crimes in his jurisdiction offered this, particularly
useful take on his position within the drug war: "I think the most classic
statement I've made in a while—you know, Judge—stopped me a while
back, and he goes, kind of cross, 'So Mr. [District Attorney], are you still
trying to win the war on drugs?' and I said, 'No, your honor, I am far
more modest than that. I am only trying to win the war on drugs in [this
county]. And if I can press them out of here, they will go to Wichita,
or they will go to Lawrence, or they will go to Kansas City.'" That his
aim is to "press them out of here" reveals much about this particular
prosecutor's drug-war politics. This is a stripped-down affair: he knows
the battlefield and enemy, this is a war, and he intends to win. In this
brief statement, we can see how state power is enlisted to police real and
imagined boundaries. There are, on the one hand, material boundaries

of jurisdiction and, on the other, the contested boundaries of morality, both of which are always at play within the drug war. More subtly, however, by setting the parameters of his drug war, the prosecutor reveals how the power of his office and state power more generally are put to work fashioning a particular understanding of place, for war is always understood and remembered by its towns and terrains, its vanquished as well as its victors. Continuing themes from previous chapters, the aim here is to show how contemporary understandings of the rural United States are entwined with and produced by the methamphetamine and drug-war imaginaries.

Browse a few of the many lists of top crime films found online, and you are sure to find *Goodfellas*, *Chinatown*, *Scarface*, and at least the first two installments of *The Godfather* trilogy among them. Some themes— organized crime, gunplay, murder—are immediately obvious. Perhaps less apparent is that the majority of these films share the city as their canvas: New York, Los Angeles, Boston, Miami. In fact, outside of *In Cold Blood*, *Badlands*, and *Bonnie and Clyde*, most celebrated American crime films are almost exclusive to the city. This is a useful heuristic for insights into normative conceptions of the city, contemporary criminological thought, and the social imaginary of crime more generally.

Just as *Breaking Bad* failed to include the rural in its contribution to the methamphetamine imaginary, we can say with some certainty that within the broad cultural imaginary, crime is decidedly urban in its texture.[1] The same might be true for academic criminology, a discipline that from its earliest days has focused on the delinquency of inner-city youth and the criminogenics of slums and ghettos. For some time now, however, a few criminologists have attempted to create space for "rural criminology" with admirable determination. These scholars—namely, Kerry Carrington and Russell Hogg in Australia, Walter DeKeseredy, Kenneth Tunnell, Ralph Weisheit, Joseph Donnermeyer, and Wayne Osgood in the United States—have done much to make the rural a serious topic of study within criminology proper.

Despite the important writing by these scholars and the influential work of a few geographers, criminology has yet to decide some fundamental issues, namely, *what* and *where* the rural is and *how* to go about locating it as a discrete object of study in its own right. This is not terribly surprising, as even those scholars gathered under the edifice "rural sociology" take up a number of competing and sometimes contradictory epistemic positions. As the sociologist Michael M. Bell has put it, it is annoying, if not alarming, that American rural sociologists have never settled on just what the rural is.[2] So for argument's sake, let us begin with a recent conceptualization of "rural" offered by two of the most active criminologists in this area. Working toward, in their words, "a new left realist perspective" of rural crime, DeKeseredy and Donnermeyer write,

> Not all rural communities are alike and . . . *rather than overloading the definition of rural to reflect social and cultural features that promote idyllic images and suppress the rural realities of crime*, we offer a nominal conceptualization of "rural." Here, rural communities are places with small population sizes and/or densities that exhibit variable levels of . . . collective efficacy, which is "mutual trust among neighbors combined with a willingness to act on behalf of the common good, specifically to supervise children and maintain public order." Still, we make no assumptions about collective efficacy in rural areas because it may facilitate the commission of some types of crime even as it constrains other forms of offending.[3]

It seems to me that there are a number of problems and contradictions in DeKeseredy and Donnermeyer's conceptualization that, if dealt with, can help fashion a broader, more theoretically rich rural criminology and ontology of the rural more generally.

First and foremost, the pair's aggressive dismissal of "social and cultural features that promote idyllic images and suppress the rural realities" seems to suggest that paying attention to culture and meaning leads invariably to the sort of writing that champions distorted images of rural life and ignores "real" harms suffered by rural people. This is particularly surprising given recent writing by the pair aiming to show how (mis)representations of rural people as unrefined outsiders mask "the real issues about crime, violence, and gender relations in the rural context."[4] It is equally problematic in my view to dismiss "social and cultural features" for quantitatively driven "nominal" understandings of complex social relations.

Useful here is Michael Bell's understanding of first rural spaces, understood as those defined by numerical, spatial, and binary objectivity, those that can be found on a map and assume meaning in relation to urban spaces.[5] However, the first rural view is insufficient as it leaves the thinking, writing, and hence the reality of the rural in the shadow of its urban binary. More fundamentally, because first rural definitions are the work of various state agencies, locating and understanding the first rural is often a confusing and problematic endeavor. For instance, Ken Tunnell draws attention to the inadequacy of first rural definitions in their ability to make sense of things as seemingly cut-and-dried as a farm. In Kentucky, depending on the terms employed, the number of farms would drop from 83,000 to 5,900 and, with yet another definition, would fall again to 3,030.[6] For a family farm or small rural town whose future is chained to state and federal definitions of place, we can see how first rural understandings may replicate and exacerbate existing structures of inequality. Even more fundamentally, first rural and state definitions matter little in our shared and everyday understandings of place. For certain, those who live on the Montana high plains, like those who walk crowded city streets, understand their sense of place and everyday lives not through the lens of staid federal definitions or esoteric notions of efficacy but through affective landscapes sketched by city skylines, unpaved country roads, and local foods, dialects, and history.

In the effort to address these shortcomings, this chapter sets out the value of cultural criminology and the disciplines from which it draws in thinking and writing about crime in the rural. In doing so, I hope to broaden cultural criminology's already-expansive yet decidedly urban terrain and sketch a cultural criminology of the rural. This is not the first effort of this kind. Ken Tunnell has done much to bring issues of rural culture and crime to the fore. Picking up this charge, the aim here is to establish a particular epistemological position in relation to orthodox criminological and even more critical approaches to rurality and crime. What cultural criminology is perhaps best known for is its foregrounding and rather militant focus on cultural production and the politics of meaning.[7] This is also a politics of method, as situation, experience, observation, images, and texts are the primary objects of analysis. Paying attention to the "subjective, affective, embodied, aesthetic, material, performative, textual, symbolic, and visual relations of space," I intend here to theorize rural landscapes as, in the words of Elaine Campbell, "relational, improvised, contingent, constructed and contested through an array of creative and dynamic cultural practices," rather than only through fixed and disparate parameters of state definitions.[8]

Keith Hayward orchestrated a conversation between the spatial legacy of the Chicago School and cultural geography to outline the spatiality of cultural criminology or, as he describes, its "five spaces."[9] Hayward's multifaceted aim—to show how "the new cultural geography" can strengthen contemporary area/environmental criminology, to help criminology along its way to a more thoughtful engagement with questions of how power and meaning overlap with everyday understandings of space, and to consider how cultural landscapes function as systems of reproduction, meaning, and affect—is an understanding of place beyond the rational parameters of population counts and postal code. Juxtaposed against the flat first rural, we can see how Hayward's understanding of space lends itself to a more engaged study of rurality and the ways in which the methamphetamine and drug-war imaginaries are at work fashioning everyday understandings of space and place.

For instance, in 2013, an elite academic journal published an article seeking to explain "crime in rural communities" via "the first direct test" of a particular configuration of social disorganization theory.[10] Though variation in rural crime is the article's primary concern, its authors get to the important work of discussing "the rural" somewhere in the fifth or sixth of its eighteen pages. After a lengthy and complicated discussion of the history of a particular social survey, its many iterations. and the myriad ways in which the survey classifies social space, the authors describe how they selected respondents from the survey and hence defined *rural* by two key criteria—population density and postal code. Then, after eliminating a sizable portion of their "postcode sectors," because "they contained fewer than 20 respondents" or because they were perhaps too rural, the authors conclude that the original conception of social disorganization does not adequately explain rural crime. To close, they speculate that "other or additional variables" are needed, or maybe there is just "more than one type of 'rural' community."[11] Though the authors were admittedly hampered by the same limitations suffered by "earlier urban-centered social disorganization research," at no time do questions of meaning, affect, power, culture, or politics appear in the discussion. Rather, it appears that gathering better data or constructing better variables is the solution to understanding the lived complexities of rural crime.

To show how local culture and state power collide to produce a distinct social order, this chapter draws together points of the previous chapters, weaving them into a single narrative to detail various social locations where meaning is made, remade, consumed, and contested. Stitching together state definitions, crime-control projects, the work of police, and the words of everyday people, the hope is to detail how meth's specter affixes a particular understanding of crime on rural spaces, misrecognizing signs of physical and corporeal decay for evidence of meth's supposed siege on rural landscapes and the moral disintegration of rural people.

In doing so, we accomplish another yet no less important aim. That is, by drawing attention to the cultural and political economies of police and state power, we confront cultural criminology's supposed "myopic subjectivism," said to romanticize transgression in lieu of serious engagement with the immutable ills of global capitalism.[12] The goal in theorizing the methamphetamine and drug-war imaginaries has been to illustrate how meaning, fantasy, affect, spaces, and bodies are produced, thereby revealing the ways in which state power operates through circuits of cultural relations. The so-called rural meth epidemic is a distinct cultural production—whether active fabrication or unintended consequence—of state power. As such, state power travels through affective fields acting on the spaces of the rural and the bodies of rural subjects. The various efforts to police the "rural meth epidemic" animate a particular criminalized and penal subjectivity—a carceral habitus—of rural crime.[13]

Situating culture at the center of inquiry is no soft postpolitical project, then, nor is it an attempt to romanticize inconsequential subcultural formation. Rather, it is the recognition that meaning is born of tensions between attempts to define and control from above and everyday interactions and cultural production from below.[14] In other words, something like "rural crime" is a product of the cultural work of everyday people as they navigate and negotiate state power. As such, any attempt to establish a "rural criminology" must attend to materialist first rural and symbolic "idealist" understandings of place simultaneously.[15]

Doing this leads us closer to an understanding that the rural, particularly pastoral visions of wholesome green spaces or the "rural idyll," is an ideological production in its own right. Which is to say that the contemporary understandings of idyllic rural places is a hegemonic representation that takes form in relation to and in tandem with late-modern industrial and consumer culture. In this way, we understand the rural as a manufactured landscape and small rural towns as *imagined* communities par excellence, the product of a particular moral ordering, crucial to the production of race and nation. Here, the rural idyll is everything that impure city geographies are not. But by engaging the methamphetamine imaginary, we are better able to apprehend the changing texture of life in the rural United States.

In early 2004, the journalist Fox Butterfield penned "Across Rural America, Drug Casts a Grim Shadow" for the *New York Times*. In the article, which outlined how methamphetamine was said to be overrunning beleaguered rural towns across the United States, Butterfield makes the following point: "To the experts, methamphetamine is both a symptom of rural decline, as people give up on faltering farms and factories, and a cause that makes the decline worse. In this dual role, methamphetamine acts much like crack did in big cities in the 1980's, said Mark Kleiman, a professor of public policy at the University of California at Los Angeles."[16] The first part of Butterfield's thesis is the familiar drugs-as-diagnostic ideology, a perversion of the famous maxim often attributed to the Russian novelist Fyodor Dostoevsky, which holds that the degree of civilization in a society can be judged by entering its prisons. In crowded inner cities and sleepy rural towns, so the logic goes, people turn to drugs to support themselves and cope with the pains of living in a society that has left them behind. Drug problems, then, mark the space of decline, the frayed edges of an unraveling social system. But Butterfield does not stop there; citing a well-known drug policy analyst, Butterfield suggests that methamphetamine is not only an indicator but also a *cause* that makes community decline worse. So which is it? Is meth a viable business opportunity, a coping mechanism, or is it the catalyst of decline, which then necessitates entrepreneurialism and coping strategies? Methamphetamine's "dual role," as Butterfield describes it, is an impenetrable tautology. Yet, as we have seen, this tautology is precisely the logic underpinning the methamphetamine imaginary. Was the impetus of Walter White's break of the instrumental "for the family" variety or an affective "for me" indulgence? Whatever the order, methamphetamine was key to Walter White's eventual downfall. Butterfield also has it both ways, but what is unique is his recollection of the Reagan-era crack-cocaine template and the manner in which he maps it onto rural landscapes.

Methamphetamine has haunted the sparsely populated corners of the United States in this way for decades. On streets and in the news—from homes falling in under their own weight, the similarly decaying bodies of emaciated meth zombies, and heart-wrenching reports of meth-driven child abuse—some people see the drug as the culprit of all manner of physical and social decay in America's "heartland." Yet we should not take the warnings of meth-driven rural decline at face value, nor should we dismiss them outright. It is also important to acknowledge that there are *other* methamphetamines. That is, focusing on the rurality of the methamphetamine imaginary does not necessarily speak to the cultural life of methamphetamine in other geographies.[17] Nevertheless, the drug is wed to images of poor whites and the hardscrabble lives they eke out on forgotten rural landscapes. Take, for instance, the 2010 film *Winter's Bone*, which chronicles the travails of Ree Dolly (Jennifer Lawrence), as she tracks down her meth-cook father, who left the family high, dry, and on the brink of eviction. Launching Lawrence's meteoric career, *Winter's Bone* was lauded by critics, winning the Grand Jury Prize of the Sundance Film festival and four Academy Award nominations. The film was shot on location in the "frozen Ozarks" of southwestern Missouri, and its rural landscapes play a role just as central to the film's narrative as does the tough-as-nails Dolly. As National Public Radio (NPR) described, *Winter's Bone* "is set in the bleak chill of southwest Missouri in its starkest season, when the trees are black spikes and the hills are bleached silver and rust." This "painfully poor" country, "where the illegal methamphetamine trade flourishes, . . . shapes the bodies and lines the faces of the people who live there."[18] Like Walter White's turn to methamphetamine, *Winter's Bone* helps imagine the destitute and jobless rural poor's turn to the illicit methamphetamine economy as a means, perhaps the only means, of survival in a hostile political economy. While set in the present-day Ozarks, the narrative of isolated, violent backwoods folk who scratch out a living plying their outlawed wares is far older. In fact, outside of methamphetamine, *Winter's Bone* revisits long-standing battles between "revenuers and moonshiners,"[19] underscoring the importance of rurality in the construction of a distinct sort of outsider/criminal subjectivity. In this way, moonshine and meth are simply veneers used to disguise, if not rationalize, the poverty and social exclusion of particular rural geographies.

Another of the many contemporary retellings of backward/backwoods outsiders is the popular FX series *Justified*. Set in the eastern Kentucky Appalachians rather than the southern Missouri Ozarks, *Justified* is a boilerplate cop drama dressed up with the exoticism of rural depravity, deprivation, and decline. Here, the gamut of pathological traits—drugs, violence, dependency, promiscuity, racism, incest—is written into the characters and hence the imaginary of the rural mountain poor. Of course, all of this "justifies" the further marginalization, brutalization, and in many instances outright execution of rural outlaws at the hands of the show's hero US marshal, Rayln Givens (Timothy Olyphant), a steely eyed, Old West–style gunslinger born anew. And though the program's numerous underworld villains traffic in nearly every substance commonly associated with poor rural whites—moonshine, marijuana, OxyContin—*Justified* routinely uses methamphetamine as a biopolitical cue of the worthiness of its characters. This diagnostic logic appears in the very first scene of the very first episode, when Givens's boss confronts him on a fatal shooting:

BUCKS: Guess [the dead suspect's] attorney is going to have a few questions.

GIVENS: Nothin' I can't answer.

BUCKS: You might think that you cornered him, didn't give him a choice.

GIVENS: Oh, he had a choice.

BUCKS: How's the hat? I was wondering if it shrunk ya know, got a little too tight, ya took it off your head and now you're suffering from sunstroke. You do know we aren't allowed to shoot people on sight anymore.

GIVENS: I didn't.

BUCKS: And haven't been for . . . oh I don't know maybe 100 years.

GIVENS: He pulled first.

BUCKS: It's not about who pulled first. You remember that meth-head last year, the one who pulled a shotgun. That ended up on what? Page 9. This. This bullshit. This is going to be on the nightly news.[20]

Clearly, this dialogue establishes the lethal authority of Givens as a sort of John Wayne 2.0, who dispatches the bad guy "on sight." This is an important bit of ideological production, as it accesses and reaffirms the very simple binary narrative that police and the police power (good) always win out over criminals (bad). More subtly, that the man's death would end up on the nightly news rather than being relegated to the obscurity of page 9, like that of the "meth-head" Givens previously gunned down, seems to suggest that the dead man's identity positioned him above the "meth-head" on an imagined hierarchy of worth, culpability, and grievability. Meth heads, like zombies, are the lowest common denominator, disposable enemies littering *Justified*'s threatened ruralities.

Unlike *Breaking Bad* and other programs such as *The Wire* that revolve around the illicit drug trade, *Justified* is unique in that its landscapes are decidedly rural and its characters, particularly its villains, mostly white. In fact, not until season 3 does the plot stray from its predicable roster of corrupt cops, backwoods moonshiners, and white-power skinheads to introduce a nonwhite antagonist. Played by Mykelti Williamson, Ellstin Limehouse commands the black portion of *Justified*'s segregated criminal underworld from his butcher shop and barbecue joint. Importantly, the program's only nonwhite villain does not dabble in the moonshine, OxyContin, or methamphetamine trade like the other characters Givens battles. The point is that in the imagined underworlds of *Winter's Bone*, *Justified*, and numerous other such stories, methamphetamine is apparently the business of white people.

Of course, the example of the methamphetamine imaginary's rurality that is particularly useful here is the *New York Times* best seller *Methland: The Death and Life of an American Small Town*. Written by the journalist Nick Reding, *Methland* chronicles the drug's siege on Oelwein, a small farm town in northern Iowa. Already in its seventh printing since its release in 2009, Reding's warning of drug-driven rural decline has proven incredibly popular. It won numerous awards, and there is now even some talk of a film based on the book.[21] Reding, who admittedly settled on Oelwein because a few of its citizens were willing to speak with him, researched the book in a manner he calls "live-in reporting" over about three years, 2005–2007. Reding admits, however, that he "lived in" Oelwein only about two and a half months over the course of three years.[22] Reading like ethnography at some points and crime fiction at others, *Methland* contains 255 pages of life, death, and meth without a bibliography and surprisingly even a single footnote.

Conjuring imagery perfectly opposed to yet oddly reminiscent of Elijah Anderson's famous trek down Philadelphia's Germantown Avenue in *Code of the Street*, the book's opening pages bring us through picturesque Iowa farmland and the tree-lined streets of small towns dotting its landscape—dread floating on the breeze:

> Against the oppressive humidity, the night's smells begin to take shape. Mixed with the moist, organic scent of cut grass at dew point is the ether-stink of methamphetamine cooks at work in their kitchens. Main Street, just three blocks distant, feels as far away as Chicago. For life in Oelwein is not, in fact, a picture-postcard amalgamation of farms and churches and pickup trucks, Fourth of July fireworks and Nativity scenes, bake sales and Friday-night football games. Nor is life simpler or better or truer here than it is in Los Angeles or New York or Tampa or Houston. Life in the small-town United States has, though, changed considerably in the last three decades. It wasn't until 2005—when news of the methamphetamine epidemic began flooding the national media—that people began taking notice. Overnight the American small town and methamphetamine became synonymous. Main Street was no longer divided between Leo's and the Do Drop Inn, or between the Perk and the Bakery: it was partitioned between the farmer and the tweaker.[23]

In thoroughgoing detail, Reding sketches the affective rhythms of meth-ravaged small towns, soberly warning that in some places, you can smell the meth in the air, an absurdity for even the most drug-plagued neighborhoods. Divining tensions between the wholesome ideal of rural life and the dread of big-city crime, between Oelwein and Chicago, between "the farmer and the tweaker," Reding adds a new spin to a timeless story—the collapse of traditional life. In an interview with NPR, he elaborates this binary further, responding to criticism that the mainstream media's treatment of the methamphetamine issue, much like his own, is largely overblown:

INTERVIEWER: What would you say to those who have reported in recent years that the meth epidemic was wildly overblown, contributed
to this sort of frenzy of panic about meth?

REDING: I would say that I never saw any of them when I was walking down the street in Oelwein—or in any of the other places that I
spent four years going back and forth to. The thing that the media
could justifiably be criticized for is missing the point with meth. The
point is really not entirely that people make it in their homes. The
point, I think, is that it stands for something much bigger in American culture, which is the demise of small-town America. So, in some
ways, I think the criticism that meth has been overblown, that misses
the point in the same way that media attention to the drug has been
missing it all along.[24]

Like Butterfield, Reding sees meth as a harbinger of change and Oelwein as the canary in the coalmine. As he imagines it, Oelwein is the
site of decline, the liminal space between what the late Marxist cultural
theorist Raymond Williams described as the "pastoral" and "counter-
pastoral"[25] or what the cultural geographer David Bell calls the "idyll"
and "anti-idyll."[26] Just as the rural idyll, with its lush green rolling hills,
is an imaginary of desire in relation to the city's blight, the anti-idyll,
with its landscapes spoiled by meth-lab trash dumps and bestial meth
zombies, reminds of the promises and progresses of modernity.[27] While
Reding leaves little doubt that his book is about methamphetamine, he
also urges his readers to understand *Methland* as a story about how people cope with change in "the era of the global economy":

What it took three and a half years to understand . . . is that the real story
is as much about the death of a way of life as it is about the birth of a drug.
If ever there was a chance to see the place of the small American town in
the era of the global economy, the meth epidemic is it. Put another way, as
Americans have moved increasingly to the coasts, they have carried with
them a nostalgic image of the heartland whence their forebears came, as
worn and blurry as an old photograph. But as the images have remained
static, the places themselves have changed enormously in the context of
international economics, like an acreage of timber seen in two photos,
one in spring, the other in winter.[28]

While I do not necessarily agree that *Methland* documents the birth of a drug, nor am I quick to adopt the language of epidemic, I agree that for some, methamphetamine signals the death of a way of life, an image of apocalypse drawn from an active and collective social imaginary. As Thomas Frank's *What's the Matter with Kansas?* famously argues, threats to traditional life packaged as abortion, "illegal immigration," and "gay marriage" stir a politics of backlash[29] and encourage poor and working-class (mostly) white people to support reactionary politics and policies to their detriment. This cultural anger, Frank writes, is organized for economic ends, and "it is these economic achievements—not the forgettable skirmishes of the never-ending culture wars—that are the [conservative] movement's greatest moments."[30] So on this much we agree. Part of a vibrant, perhaps never-ending culture war, methamphetamine marshals a palpable cultural anger, helping to eclipse or rather disavow long-standing social and economic inequalities.

Where clarification is needed is on the point of change. Reding's mistake, as I see it, is to assume that the nostalgic images of the heartland, which he says have worn so blurry, were ever real to begin with. That is, Reding's argument is predicated on the "death of a way of life" that may have never existed outside of the paintings of Norman Rockwell and episodes of *The Andy Griffith Show*. The lives of family farmers across the rural Midwest and miners in deep Appalachia have always been hard fought and uncertain. To assume "enormous change" even in the context of shifting "international economics" is to idealize a distorted image of small-town life, one that overlooks in dramatic fashion the inequalities inseparable from wage labor in local agricultural and extractive economies. Indeed, as the archivist and historian Otto Bettmann wrote more than forty years ago, "It is difficult to think of country life without illusion. We are always tempted to invest it with virtues that appear to have been corrupted by urban culture. And rural folklore, shamelessly exploited, intensifies images of idyllic simplicity and bedrock values. Country living presents visions of nostalgia to soothe city nerves. But these visions are grossly inaccurate especially when applied to the good old days."[31]

To be clear, my concern is not necessarily that "the good old days" never existed but rather the way that the imaginary of rural decline operates in the present. How do we understand this largely illusory concept? How do we know the rural? On the one hand, there are materialist first rural boundaries of place that speak the language of population density and census tracts.[32] For those who are on the outside peering in, the rural is everything the urban is not; it is, as Joe Bageant has described, "the stuff between cities."[33] On the other hand, there is a "second rural" fashioned of culture, an idyllic past and ghosts of place.[34] This is a rural of phenomenon, symbol, and imagination. This is where a critical reading of *Methland* is useful, as the book operates as an imagined community, a contemporary point of reference that invigorates the long-standing narrative of rural decline.[35] The frenetic connectedness of technological progress—highways, cell phones, and internet shopping— has in many ways obliterated the once-solid boundaries between city and country. And so, in an age when transportation and electronic mediation bring people from vast distances together, boundaries of the rural are increasingly defined in cultural terms. By bringing Methland into being, Reding animates and reaffirms the rural idyll and anti-idyll through the unique lens of the methamphetamine and drug-war imaginaries. But again, this is not simply an issue of cultural representation. Returning to Butterfield's *New York Times* exposé, we can see the materiality of the methamphetamine imaginary at work: "In Nebraska, crime has increased four fold since methamphetamine became a serious problem in the mid-1990's, as migrant workers brought in to work in the meatpacking plants began dealing the drug, said Glenn Kemp, the drug investigator for the Adams County Sheriff's office in central Nebraska. 'We never had a big crime problem in Nebraska till meth,' Mr. Kemp said. 'But now we have a lot of stabbings and shootings in our little towns and every homicide goes back to meth.'"[36] Never mind that crime did not increase fourfold since the mid-1990s.[37] Never mind that Adams County had just three murders in the four years leading to Butterfield's article. And never mind that despite my best efforts, I could not verify if all or any of these crimes had anything to do with methamphetamine.

Through the meth talk of journalists like Butterfield and Reding and police like Kemp, the "grim shadow" of meth-driven crime and violence is nevertheless cast, animating a thousand Methlands across the less traveled landscapes of the rural United States. Springing to life through the cultural work of police and the pronouncements of politicians and in the minds of the people who elect them, Methland exists somewhere "out there" in the space between cities. Key to this cultural architecture is Reding's understanding of place and more specifically the *heartland*: "By the time I went to Iowa in 2005, I'd already spent six years watching meth and rural America come together. The first time I ran across the drug in a way that suggested its symbolic place in the heartland was not in Iowa but in Idaho, in a little town called Gooding." As Reding describes it, the methamphetamine problem is not only uniquely rural but a matter for the heartland specifically. But where and, more importantly, what is this heartland? As it is commonly understood today, *heartland* has its origins in the writings of the English geographer Halford John Mackinder. In *The Geographical Pivot of History*, a published address that he delivered to the Royal Geographical Society in 1904, Mackinder advanced what he called Heartland Theory. The theory imagined the earth's landmasses as three island groups, the largest of which, the World-Island was made up of the European, Asian, and African continents. Two other groups, the Offshore islands and the Outlying islands, were made up of the British Isles and Japanese islands, and the American continents and Australia, respectively. At the center of this global configuration lay the heartland, stretching from the Volga to the Yangtze and from the Himalayas to the Artic. With the heartland holding nearly half of the earth's known natural resources, Mackinder believed it key to world domination. In summarizing his theory, he recalled the story of a Roman general who in the midst of glorious triumph had a slave whisper the reminder, "You are mortal"; likewise, Mackinder warned that contemporary leaders in discussions with trampled enemies should have the maxim "who rules East Europe commands the Heartland: who rules the Heartland commands the World-Island: who rules the World-Island controls the world" whispered in their ears.[38] A tremendously influential imperialist doctrine, the heartland was implicated in both world wars, with several proponents of the theory counted among Nazi leadership.[39] The heartland being the center, core, and the very heart of a place is important given that it routinely appears in discussions of methamphetamine. In formal hearings concerned with "fighting methamphetamine in the heartland"[40] and prime-time television news programs reporting on the "scourge of the heartland,"[41] methamphetamine is intimately linked with the symbolic core of American social, cultural, and moral life. And so this is not just another drug epidemic and Methland not just some small town in Iowa but the front lines in a battle for the heart of America itself.

Of course, *heartland* relates to another worrying but important term, *homeland*. As Amy Kaplan argues, *homeland* has a "folksy rural quality, which combines a German romantic notion of the folk with the heartland of America to resurrect the rural myth of American identity."[42] Appealing to nationalist and nativist sentiment, *homeland* does the cultural work of imagining national borders and conveys a sense of common origin, birthplace, and birthright. In fact, the choice of *homeland* as the moniker for the nascent Department of Homeland Security drew considerable criticism at the time because of these palpable connotations and, again, links to Nazi Germany. From the late 1920s on, German and Austrian defense forces were known as Heimwerh or Heimatschutz, taken from the German word *heimat* for "home" or "homeland." These proto-Nazi forces were thus tabbed the "home guard" or "homeland defense," not far from the controversial Department of Homeland Security that emerged in the United States several decades later.

In the book *Blood and Soil: A World History of Genocide and Extermination from Sparta to Darfur*, the historian Ben Kiernan describes a core Nazi ideology, *Blut und Boden*, which refers to the purity of racial heritage and birthright of German lands—*blood* and *soil*.[43] Key was the idea of the soldier peasant, an ideal German subject of pure birth and, because of his connection to pastoral German lands, a subject uncorrupted by the city. As with *heartland*, the use of *homeland* in the context of a "rural methamphetamine epidemic" suggests that the drug is laying siege on the most honored people and land.

When the Bush administration introduced Tom Ridge as the first director of the Department of Homeland Security less than a month after the September 11 attacks, the cultural logic of heartland/homeland was again front and center. As Ridge described,

> We will work to ensure that the essential liberty of the American people is protected, that terrorists will not take away our way of life. It's called Homeland Security. While the effort will begin here, it will require the involvement of America at every level. Everyone in the homeland must play a part. I ask the American people for their patience, their awareness and their resolve. This job calls for a national effort. We've seen it before,

whether it was building the Trans-Continental Railroad, fighting World
War II, or putting a man on the moon.[44]

With an effort requiring "the involvement of America at every level,"
Ridge enlists the insecure imaginary as direct governing practice, urg-
ing the public to do what it can to protect the homeland, liberty, and the
American "way of life."

Though *heartland* appears only twice in *Methland* and *homeland* only
a couple more, Reding builds and draws on this sort of heartland/home-
land imaginary throughout. This begins with the first person Reding introduces to his readers. Nathan Lein, the assistant prosecutor for Fayette
County, is a walking contradiction of sorts. At six foot nine, 280 pounds,
this "card-carrying Republican" criminal prosecutor, who admittedly
had "done every drug known to man, including methamphetamine," is
also a contemporary "deadhead," rarely missing a performance of the
"hallucinogenic-hippie band Widespread Panic" within 400 miles.[45]
Growing up on a farm near Oelwein, Lein attended college and then
law school elsewhere and was later lured back by the town's mayor to
help "clean up meth in Oelwein."[46] Described as a dedicated, salt-of-the-
earth public servant doing his best to stem the rising tide of the meth
epidemic, Lein stands in for all the frontline soldiers of the drug war. Yet
what is interesting about Reding's take on Lein is the character's connection to the land and what his position as a state prosecutor, given the
mandate to "clean up meth," means by implication. We catch a glimpse
of this in Lein's consternation about taking over the family farm:

> Whether Nathan will take over his parents' place one day is one of the
> defining questions of his life, and one that for now, remains sorely un-
> answered. No one understands the ins and outs of the Lein place like
> Nathan. Nor is there anyone for whom that *ground* has more meaning.
> Land is something you crave or you don't; if you're born with a desire
> for it, you intrinsically understand why people like the Leins break their
> backs every day, at the ages of sixty-nine and seventy, to keep it. Doing
> so is less a question of vocation or aesthetics than a question of *blood*.[47]

"It gets in your blood" is a common refrain describing how a vocation and way of life is inherited across generations. When we consider

families such as my own, who have nurtured the same land for generations, the metaphor has its place. However, in the context of *Methland*,
one is left with an oddly nationalist sentiment. For Nathan Lein, a local
who returned home and assumed the state's authority in order to "clean
up Oelwein," that the "ground has more meaning" suggests something
more, perhaps a birthright. Featuring Lein, Reding effectively conveys
imagery of an honorable few defending hallowed ground from descent
into chaos. This continues in Lein's description of his first days as a
prosecutor: "Talk about a nightmare. . . . We'd lost all the bases of civilized culture around here. It was third-world. People began referring
to Oelwein as 'Methlehem.'"[48] In Lein's mind, he returned home and
stepped into a nightmare; more than the fight for Oelwein, the battle
against meth was a fight for civilization itself. Lein describes how he
went "from totally apathetic to totally gung-ho in about a week," committing wholeheartedly to the drug war. "We were going to fix this
place," he recalls. "I really believed that. In some ways I still do." In Lein's
battle to retain "civilized culture," we can see how the drug war is not
necessarily a war fought to eradicate drugs but one to "civilize" subjects,
and as such, we might better understand the drug war as a war fought
for a way of life and a distinct understanding of social order.

Lein had already been at war for a few years when Reding moved
to Oelwein in 2005 to start on the book. To set some context, he notes,
"between 1998— . . . when there were only 321 labs busted in Iowa—and
2004, there had been an increase of nearly 500 percent. And that's really
only the tip of the iceberg."[49] This assertion is somewhat misleading,
as the DEA reports 478 labs seized in 2004, a far spot off a 500 percent
increase. However, if one adds the other two DEA categories, chemi-
cals/glassware (243) and dumpsites (711), to the number of actual seized
labs, as Reding presumably does, then the new total (1,432) may in fact
represent a 500 percent increase in "meth labs" across the state.[50] At
this time, Lein estimated that 95 percent of his cases were because of
the drug in one way or another. Manufacture, possession with intent to
distribute, even child abuse and rape all led back to methamphetamine,
a flood of cases in which Lein admits he had to offer a plea in "ninety-
eight out of a hundred." As populations decline and tax revenues fall,
Reding says, "certain basic civic functions become indulgences. Keeping the streetlights on at night is no longer a given." All this, he argues,

makes criminal trials and lengthy sentences economically unfeasible. With the county jails brimming and rehab programs nonexistent, "there was simply no place to put meth addicts."[51] Of course, the state's practice of offering plea agreements in the vast majority of criminal cases is long-standing and has little to do with methamphetamine or space available in local jails and rehabilitation programs. Nevertheless, the idea that almost all of the cases were attributable to the drug effectively conveys a criminal justice system absolutely overrun by the burgeoning epidemic, reaffirming Methland as ground zero in the fight for a way of life and civilization itself.

All of this, at least initially, Reding says was driven by small-scale "mom-and-pop" cooks, or "batchers" (one batch at a time). "Like the moonshiners of the early twentieth century," Reding writes, these "Beavis and Butt-Head" cooks "were the last of a breed, not just of rebellious criminals, but of small-business people, . . . who touted their place as entrepreneurs in the increasingly weak economy of Oelwein." Referring to the 1990s cartoon that featured two grossly ignorant teen boys who lived in utter squalor, Beavis and Butt-Head are a cultural template for "Nazi Cold" and "Red P" cooks, who did their business out of trailer homes and amid the detritus of previous runs. "Lab," as Reding later describes, "is largely a misnomer" as all that is required to make "Nazi dope" is some anhydrous ammonia, cold pills, lantern fluid, and "a ninth-grade knowledge of chemistry."[52] Here Reding underlines the cultural understanding of meth production as a grimy, haphazard, and dangerous process that basically any backward derelict could undertake. In fact, one might think of the filth and general imprecision characterized by the dash of chili powder that Jesse Pinkman added to each of his batches as representing this type of meth cook. These people cooked meth where they cooked dinner, and some, in order to evade police and dissipate the smell, road around on bicycles with "one pot" batches roiling in two-liter soda bottles. These were not chefs; they were fast-food fry cooks, more akin to Jesse Pinkman than Walter White.

Once up and running, Beavis and Butt-Head, mom-and-pop batchers instigated untold chaos and calamity, documented by Reding in story after horrific story. From children who unknowingly brought meth-tainted cookies to a school-sponsored bake sale, to a boy who melted one of his testicles off while stealing anhydrous ammonia, meth was the monster terrorizing the little town.[53] Though stories such as these are eminently entertaining and do the horrifying trick, they should not escape careful scrutiny. While an Iowa school district did indeed ban homemade treats in 2005, it did so based not on an actual case of meth-tainted food but on the fear that this sort of thing *could* happen. Apparently, this fear was instigated by a training given to school officials by a "methamphetamine specialist" with the Iowa Department of Human Services, in which he reasoned, "If the parents are brewing up the meth in the microwave or storing it in the refrigerator or stove, that toxin could be transferred to the food."[54] And while reports of anhydrous ammonia melting skin are certainly plausible, the particular circumstances of this second- or third-hand story retold by Reding are difficult to verify. Nevertheless, as he admits, "It's stories like this, told and retold every day among farmers at Hub City Bakery or while shopping at VGs, that had begun to fray the sense of civility in Oelwein by summer 2005."[55] Here the meth talk of police, prosecutors, town doctors, and everyday people informs the methamphetamine imaginary and the lived realities, the very structures of feeling, of small-town life.

With civility frayed, it was not long before community leaders including the mayor and Lein authorized local police to "pull over cars for almost any reason in hopes of finding meth."[56] Hoping to dissuade cooks of the two-wheeled variety, some people even lobbied the city council to prohibit riding bicycles within the town's boundaries. Quickly, methamphetamine became the sole criterion for a uniquely small-town version of the NYPD's notorious "stop and frisk." And as this sort aggressive policing did in New York City, it soon led to complaints of eroding civil liberties and allegations of police brutality from the unfortunate souls caught up in the sweep. One such case began when police arrested a man named Jason Annis at his sister's home, with a meth-filled needle allegedly "sticking out of his arm."[57] Annis was booked into the local jail on a variety of charges, and video cameras caught an Oelwein police officer slamming him to the ground so hard that it shattered the orbital bone and cheekbone on the left side of his face. A federal court of appeals eventually dismissed a civil lawsuit brought by Annis in 2008. In the meantime, he had pleaded guilty to manufacture of methamphetamine, attempted manufacture of methamphetamine, and being a felon in possession of a firearm. And though the firearm that weighed heavily on his sentencing was an incomplete and inoperable relic, the courts nevertheless imposed a sentence of 235 months, which was the minimum allowed by federal sentencing guidelines. As it stands, Jason Annis will be released no sooner than December 3, 2021.

Here Reding, to his credit, offers some criticism of the tactics employed to fight meth in Oelwein, suggesting that cases such as Annis's reflected the desperation and panic brought on by a worldview that blamed meth and meth users for more complicated problems. Even Lein, Reding suggests, whose conservative childhood and classically liberal education allowed for some amount of reflexivity, "was quick to talk about the 'shitbags' and the 'scum' whose addiction made everyone else pay the price."[58] After all, as a representative of the people, Lein was sworn to protect his hometown and exact some revenge on the "shit bags" and "scum" on their behalf. Lein says, "Dealing with meth logically is a difficult sell to the people of this town. I understand why. It's hard, knowing that same dirt-bag is going to be in court tomorrow for the third time this year. I mean, I'm sorry, but I leave work and go to the farm and work more. And sometimes I look at the guy who can't stop doing crank, and I just think, 'Fuck. It'd be easier to shoot the son of a bitch.'"[59] Whether the reaction is driven by panic or desperation, taking Annis's brutalization at the hands of police and the draconian sentence handed down by the courts as an example, one could say that Oelwein's authorities were stopping just short of shooting any "son of a bitch" they deemed enemy.

About halfway through the book, Reding again insists that his focus was not so much methamphetamine as it was what the drug represents:

> Rural America remains the cradle of our national creation myth. But it has become something else, too—something more sinister and difficult to define. Whether meth changed our perception of the American small town or simply brought to light the fact that things in small-town America are much changed is in some ways irrelevant. In my telling, meth has always been less an agent of change and more a symptom of it. The end of a way of life is the story; the drug is what signaled to the rest of the nation that the end had come.[60]

So it could be that Reding sees methamphetamine not as an agent of change or cause of rural decline but as a symptom, an indicator, a signal that the "end had come." But the question remains, even if Reding wanted to tell the story of the end of a way of life, which is a problematic thesis in its own right, why tell it through the lens of methamphetamine? Why name the book *Methland*? The answer to this question is the same as when it is posed about *Breaking Bad*. The steady and mounting pressures faced by working people across the rural Midwest are not nearly as compelling as is the story of poor backward, backwoods people wrecking their own lives and the lives of others with some white-trash concoction. There is no Walter White and no *Methland* without methamphetamine.

To be sure, not everyone appreciated this take on the methamphetamine problem. In a review of the book for the *New York Times*, aptly titled "Methland vs. Mythland," Timothy Egan, no stranger to the rural himself, wrote,

> Like a brief, intense summer squall, a media storm passed over small-town America a few years ago, stripping away what was left of the myth of the rural idyll to reveal a cast of hollow-cheeked white people smoking meth behind the corn silo. It was going to destroy the heartland, this methamphetamine epidemic, just as crack cocaine had done to the inner city. There was no George Bailey in this version of Bedford Falls. No John Mellencamp melodies on the soundtrack. Just toothless boys on bikes peddling some nasty stuff cooked up from cold medicine and farm products. And then it all passed, as these things do, the damage done, leaving the impression of rural America as a broken land, scary.[61]

Despite Reding's stated intentions, his vision of the contemporary rural United States was no "wonderful life"; there were "no little pink houses for you and me," just bombed-out trailer homes, dive bars, deserted factories, and methamphetamine. After reading the book, one local pleaded, "I don't want Oelwein to be labeled that way. That label sticks."[62] But to say that Reding simply labeled Oelwein Methland is to grant the book and its author power they do not necessarily possess. Considering that Reding's first book sold about 3,000 copies before going out of print, while *Methland* commanded five printings in hardback in just the first two months of publication, it might be more accurate to say that Reding tapped into a cultural imaginary much deeper and wider than a simple drug fad.[63] It is not so much that Reding created a label that stuck but rather that he accessed an already-existing preconceit, a historically determined horizon of preunderstanding that structures life as it is. So it might be that no matter how nuanced and heartfelt Reding's work or the counternarratives of the people of Oelwein and other similar small towns prove to be, they offer little challenge to the ancient story of the spoiling of unspoiled lands and disintegration of honored traditions. Drawing on the familiar urban drug-war imaginary, *Methland* provided, for those who were unfamiliar with methamphetamine and the rural Midwest, a salacious and entertaining narrative of the self-destructive rural poor and, for those who call the rural home, a framework to understand increasingly uncertain social conditions.

On this point, we should recall Fox Butterfield's troubling tautology that sees methamphetamine in a "dual role," as both a symptom of rural decline and a cause that makes the decline worse. So for true believers like Nathan Lein, methamphetamine maps the front lines of the battle for his community and perhaps civilization itself. However misplaced, the logic is quite clear: eradicate meth users and save the community. On the other hand, viewing methamphetamine as a symptom of decline negates full engagement with and critique of the social circumstances of which methamphetamine is supposedly symptomatic. This becomes even more evident considering that even townsfolk critical of the book did not challenge Reding's take on the meth problem and instead took issue with his description of the community and its future prospects. As one columnist wrote shortly after the book's publication,

> After 30 years of economic downturn, culminating with the loss of union jobs from Iowa Ham and the exodus of a factory owned by Bloomington-based Donaldson Co., some Oelwein residents feel further victimized by seeing their town's dark side become national news. Few news outlets have mentioned the hundreds of new, good-paying jobs in Oelwein, the new library and sewer systems, the new swimming facility, the geothermal heating and cooling systems of the school buildings, the beautification of the town's main street, or even the fact that meth lab busts are down dramatically.[64]

Here the critique is not about the veracity of the "epidemic" or Reding's work but that he aired Oelwein's "dark side." Problematic is that the so-called dark side of methamphetamine is seen as the taken-for-granted consequence of decades of economic downturn, job loss, and capital departure. That new jobs and infrastructure and a decline in the number of labs is offered as a counter to Reding's sketch of Oelwein only serves to underscore the misplaced faith in methamphetamine as symptomatic of community dysfunction. If the material conditions and economic future of small rural towns like Oelwein are the abiding concern, the target of critique should always be placed squarely on the political and economic structure. To fetishize methamphetamine as cause or correlate of social change and community decline is to disavow and reaffirm the ideological structures that perpetuate social exclusion and uneven economic development.

Conceptually, then, we might think of the assumptions of character and culture, of people and place, built into the imaginary of Methland as an (im)moral geography.[65] This is not to suggest an objective morality but rather a critique of power's designation of some places and bodies as moral and others as immoral. Take, for example, the divisive moral geographies of a "real America" imagined by Sarah Palin during the 2008 presidential race. Speaking on the campaign trail, she professed,

> We believe that the best of America is in these small towns that we get to visit, and in these wonderful little pockets of what I call the real America, being here with all of you hard working very patriotic, um, very, um, pro-America areas of this great nation. This is where we find the kindness and the goodness and the courage of everyday Americans. Those who are running our factories and teaching our kids and growing our food and are fighting our wars for us. Those who are protecting us in uniform. Those who are protecting the virtues of freedom.[66]

Palin's "real America" has meaning only in relation to those "unreal" spaces apparently populated by those who do not meet her meritocratic benchmarks of "kindness," "goodness," and "everyday American courage." Reproducing stark and familiar binaries, her moral geography is quite clear—the "real" center versus the "unreal" fringes, its hardworking, patriotic core and its feckless and disrespectful margins. This is precisely Reding's narrative, the time-honored and wholesome spaces of "real America" overtaken by the denigrated immoral geographies of Methland. By early 2016, conservatives had returned to this narrative and put it to work in the analysis of the troubling support for the presidential candidate Donald Trump. Only now, rural communities in "white upstate New York," eastern Kentucky, West Texas, and elsewhere were not invoked as "real America" but instead were blamed for buoying Trump's vitriolic campaign. Writing for the *National Review*, the columnist Kevin Williamson insisted that despite the challenges faced, the white working class had "failed themselves."

> If you spend time in hardscrabble, white upstate New York, or eastern Kentucky, or my own native West Texas, and you take an honest look at the welfare dependency, the drug and alcohol addiction, the family anarchy—which is to say, the whelping of human children with all the respect and wisdom of a stray dog—you will come to an awful realization. . . . The truth about these dysfunctional, downscale communities is that they deserve to die. Economically, they are negative assets. Morally, they are indefensible. . . . The white American underclass is in thrall to a vicious, selfish culture whose main products are misery and used heroin needles. Donald Trump's speeches make them feel good. So does Oxy-Contin. What they need isn't analgesics, literal or political. They need real opportunity, which means that they need real change, which means that they need U-Haul.[67]

With a particularly ruthless spin on Charles Murray's 1993 *Wall Street Journal* essay,[68] Williamson invokes a distinct vision of the derelict and dependent "white American underclass" and an adjoining vision of the rural as a space beyond repair. Michel Foucault, writing on what he called the "political dream of the plague," described how disease, the leper colony, and the plague city serve powerful disciplinary and police functions:

> There was also a political dream of the plague, which was exactly [the] reverse [of the literary fiction of the festival that grew up around the plague]: not the collective festival, but strict divisions; not laws transgressed, but the penetration of regulation into even the smallest details of everyday life through the mediation of the complete hierarchy that assured the capillary functioning of power; not masks that were put on

and taken off, but the assignment to each individual of his "true" name, his "true" place, his "true" body, his "true" disease. The plague as a form, at once real and imaginary, of disorder had as its medical and political correlative discipline. Behind the disciplinary mechanisms can be read the haunting memory of "contagions," of the plague, of rebellions, crimes, vagabondage, desertions, people who appear and disappear, live and die in disorder.[69]

Following Foucault, we might also think of Methland as an imaginary enclosure at work on a couple of levels. Whereas the leper colony served as a zone of exclusion, a place where diseased bodies were exiled and contained, the plague city functioned as a disciplinary mechanism of inclusion. Here, residents must constantly examine themselves and one another for signs of impurity, thereby actively producing normality for state authorities. As such, the imaginary of Methland and drug epidemics more generally is a function of the police power and aims to fabricate a distinct and pure social order. For those who are on the outside of the rural imaginary, Methland is a leper colony, enclosing the depravity of a rural drug "epidemic," walling off the atavistic rural others of "fly-over" country from the more refined and desirable territories of the United States. And from the interior, Methland as imaginary enclosure functions as the plague city, sorting moral bodies from those people and things cast out and rendered other, what the cultural geographer David Bell has called the rural abject.[70] On both accounts, Methland signals the demise of "real America" and thereby reaffirms both rural and urban ideals.

It is important to be clear that even if the rural exists in the imaginary, it still has considerable power materially. Today, battles between corporate agriculture, oil and gas companies, and local people that reject companies' production and extraction methods are largely fought on landscapes of the rural. Despite accounting for 16 percent of the population, places outside America's cities account for about 40 percent of America's military personnel. Here we can say that American imperial power and rural power are intimately entwined.[71] Thus, the rural is an active producer, both symbolically and materially.[72] Just as first rural definitions invest *urban* and *rural* with particular meanings, state definitions that force people into rigid categories and the boxes of census and medical questionnaires animate race in the everyday. Yet these categories are by themselves empty signifiers; it is the cultural work of everyday people that makes *race* and *rural* material realities. This is important, as ideas of innate racial or spatial inferiority do not necessarily precede or legitimize domination and inequitable social relations. Rather, long-standing systems of inequality and domination give the appearance of racial and cultural inferiority. For this reason, we can say that race is not a fixed category, "not an idea but an ideology," the product of specific cultural and historical relations.[73] Disparate racial subjectivities and (im)moral geographies are constructions produced in tandem. On this, it useful to return to Foucault's plague: "Underlying disciplinary projects the image of the plague stands for all forms of confusion and disorder; just as the image of the leper, cut off from all human contact, underlines projects of exclusion."[74]

Just as lepers and other impure and abnormal bodies (beggars, lunatics) were subject to disciplinary partitioning, drug epidemics of various kinds produce their own abject carceral subjects and subjectivities. Here, intraracial and intraclass contempt, boundaries between different forms of whiteness, body, and appearance are marshaled and reinforced by the cultural work of everyday people as they negotiate state and nonstate crime-control projects. Like Mary Shelley's Dr. Frankenstein, who stitched his monster together from the bodies of the dead, the particularly racialized and abject figure of the "meth zombie" is animated by the work of crime-control projects and comes alive and is affixed to particular geographies in the methamphetamine and drug-war imaginaries. For instance, a pair of mug shots first published by Faces of Meth and then aggregated and circulated by the Meth Project on its Facebook page imagines the unfortunate arrestee as a modern-day leper—a meth zombie (fig. 5.1).

If we understand these images simply as static representations, they more easily dissolve into the dizzying expanse of late-modern mediascapes. But if we begin with the assumption that the image is dynamic and performative, able to actively produce social relations, then these images take on another complexion altogether. For our purposes, then, it might be helpful to think of Faces of Meth and the Meth Project's advertisements as does Rachel Hall—as wanted posters.[75] That is, like the handbills and wanted posters of old, antimeth advertisements must be understood as instruments of power that instruct an anxious public to be on the lookout for outlaw subjects. For Hall, the wanted poster transforms passive consumers into active spectators—vigilante viewers. But this transformation

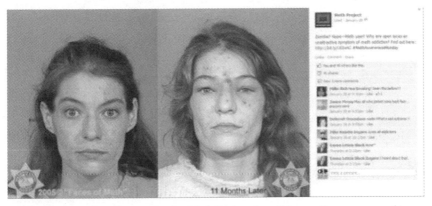

Figure 5.1. A social media post by the Meth Project describing meth users as zombies.

is not brought about by promises of a cash bounty. Rather, public-service announcements, mug-shot magazines, and locally crafted antimeth billboards warn of the dangers that lurk in the periphery, enlisting vigilante viewers in policing social and moral boundaries. These antimeth materials also produce a spatial boundary, a demarcation, reminding residents and passers through of the problems haunting local geographies.

Of course, these visual materials do not simply demarcate physical space but also warn of menacing defiled bodies that lurk in periphery. It is a long-standing pejorative assumption that the rural poor are a homogeneous lot of degenerates who dwell in filthy shacks and spawn "endless generations of paupers, criminals, and imbeciles."[76] As such, on landscapes marked by antimeth billboards, public-service announcements, and crime-control projects, the rural poor—white trash, hillbillies, rednecks— take on new meanings. Embodying powerful race and class assumptions, meth zombies are the ideal rural abject, spectral subjects that circulate in the excluded margins of the dominant economic, moral, and juridical order. Appropriating space in this way, the visual materials of state and nonstate antimeth projects draw certain bodies and territories within the material boundaries of the methamphetamine and drug-war imaginaries.

Like residents of a plague city, vigilante viewers on the watch for abject others read the physical appearance of friends, neighbors, and strangers on the street as a proxy for moral character. The observation that authorities develop aesthetic criteria to create and enforce social hierarchy is in no way new to cultural criminology or criminology proper for that mat-

Figure 5.2. A Meth Project "meth mouth" billboard.

ter. Indeed, early positivist criminologists had much interest in the face and mouth, in particular, as the physiognomist Samuel Wells wrote more than a century ago: "The mouth tells tales. The mouth not only reveals much of a man's character, but something of his history, also. Someone has said that 'our other features are made for us, but we make our own mouths'; and though the first part of the proposition is not wholly correct, the last is emphatically so. We do most certainly make our own mouths, and when made they are sure to tell tales about us, no matter how closely we keep them shut."[77] Through an arcane relic of misguided pseudoscience, the physiognomic fixation on the face and the logic that "we make our own mouths" is alive and well in discussions of the dramatic dental decay supposedly caused by methamphetamine—meth mouth. As an advertisement from the Meth Project powerfully conveys, the gross physical decay caused by meth stains not only the body but also the morality of users, with a mouth of their own creation (fig. 5.2).

Of course, police on the rural beat support and reproduce the aesthetics of rural abjection. As one police officer in a town of less than 2,000 residents explained, "But as far as appearances, for lack of a better term, grungy. Very few meth people care about their appearance. Behavior in general, they're either antsy, they're jumpy, they avoid people. They'll go places where there's people, but they'll avoid the contact. And then you got the anger when they don't get their way associated with it." For this officer, aesthetics is the first, perhaps only, diagnostic logic necessary to judge the bodies and thus the lives of the people he polices every day. While a more critical read might be to view the appearance of these anxious, antisocial, "grungy meth people" as the visible signs of poverty, degradation, and the shame of living on the margins of a highly exclusive society, he seizes on "appearance" to support his own vision of racial hierarchy and social order.

Another hit television crime series, *Orange Is the New Black*, and one of its key antagonists, Tiffany "Pennsatucky" Doggett, draw out the cultural force of meth mouth further. Pennsatucky, her nickname a slur for people from the rural areas of Pennsylvania, is a scrappy un-predictable woman, known best for her mouth full of meth-ravaged teeth. Combined with her thick "hillbilly" accent and befuddling evan-gelical sermons, Pennsatucky's meth mouth marks her as an obscene caricature of the atavistic drug-addled rural poor. Commenting on the class politics encoded in Pennsatucky's "poor teeth," the journalist Sarah Smarsh writes, "A century ago, du Bois wrote: 'The problem of the 20th century is the problem of the colour line.' The problem of the 21st cen-tury is that of the class line. For the American Dream to put its money where its mouth is, we need not just laws ensuring, say, universal den-tal care, but individual awareness of the judgments we pass on people whose teeth—or clothes, waist lines, grocery carts, or limps—represent our worst nightmares."[78] While Smarsh and others such as Naomi Mu-rakawa[79] have drawn critical attention to the myths of meth mouth, and medical research[80] has challenged its most basic assumptions, the ema-ciated meth zombie, with its rotting teeth and decaying flesh, lives on as a powerful marker of abjection and social decline. Here the metham-phetamine imaginary that is always a part of the police power actively produces a distinct social order, the (im)moral geographics of Methland and contemporary understandings of the rural United States. As Smarsh puts it, "if you have a mouthful of teeth shaped by a childhood in pov-erty, don't go knocking on the door of American privilege."[81]

Without other ties to local terrains, however, monstrous meth zom-bies may remain a shadowy figure haunting the dark recesses of the in-secure imagination. Again, categories produced and guaranteed by the state help link the meth epidemic to specific places and animate Meth-land and the methamphetamine imaginary in the real and everyday. For instance, the DEA's National Clandestine Laboratory Registry publishes meth-lab incidents by state and in many cases by street address.[82] These databases allow researchers, law enforcement, and the media to speak of certain cities and states as methamphetamine hot spots. In one such instance, a news outlet warned, "Meth labs can turn up anywhere. Last year, one was found in a building of million-dollar-plus apartments on Manhattan's West Side. But the root of the problem lies in America's heartland. In states like Missouri, Arkansas and Oklahoma, thousands of meth labs are discovered each year."[83]

As we have seen in chapter 3, like other state figures, meth-lab statistics are highly subjective and prone to politicization and thus should not escape careful scrutiny. Police agencies record "meth-lab incidents" in three categories: chemicals only / equipment only, dumpsites, and lab seizures. However, when reporting the condition of methamphetamine problems to the public, police and members of the media, such as Nick Reding, often conflate these counts into a single category and thus potentially misrepresent waste or equipment from meth production simply as "lab seizures." For example, the 2013 Iowa Drug Control Strategy reports "412 labs seized" in the state in 2011,[84] yet data submitted to the DEA by Iowa law enforcement report "415 total incidents," of which 38 involved chemicals/equipment, 194 dumpsites, and 183 lab seizures.[85] In the public's imagination, however, it is likely that all 412 or 415 "incidents" appear as familiar scenes of armed police entering a home clad in HAZMAT gear, rather than the less spectacular image of trash dumped in the ditch alongside a country road. Innovated following federal restrictions on pseudoephedrine, "one pot" or "shake and bake" production methods allow for production on a small scale, usually enough for one or two doses. The "one pot" in question is typically a two-liter soda bottle filled with a concoction of chemicals and a handful pseudoephedrine pills. However, in media reports, these "one-pot meth labs" are simply "meth labs"—in the case of Iowa, 109 of its 183 labs in 2011 were of the "shake and bake" variety—further distorting meth problems along the arc of epidemic and emergency. Even when local news report on "2 'one pot' meth labs found" at a local motel,[86] the term "lab" undoubtedly conjures images of a "Beavis and Butt-Head" setup or even Walter White's sophisticated equipment, network of distributors, and users, when in reality what law enforcement "seized" was two discarded soda bottles in a dumpster behind a motel. By comparison, consider

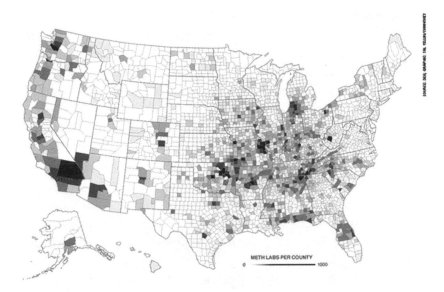

Figure 5.3. The (im)moral geography of "meth lab homes" as imagined by *Scientific American*.

how this would play out with marijuana. In such a case, a small amount of marijuana paraphernalia or perhaps a few plants could be reported by law enforcement and news media as a "grow operation."

Again, the particulars of how the state defines and counts labs are crucial, as the count serves as a proxy for the social health of a particular place. So, for instance, as the following excerpt from an article in *Scientific American* demonstrates, the number of labs routinely crowns places like Missouri with the inglorious distinction "meth capital of the world": "And although meth houses are more concentrated in certain states— Missouri is the meth capital of the world, with 1,471 labs discovered in 2008 alone—there are meth houses in all fifty states."[87] This distinction is as fluid and dubious as the definitions of meth labs themselves. Over the past thirty years or so, various media sources have crowned a range of places in Pennsylvania, California, Missouri, Florida, Oklahoma, Tennessee, Louisiana, Colorado, Idaho, and Oregon the "meth capital of the world."[88] Adding yet another confounding dimension, a series of articles tabbing Tulsa County, Oklahoma, ground zero of the "meth epidemic" described the specter of meth labs—both "seized labs" and those undiscovered by police—as "meth lab homes."[89]

Not willing to rely solely on official state data, several groups have formed to locate and respond to homes used in methamphetamine production. As Dawn Turner, owner of the web-based service Meth Lab Homes, claims, the "DEA's list can't be relied upon because it's completely voluntary," suggesting that as many as one and a half million "meth homes" go undiscovered by police.[90] Some state agents support this claim, as a spokesperson for the Oklahoma Bureau of Narcotics and Dangerous Drugs Control warned: "There have been nearly 84,000 meth lab seizures since 2004, according to the Drug Enforcement Administration. But only a fraction of meth labs, as few as 5%, get discovered by authorities."[91] If this statistic is correct, and the thousands of labs identified over the past decade represent just 5 percent of the actual population, then "epidemic" is perhaps an appropriate diagnosis after all.[92] However, as with officers' assumption that the poor are "grungy meth people," the notion that some 95 percent of meth labs go undiscovered has important implications. If we follow this implicit logic, the epidemic is a taken-for-granted fact, and even if the yearly tally of labs falls off, the assumption is that a far greater number remain. As such, "meth labs" and "meth lab homes," these important spatial markers of rural crime, are illusory, everywhere and nowhere at once—spectral. For instance, when I asked a rural police officer what he would show me to illustrate meth's effects on his town of some 5,000 residents, he introduced me to Chuck's, a local convenience store:

> I'm training recruits right now, and they asked me, they said, "Well, where is it that kids go to hang out and do rotten things?" I'm like, "Chuck's." And that is it. I mean, obviously everybody does stuff in their house, and I can show you neighborhoods—the broken window theory. I could show you those neighborhoods and say, "Obviously we've got problems here, here, here, here." But if you want to see the people, the impact on the people, go hang out at Chuck's, watch the world go by, and say, "Wow, this is messed up."

Interesting is the officer's faith in broken windows theory and his ability to diagnose the aesthetic features of certain neighborhoods in his community as "problems here, here, here, here." Yet it is his familiar worldview—problematic people make up problematic spaces—that is particularly important. For the officer, a host of social ills—drug use and poverty—are concentrated on an unremarkable convenience store in an out-of-the-way town in southeastern Kansas, allowing him to read its patrons as indicators of the health of his community.

At yet another rural farm town, another officer said the following in response to my question about a hypothetical tour for a visiting politician: "Yeah. We don't have a bad side of town. We have some parts of town that are obviously lower economically speaking than others, but it's all over town. I mean, you could have a nice house, great family, obviously making their way in the world right next door to a meth house. That's how it is in [here]. Right next door or just down the street is a meth house, just in the middle of normalcy. In the middle of a nice neighborhood, you have a meth house." Importantly, not having "a bad side of town" shows how every uncared-for home is viewed through the lens of criminality and moral decay, becoming a "meth house" whether it is or not. Imposing what Jeff Ferrell calls "aesthetics of authority," police speaking on behalf of and to the public delimit moral boundaries and actively produce geographies of exclusion.[93]

In some cases, police spoke of the rural abject and ramshackle homes as almost interchangeable. The police chief of a small rural town remarked,

> Probably the housing would be number one. If we could find some of the folks who are users, that would be number two—if we could lure them out of the house because roaches don't come out in the daylight—to actually see the effects on the human body, because it's quite obvious. I mean, oh, my gosh! I know people who are ten, fifteen years younger than me and they look easily twenty years older. I mean, just horrible: loss of teeth, skin that just hangs on a skeletal frame. I would show you houses and people.

Comparing meth users to cockroaches reveals more about the humanistic leanings of police and state power than it does about the condition of the community or the supposed corrosiveness of methamphetamine. Here in a blur of decay and disorder—corporeal and physical—emerges what Gilles Deleuze and Félix Guattari have called a "face-landscape correlation," fixing the "Face of Meth" crimes on rural spaces.[94] Through

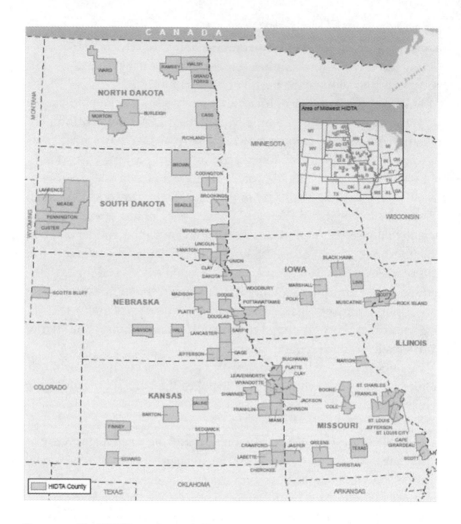

Figure 5.4. The HIDTA cordon sanitaire.

the aesthetic authority of the police power, the visible signs of social inequality become stigmata of sorts, allowing police and public to read the façade of small towns as an indicator of the health of the community on the inside.[95]

For a final vantage, it is perhaps useful to step back and look at the rural from the outside and again through the lens of drug control. The map in figure 5.4 displays the Midwest as defined by the High Intensity Drug Trafficking Areas (HIDTA) of the DEA. From the perspective of the DEA, a state agency invested with the power to shape—indeed to name—things for the public, might these neatly defined HIDTA enclosures and the individual counties highlighted also delimit the immoral geographies of Methland?

Conceptually, then, for those who are peering into the unfamiliar terrains of the rural Midwest from the outside and on either coast, might this map function as a social container or what Hayward calls a "cordon sanitaire," enclosing the meth epidemic and the cultural poverty of poor rural folks? Much like the "hot spots" of urban policing, these "high intensity" areas carry a dual meaning. With the DEA's designation come both the implication of more drug activities and the promise of heightened policing intensity. And so it goes: "ask and it will be given to you; seek and you will find." Just as Jock Young observed decades ago, increased policing is sure to produce at least the cultural understanding of heightened drug activity.[96] Thus, we can say that the police power is in the business of amplifying deviancy or, perhaps more aptly, actively producing social relations, social order, and in turn, a distinct material rurality.

Paraphrasing Leon Trotsky, Raymond Williams once said, "the history of capitalism is the history of the victory of the town over the country."[97] This is still very much the case. From state agents and academics who see the rural only through the rational parameters of count and code to police who elaborate, if not exaggerate, the dangers of methamphetamine to legitimize their work, the rural as the idyllic/anti-idyllic underside of the urban is an ongoing cultural accomplishment. Though the perfect data and measures prove illusory, the rural exists even if only in the imaginary as heartland, homeland, and Methland. As this chapter has described, by breaking with the parochial disciplinarity of mainstream social science, cultural criminology offers an epistemological and political alternative to the bloodless outline of the rural fashioned by administrative criminology and state power. In the pages of best-selling novels, mediated crime-control projects, and the knowledge work of police, the affective wash of rurality and indeed the rural itself are forged. Moving beyond the internal boundaries of the rural, chapter 6 continues these themes, illustrating how the methamphetamine and drug-war imaginaries are put to work fabricating national boundaries and a particular sort of global social order.

Drug War, Terror War, Street Corner, Battlefield

The war on drugs is a long-term fix to capitalism's woes, combining terror with policymaking in a seasoned neoliberal mix, cracking open social worlds and territories once unavailable to globalized capitalism.
—Dawn Paley, *Drug War Capitalism*

Hoping to assess illegal-drug use from the perspective of local police, in late 2011, the Kansas Bureau of Investigation distributed questionnaires modeled after the DEA's *National Drug Threat Survey* to the state's municipal police and sheriff departments. When police were asked, "Which drug is the greatest threat to the community you serve?" like police discussed in chapter 5, nearly 70 percent named methamphetamine (229 of 339). Likewise, when they were asked, "Where do the drugs that are trafficked into your community come from?" nearly 60 percent offered some variant of "Mexico" or "south of the border" (199 of 339). Finally, when they were asked what policy remedies they would pursue, along with increasing mandatory penalties, expanding undercover operations, building multistate task forces, and simply putting "more police on the streets," many unsurprisingly pointed to "the borders," warning that "shutting them down" was the only way to "cut off the supply" of drugs into their community.[1]

Today, fears of "Mexican meth" are in full bloom. In the widely circulated 2015 essay "Not Mayberry Anymore," the journalist Sharon Cohen told the familiar story of small-town police—in this case those working the oil-field boom towns of North Dakota, Montana, and Canada—overrun by petty criminals, sex workers, and of course meth dealers and users: "The gusher of oil and money flowing from the Bakken fields has made policing more demanding and dangerous, forcing small-town officers, county sheriffs and federal agents to confront everything from bar fights to far reaching methamphetamine and heroin networks and prostitution rings operating out of motels." Police of the Bakken oil-fields boom towns knew they were in a bad way when, according to Cohen, they started to notice license plates from Sinaloa, Mexico, showing up, a sign that "one of the world's most violent drug cartels" had arrived. Though admittedly police had made only "indirect ties" to the Sinaloa Cartel, and it was just as likely that the Mexican newcomers had, like thousands of others, simply been drawn to the area by promises of work, the narrative of invading drug cartels won out.[2]

The belief that the bulk of the methamphetamine in the US now comes from Mexico seems to have grown with the widely advertised successes of the Combat Methamphetamine Epidemic Act. In September 2007, not long after the new pseudoephedrine restrictions were imposed, then Montana senator Max Baucus convened a congressional hearing titled *Breaking the Methamphetamine Supply Chain: Meeting Challenges at the Border*. Opening the hearing, Baucus remarked, "In the fight against meth, our resolution to succeed is so important. It is one year after enactment of the Combat Methamphetamine Epidemic Act, and there is evidence that we are making progress. Partly as a result, last year meth lab seizures declined 42 percent nationwide. The Combat Meth Act is disrupting supply, and I am proud to have co-sponsored the law. We now must do more."[3] As we have seen with the Matt Samuels Chemical Control Act discussed in chapter 3, the successes attributed to the Combat Methamphetamine Epidemic Act were not met with complacency but with a reimagining or refiguring of the threat and were celebrated with a vigilant call to "do more." Insisting that "meth is still the number-one law enforcement problem in the Nation," Baucus continued,

> Last September, this committee heard testimony on the significant re-duction in the number of local mom-and-pop meth labs, and that was because of restrictions on the sale of products containing ephedrine and pseudoephedrine. . . . But now an estimated 80 percent of meth con-sumed in the United States originates in Mexico. It is smuggled in. So today we will hear how Federal, State, and local law enforcement are col-laborating to shut down meth smuggling at the border, and we will hear of efforts to control the legally produced chemicals that are used for meth production. The fight against meth is not over. We need to continue meth

education, prevention, and treatment, and we need to redouble our re-
solve to break the meth supply chain at the border. In the battle against
meth, we must maintain our resolution to succeed. That resolution remains vitally important, and, with that resolution, let us bring to an end
the problem of methamphetamine.[4]

For Baucus and others, "the fight" is indeed not over. Just as a flow of
water finds the path of least resistance, it seems the new law simply
enabled or made profitable trafficking from Mexico. We must recall,
however, that even at the height of concern over "Beavis and Butt-Head"
domestic labs, meth was already being moved into the United States in
sizable quantities from Mexico and elsewhere. In fact, as early as 1996,
the DEA had shifted its efforts to police methamphetamine away from
the "outlaw motorcycle gangs" that were once said to be the primary
traffickers of the drug and onto the Mexican "organizations" that were
thought to also control the flow of other illegal drugs into the United
States. According to the DEA, the nascent methamphetamine trafficking organizations were made up of Mexican nationals and Mexican
Americans who were able to "operate on either side of the border" and
aided by insurgent "illegal aliens" in the United States. As the DEA
understood and reported, "well-established families involved in smuggling contraband for decades," such as the Amado Carrillo Fuentes
group, which later formed the foundation of the Sinaloa Cartel, had
decided to use existing infrastructure to expand into the methamphetamine business.[5] Along with increased drug seizures, the DEA pointed
to turf wars near the border in San Diego that wrought "26 murders in
just a 6 month period in 1993" as evidence of the Mexican foray into the
meth business.[6]

All of this is not to adjudicate the temporal origins of methamphetamine in the United States but to show that from the position of the
DEA, Mexicans have trafficked the drug for decades, and thus any description of it as new or exceptional must be met with measured skepti-
cism. What is most important to note about today's renewed focus on
Mexican meth is the ways in which this discourse activates and invigorates the politics of security, race, border, and nation through conjoined
drug-war and terror-war narratives. As many people have noted, "the
border," like "the rural," is not simply a line drawn on a map but an on-

going cultural accomplishment fashioned in no small part by the efforts to control flows of bodies and materials, particularly drugs, across them. As the historian Paul Gootenberg writes,

> A major . . . fallacy in this state-border dynamic is seeing borders as static given "things" (something like a wall), rather than liquid—fluid spatial relationships under constant ebb and flow. Borders were historically constructed from fuzzy or contested frontiers, over most of the last century. The border controls that exist today (information-gathering, physical barriers, surveillance, intricate fiscal and legal operations) were barely in in place seventy-five years ago, and before that, not even the individual passport was common.[7]

Just as the methamphetamine imaginary helps to weave the cultural fabric of the contemporary rural United States, in police and politicians who believe that the only effective drug-control strategy is to "shut down" the US-Mexican border, we can see that the methamphetamine imaginary is an important part of a discursive and material regime that mobilizes state power, thereby shaping and animating the physical boundaries between nations. However important drug control is to fabricating the US-Mexican border, the efforts of the United States to police methamphetamine and to wage the drug war extend far beyond its sovereign boundaries. On this, it is useful to recall the conflation or deliberate melding of the drug war and the terror war offered by George W. Bush in his signing statement attached to the Combat Methamphetamine Epidemic Act. Said to provide tools crucial to national security, the act diagrams a battle against an expansive category of actors— international terrorists aligned with local drug dealers—increasingly defined by the term *narcoterror*.[8]

Sometimes attributed to the former president of Peru, Belaunde Terry (in 1983), the term originally described groups such as Colombia's Medellín Cartel that used violence to dissuade government interference.[9] No doubt influenced by the September 11 attacks and the Afghan heroin trade that blossomed after US forces unseated the Taliban,[10] the DEA now advances a broader and perhaps simplified understanding of narcoterrorism as "terrorist/insurgent organizations that use drug trafficking proceeds to advance their political agenda."[11] However, as others have argued, narcoterrorism is a problematic category as it assumes a relationship between "terrorists" and drug traffickers, which is not often supported by evidence. What is more, the term tends to overestimate the importance of the drug trade in funding terrorist activities and diverts attention from broader systems of corruption and state-sponsored violence.[12] Taking the lead of the geographer Trevor Paglan, who shows how the iconography of American "black ops" groups offers a unique and particularly revealing look into the unspoken thoughts and murky politics of state power, we can see how the insignia of the DEA's Counter-Narcoterrorism Operations Center, depicting a fierce black eagle swooping in toward its prey—an opium poppy and a Kalashnikov set in the center of rifle-scope sights—discloses this rather uncomplicated view of its opponent.[13]

While some people caution against conflating the wars on drugs and terror,[14] military, police, and government agents of all kinds increasingly position narcoterrorists as the primary, perhaps universal, enemy in a borderless war for national security. For instance, in a "strategic military assessment" of "Texas border security" commissioned by the state's Department of Agriculture, the former "drug czar" and four-star general Barry McCaffrey and the two-star general Robert H. Scales warn of a convergence of "crime, gangs and terrorism" operating on the state's southern border:

> America's fight against narco-terrorism, when viewed at the strategic level, takes on the classic trappings of a real war. Crime, gangs and terrorism have converged in such a way that they form a collective threat to the national security of the United States. America is being assaulted not just from across our southern border but from across the hemisphere and beyond. All of Central and South America have become an interconnected source of violence and terrorism. Drug cartels exploit porous borders using all the traditional elements of military force, including command and control, logistics, intelligence, information operations and the application of increasingly deadly firepower. The intention is to increasingly bring governments at all levels throughout the Americas under the influence of international cartels. . . . History has shown that a common border offers an enemy sanctuary zone and the opportunity to expand his battlespace in depth and complexity. Our border with Mexico is no exception. Crimi-

nality spawned in Mexico is spilling over into the United States. Texas is the tactical close combat zone and frontline in this conflict. Texans have been assaulted by cross-border gangs and narco-terrorist activities. In response, Texas has been the most aggressive and creative in confronting the threat of what has come to be a narco-terrorist military-style campaign being waged against them.[15]

The terrifying state of affairs described by McCaffrey and Scales sees the drug war taking on the "trappings of a classic war," transforming US borders into "battlespaces" of a "narco-terrorist military-style campaign" waged by enemy forces from the "southern border, . . . across the hemisphere and beyond." This sort of asymmetrical, irregular war against sundry narco-forces is of increasing concern for military and security advisers.

In another report, an analyst cites a marine who described a firefight with "drug intoxicated insurgents" in Fallujah: "My guys put five [machine-gun] rounds into a guy who just stood there and took it and then took off running."[16] Another marine offered his own take on drug-induced zombies, in this case insurgents under the influence of "amphetamines" and "crack," comparing the firefight to the zombie film *Night of the Living Dead*: "Body shots were not good enough. . . . People who should have been dead were still alive."[17] The simplified, often alarmist view of runaway violence, roiling just south of the American border, what Dawn Paley calls "cartel wars discourse," is increasingly important to US policy in the area.[18]

Since 2006, when Mexican president Felipe Calderón declared his "war on the drug cartels," there has been a well-publicized rise in violence, with some estimates placing the death toll upward of 160,000. In discourse and the broader drug-war imaginary, the violence no doubt takes the spectacular form of publicly staged victims, so called "body messages"—decapitated heads, bodies hanging from bridges. One needs only recall the fate of "Tortuga" (Danny Trejo) in *Breaking Bad* to position such violence within the methamphetamine and drug-war imaginaries. When in the episode "Negro y Azul," the Juárez Cartel learns that one of its high-ranking members has turned informant, it sends a particularly bold body message, Tortuga's severed head riding atop an actual tortoise, with the words "Hola DEA" written in blood across its shell. The discourse of cartel wars is bound up in a related concern for "narco-refugees" hoping to escape the violence across the border into the United States. One analyst suggests that in 2006 alone, some 200,000 people fled Ciudad Juárez for other parts of Mexico or the United States, estimating that more than half of these drug-war refugees wound up just across the border in El Paso.[19]

There is no doubt that drug-trafficking groups are involved in much of the Mexican drug-war violence; however, the discourse of cartel wars is highly problematic as it reinforces and reproduces the inequalities of the existing social order. Instead of confronting growing levels of poverty and inequality exacerbated by neoliberal policies, the complex history of US-Mexico relations, or lives wrecked by the drug war, the popular media, think tanks, and government agents reproduce the narrative of violence born of less complicated capitalist relations—cartels fighting for control of drug markets.[20] This official and state-sanctioned understanding of drug-war violence encourages the public to assume that all those who are killed in drug-war violence, other than police, are somehow involved in the drug trade and thus deserving of their fates. Perhaps more importantly, imagining "cartel wars" as "real wars" spilling across Mexican states and, worse yet, across the border reinforces a simplistic view of the problem and hence the solution: simply more—laws, walls, police, patrols—*security*.

Yet even before the "cartel wars" and renewed focus on Mexican meth traffickers, US authorities were working to link the drug with terrorism. For instance, in 2002, when the DEA broke up what it described as a large Midwest smuggling ring providing "Mexican-based drug operations" with pseudoephedrine to produce methamphetamine, it alleged that a "significant portion" of the proceeds were "flowing into the coffers of terrorist organizations such as Hezbollah and Hamas."[21] In a very real way, we again see how the drug war links local with global, making threats posed by "international terrorists" as plausible as those posed by "local drug dealers."

Thus, the ongoing concerns of US authorities with links between "drug trafficking organizations" (DTO) and "foreign terrorists organizations" (FTO) have made street-level domestic drug enforcement a key operational and tactical concern of national security. Likewise, critics see the militarization of domestic policing as important evidence of the ever-blurring lines between police and military, domestic and foreign, drugs and terror and perhaps of the first hints of the rise of an Orwellian police state.

All of this took center stage in the summer of 2014, with the killing of an unarmed teen, Michael Brown, by a police officer in Ferguson, Missouri, and the considerable show of force mobilized to attend to the ensuing protests. One of the most cited commentators on the issue again was the Cato Institute affiliate Radley Balko, who in an interview with Amy Goodman explained,

> There are the obvious problems when we see the weapons, but the uniforms matter. When police officers are wearing camouflage, it sends a very clear message to the community that they're supposed to be serving. It also affects the mindset of the police officer himself. You know, the idea that when we take domestic police officers and we train them like soldiers and we give them military gear and we dress them up like soldiers and we tell them they're fighting a war—you know, war on crime or war on terror—they're going to start to see themselves as soldiers. And that's just a mindset that's not—that really isn't appropriate for domestic policing.[22]

Balko's point, that the change in uniforms, equipment, tactics, and culture marks a crucial shift in policing a liberal democracy, is an important one. The argument goes that the "war on crime or war on terror" has so fundamentally corrupted the policing institution that not only is it no longer faithful to its ethos "to protect and serve," but it has become a militarized juggernaut, running roughshod over civil liberties.

While I agree that criminal justice continues to grow in ways that are quite disastrous for human freedom, I am not as quick to place the blame on militarization. To begin to question the diagnostic utility of police militarization, particularly as a method to critique contemporary crime control, one need only recall that Michael Brown was killed not by the machine gun of a police agent clad in full combat dress but by the nine-millimeter pistol of the patrol officer Darren Wilson, dressed in the standard blue police uniform.[23] Nevertheless, this is an argument that many people on the left and right, including policy makers of the highest order, seem to support. Speaking to the issue of police militarization just a few weeks after Michael Brown's death, President Obama stated,

Well, I think one of the great things about the United States has been our ability to maintain a distinction between our military and domestic law enforcement. That helps preserve our civil liberties. That helps ensure that the military is accountable to civilian direction. And that has to be preserved.

After 9/11, I think understandably, a lot of folks saw local communities that were ill-equipped for a potential catastrophic terrorist attack, and I think people in Congress, people of goodwill decided we've got to make sure that they get proper equipment to deal with threats that historically wouldn't arise in local communities. And some of that has been useful. I mean, some law enforcement didn't have radios that they could operate effectively in the midst of a disaster. Some communities needed to be prepared if, in fact, there was a chemical attack and they didn't have HAZMAT suits.

Having said that, I think it's probably useful for us to review how the funding has gone, how local law enforcement has used grant dollars, to make sure that what they're purchasing is stuff that they actually need, because there is a big difference between our military and our local law enforcement and we don't want those lines blurred. That would be contrary to our traditions. And I think that there will be some bipartisan interest in reexamining some of those programs.[24]

As is common, Obama cites the 9/11 attacks as a turning point, an emergency that made "exceptional" measures necessary.[25] The task now, as he sees it, is to refocus the police on its original mission.

Of course, Obama's assertion that separation between police and military is necessary in order to "preserve civil liberties" is based on a classically liberal understanding of security, in which domestic social order is produced by the uniformed police, while international security is maintained by the military and its power to wage war. Yet the focus on preserving the lines between police and military reveals a misunderstanding or outright denial of the nature of the police power itself. That is, to insist that police are not meant to operate or even appear as an occupying force begs the question of precisely what functions police are meant to serve. Commenting on Fergusson and the distorted understanding of policing in the US, Slavoj Žižek writes, "In U.S. slums and ghettos, police effectively function more and more as a force of occupation, something akin to Israeli patrols entering the Palestinian territories on the West Bank; media were surprised to discover that even their guns are more and more U.S. Army arms. Even when police units try just to impose peace, distribute humanitarian help, or organize medical measures, their modus operandi is that of controlling a foreign population."[26] As Žižek rightfully points out, even when ostensibly concerned with bringing "peace" or "help," police are still bound to impose it on a population, which is to say, to produce social order by force. This is where critiques of domestic policing as distorted by the wars on drugs and terror miss the mark. For certain, even if reformers were successful in removing incendiary grenades and no-knock raids from the policing oeuvre, the core project of producing order will continue unabated in the police power.

For example, it is perhaps useful to briefly think through the militarization/drug-war problematic in relation to police in the United Kingdom. While most UK bobbies are famously unarmed, they are still invested with the police power, meaning that regardless of departmental rules and regulations meant to check their power and govern their behavior, it is their prerogative to capture, cage, and kill other human beings on behalf of the state, for any number of transgressions to the established social order. And so, whether an unarmed bobby, a small-town "Mayberry" sheriff, or a militarized SWAT team on a no-knock raid, all police impose and thus produce a distinct social order with the threat of lawful violence. This is the ultimate truth of the police power, as Neocleous asserts: "It deals in and dispenses violence in protection of the interests of the state. In class society, this means no more than the police dispense violence on behalf of the bourgeois class."[27]

Of course, this logic extends to foreign fields of war, usefully represented by counternarcoterror police projects. By using force to police the drug/terror war abroad ostensibly to protect the public at home, the United States brings its understanding of social order to territories outside its sovereign boundaries. Thus, we can see that the liberal understanding of internal/domestic order produced and maintained by uniformed police and national and international security maintained by the military is largely mistaken. So, while the critique of the militarization of domestic policing and the "blurring line between law enforcement and military activities" is compelling and necessarily productive, as it helps to focus some scrutiny on the policing institution, rather than thinking of police and war as separate and laboring over the corruption of one by the other, it is best to think of war and police as always together and working in conjunction as state power.[28] It follows, then, that "drug control"—one of the major concerns of the police and more recently of the military—is not concerned with drugs at all but instead is concerned with regulating markets, determining what can be traded and by whom and ultimately fabricating and reinforcing a particular set of economic relations and social order.[29] Through this lens, police and military, drug war and terror war, are not "blurring" but rather part and parcel of a borderless war for capitalist order.[30] Indeed, as Dawn Paley describes in this chapter's epigraph, a "seasoned mix" of neoliberal economic policy like NAFTA and the violence of police and military makes the drug war a long-term fix to capitalism's woes, opening markets and regulating social landscapes ostensibly beyond the reach of American influence.

Understanding the police and war power as identical processes in service of state power offers some clarity on the drug-war/terror-war problematic and the ways in which the methamphetamine and drug-war imaginaries serve the broader economic and security interests of the United States. As I have sought to illustrate throughout the course of this book, the methamphetamine and drug-war imaginaries are best understood as ideological gestures, emerging from and in service to a broader set of reciprocal economic and security imperatives. As such, in order to theorize the recent turn toward Mexican meth and to better situate domestic methamphetamine control in a broader project that opens and regulates markets, bolsters nationalistic efforts toward border security, and extends the scope of US imperial power, in this chapter I conceptualize counternarcoterror projects in terms of *counterinsurgency* and *pacification* and begin with the following fundamental assumptions:

1. The methamphetamine and drug-war imaginaries provide an ideological basis for counternarcoterror and homeland-security projects.
2. Counternarcoterror projects are best understood as counterinsurgency projects, aiming to pacify certain territories and populations.

3. Counterinsurgency pacification projects are both destructive and productive, using violence to neutralize threats and softer ideological means to win the "hearts and minds" of the public.
4. The local and overarching social order produced and imposed by counterinsurgency pacification projects supports the broader economic and geostrategic security interests of the United States.
5. Counterinsurgency pacification projects identify, work to neutralize, and then reimagine threats and are thus perpetual.

A Drug War for Order

For the US, the language of counterinsurgency and pacification has roots in military "police actions" in Southeast Asia and the Iraq and Afghanistan wars. Yet more recently, government officials and policy advisers use the terms as part of a broader discourse about cartel wars. Speaking on a rash of spectacular violence in late 2010, then secretary of state Hillary Clinton helped imagine drug cartels as an insurgency:

> We are working very hard to assist the Mexicans in improving their law enforcement and their intelligence, their capacity to detain and prosecute those whom they arrest. I give president Calderón very high marks for his courage and his commitment. This is a really tough challenge. And these drug cartels are now showing more and more indices of insurgency. All of a sudden, car bombs show up which weren't there before. So it's becoming—it's looking more and more like Colombia looked 20 years ago, where the narco-traffickers control certain parts of the country.[31]

Often spoken in the same breath as "low-intensity combat" and "asymmetrical warfare," *counterinsurgency* is somewhat of an umbrella term describing operations other than conventional army-on-army combat and includes an emphasis on intelligence gathering and ideological measures meant to gain trust, produce order, and "keep the peace."[32] What makes counterinsurgency doctrine useful to domestic police as well as to those who are in the business of counternarcoterror is that it includes an ideological means of producing legitimacy, making it particularly important and of most use when states fail to meet the needs and demands of their citizens. So, for instance, Kristian Williams has shown that the same counterinsurgency strategies and techniques deployed in war zones by the US military appear in the "antigang" and "antinarcotics" activities imposed in poor communities of color by domestic police:

> But repression does not always come dressed up in riot gear, or breaking into offices in the middle of the night. It also comes in the form of the friendly "neighborhood liaison" officer, the advisory boards to local police departments, and the social scientist hired on as a consultant. Repression is, first and foremost, a matter of politics: it is the means the state uses to protect itself from political challenges, the methods it employs to preserve its authority and continue its rule. This process does not solely rely on force, but also mobilizes ideology, material incentives, and, in short, all of the tools and techniques of statecraft. We have to understand repression as involving both coercion and concessions, employing violence and building support, weeding opposition and seeding legitimacy. That is the basis of the counterinsurgency approach.[33]

As we will see, US counternarcoterror projects do not simply rely on the force of law but employ a variety of ideological means and material incentives to gain compliance and pacify populations, the hallmarks of statecraft.

The history of counterinsurgency pacification projects begins in the late sixteenth century with a series of edicts issued by King Phillip II of Spain. Concerned that the empire's conquests were causing much disquiet among his own subjects, the king declared that all future colonial acquisitions would be termed "pacifications," which was meant to reframe colonization as an altogether different project of bringing new subjects to *peaceful* submission under Spanish rule.[34] But this was no simple change in terminology, nor did it mean that force was no longer a part of the Spanish repertoire. With pacification came the strategy of establishing cooperation with key persons who would assist in learning local cultures and terrains and winning the "hearts and minds" of indigenous people. Pacifiers were instructed to gather information and build friendships with indigenous tribes, aided by "preachers" who were to educate indigenous children, enlist them in the building of churches, and if need be, "keep them as hostages."[35] Learning customs, establishing relationships, exchanging knowledge, and satisfying some of the material needs of local peoples were tactics as much a part of the new pacification plans as was outright violence.[36] After leading pacification campaigns for a number of years, the Spanish conquistador Captain Bernardo de Vargas Machuca wrote, in arguably the first manuals on counterinsurgency warfare, that rather than waging a predetermined war, conquerors should also take steps to learn and employ the fighting methods of indigenous populations. Machuca's teachings heavily influenced French attempts to colonize Vietnam and subsequent American police actions in the region and foreshadowed counterinsurgency and "irregular warfare" doctrines some 400 years later.[37] In 1962, the Kennedy administration initiated its Overseas Internal Defense Policy, a formal and sweeping counterinsurgency pacification program merging "security and development" and aimed at halting the spread of communism in Southeast Asia.[38] It is here, in this mixture of politics and force, that counterinsurgency pacification programs developed a fundamental logic of American imperial acquisition and of the contemporary police and war repertoire.[39] Neocleous writes,

> Is [pacification] a military act? Clearly yes, in the sense that the armed force behind it is obvious. Yet it also concerns the gathering of information about the population, the teaching of trades, education, welfare provision, ideological indoctrination, and, most importantly, the construction of a market. These activities concern the practices of everyday life constitutive of human subjectivity and social order. They are the practices we associate with the police power: the dispersal of the mythical entity called "security" through civil society and the fabrication of order around the logic of peace and security. This is pacification through the policing of the everyday insecurities of life organized around accumulation and money, which would, from this point on, remain central to the colonial enterprise.[40]

Combining both hard-line military strategies and "softer" efforts to enlist community participation in disciplining populations, managing geographies, and crafting markets, contemporary counterinsurgency pacification projects are both destructive and productive—dismantling the old order and enlisting state subjects in fabricating the new. And though they fell from the US military's favor following the defeat in

Vietnam, counterinsurgency pacification projects continued, evolving in the work of US police in the following two decades of the drug war.[41] In fact, in the early 1970s, the burgeoning DEA recruited heavily from the ranks of soldiers returning from Vietnam, leaving some to continue interdiction work in Southeast Asia and putting others to work on eradication programs in Mexico. Helicopter pilots who had honed their skills flying missions low over jungle canopies in Vietnam were soon spraying herbicide on marijuana and poppy fields in Mexico as part of Nixon's "war on drugs."[42]

Deployed throughout Central and South America in the 1970s and 1980s, counterinsurgency pacification programs organized specifically under the edifice of counternarcoterror emerged more fully in the late 1990s with a multifarious plan of material aid and technical support. The plan was conceived by the administrations of Bill Clinton and Andrés Pastrana of Colombia and was dubbed Plan Colombia. In 2004, after several years of Plan Colombia operations, the US House of Representatives' Committee on Government Reform convened a hearing titled *The War against Drugs and Thugs: A Status Report on Plan Colombia Successes and Remaining Challenges*. Opening the hearing, the committee's chairman, Tom Davis of Virginia, introduced the plan with now-familiar narcoterror logics:

> Not only is Colombia one of the oldest democracies in our hemisphere, but it is also home to three terrorist groups who fund their guerrilla activities with drugs smuggled into the United States for American consumption. Colombia is a significant source of cocaine and heroin for the U.S. market. As many of us are well aware, the drug trade has a terrible and destructive impact on Americans through addiction, drug related crimes and death. Because drug trafficking and the guerrilla insurgency have become intertwined problems, Congress has granted the United States expanded authority and increased flexibility to fight narcoterrorism and reduce the flow of illicit drugs into the United States.[43]

First billed as a "Marshall Plan" for Colombia, Plan Colombia consisted of $7.5 billion distributed across three program areas—counternarcotics and security, social and economic justice, and the rule of law. The counternarcotics and security or military component of the plan received by far the greatest portion of funding—approximately $4.9 billion—focused on intelligence, interdiction, training, and eradication of coca crops. Bringing counterinsurgency war to Colombia immediately sent shockwaves through the populace, which saw the homicide rates increase significantly to some of the world's highest during each of the first three years of plan.[44]

As in Southeast Asia and later Mexico, crop eradication, particularly aerial spraying, was a key "weed and seed" strategy of Plan Colombia. Engaging in a form of chemical warfare on the poor farmers who inhabited the mountain jungles, US-backed Colombian military sprayed or "fumigated" hundreds of thousands of hectares of jungle terrains with toxic chemicals manufactured primarily by Monsanto.[45] Not only did fumigation kill coca plants, but it killed every other kind of crop that poor farmers counted on for subsistence. In no short order, crop eradication led to local food crises, forcing thousands off the land and into urban centers. In a ruthless campaign of dispossession and primitive accumulation, those who did not move voluntarily were removed forcefully, with untold numbers of peasants murdered or "disappeared."

Under the guise of a protracted counternarcoterror battle with the Revolutionary Armed Forces of Colombia (FARC) and National Liberation Army (ELN), Colombian military and police who were funded under the plan have been accused of countless human rights violations. But as a local activist told Dawn Paley, Plan Colombia was never really concerned with narcoterror or even stemming the flow of cocaine into the US but rather with repressing dissident voices and armed revolutionaries in order to make way for Western business interests: "There's a discourse about attacking production and that whole story related to coca, but really what they try to attack is the social movement. . . . If you look at the map of conflicts in Colombia, you'll find that the highest concentrations of uninformed public forces are in the zones where the social movements resist most."[46] This allegation is openly supported by some US officials such as Congressman Dennis Kucinich, who in a prepared statement during the *War on Drugs and Thugs* hearing made the following dissenting remarks:

> Most atrocious . . . is that these right wing paramilitaries, such as the United Self-Defense Forces of Colombia, that's UAC, have been routinely

assassinating labor organizers, making Colombia the most dangerous country in the world for unionists. . . . Why are so many trade unionists being killed? There's a disturbing correlation between the assignations and intimidations of public sector unionists by paramilitary groups associated with right wing business interests and the rampant privatization of Colombia. U.S. multi-national corporations are benefitting from the privatization and de-unionization of Colombia.

What a terrible irony it is that taxes paid in the United States are being spent to defeat the basic human rights to decent wages, job security and the right to organize in Colombia under the guise of the war on drugs. We have a big problem with the Government of Colombia, and it starts with the president. In a speech delivered in September 2003, President Uribe described unions and human rights non-government organizations as working "in the service of terrorism." So I think that it's going to be useful to hear a discussion on how the use of war on drugs funds for the de-unionization of Colombia and the assassination of union supporters serves the cause of the United States of America. It is not authorized by Congress, it is not U.S. policy and it should not be tolerated.[47]

Of course, counterinsurgency pacification programs are never about building peace and always have some underlying economic motivation—in this case, neutralizing the threat of organized labor and helping to lay the groundwork for neoliberal economic policy. From the perspective of the US-Colombia and Canada-Colombia free-trade agreements, which, working like NAFTA, have paved the way into the region for foreign investment and extractive industries, Plan Colombia has no doubt been a success. For instance, Plan Colombia worked directly in the material interests of the multinationals British Petroleum and the Houston-based Occidental Petroleum and in some cases provided US tax dollars to directly fund private security forces. In testimony at the *War on Drugs and Thugs* hearing, then "drug czar" John Walters admitted that nearly $100 million of Plan Colombia funding a year had gone to "airlift, helicopters and training" to help the Colombian army protect the Cano Limon Oil Pipeline that is jointly owned by Occidental and Ecopetrol. When questioned as to why US antinarcotics funding should benefit the interests of private corporations, Walters reasoned that the efforts were to prevent groups like FARC from "destroying the institutions and economic opportunities in Co-lombia."[48] Which is to say that "economic opportunities" in the form of private capital developments are crucial to Colombia's stability and thus the security of the United States. Scores of other US corporations cashed in on Plan Colombia. In 2006 alone, more than $300 million went to the private contractors Lockheed-Martin, DynCorp, and oth-ers for services such as support and maintenance of aerial-eradication aircraft and maintenance and administration of the Embassy Intel-ligence Fusion Center.[49] Cloaking long-term economic and security strategy under the edifice of counternarcoterror, Plan Colombia is just one of the many ways that the drug war is indeed a fix for American capitalism's woes, combining the force and terror of the police and war power with free-market strategies to "crack open" new social worlds and territories to private capital.[50]

Today, we can see the destructive/productive power of counterin-surgency pacification projects at work at seemingly disparate location around the globe.[51] When Rio de Janeiro won the bid to host the 2014 FIFA World Cup and 2016 Summer Olympics, it quickly set its heavily armed "Police Pacification Units" (UPP) to work dismantling the shan-tytowns and favelas that sat atop prime lands for development. Under the auspices of providing much-needed improvements, such as electric service, sanitation, and "educational opportunities," to impoverished lo-cals, the specialized police units enlisted locals in readying their neigh-borhoods for development. Backed by the Brazilian military, including the air force, the Special Police Operations Squad waged outright war on the gangs that worked the favelas in order to claim territory for develop-ment. Police Pacification Units moved in after the worst of the fighting to establish a constant police presence with the help of citizens enlisted by the government to mediate between the police and the public, to pro-vide information on resistance, and to patrol pacified territories as part of community police teams.[52] One favela resident who was interviewed by Western journalists viewed pacification positively, saying, "It's im-possible to deny the positive part of the process and a lot of people are happy because they feel more secure. . . . But there has also been a lot of collateral damage."[53] Herein lies the insidious power of pacification, as "collateral damage"—which often means civilian deaths or at the very least the transformation of public space and local social order to make way for capital developments—is the price paid for "security." Projects such as the pacification of the favelas often proceed unchallenged, as those who view them favorably invariably fail to recognize the terror and violence concealed within the state's "assistance."

But perhaps the best and most chilling contemporary example of US counterinsurgency pacification forces operating within the opaque spaces between police and military is the DEA's elite Foreign-Deployed Advisory Support Team (FAST). With the reauthorization of the Patriot Act (which also included the Combat Methamphetamine Act) in 2006, the DEA was granted broader authority to investigate and act against "international drug traffickers" if it could show a connection to terrorist activities, a move that effectively made FAST the "foreign-deployed" strike arm of the DEA. As Charlie Savage reported for the *New York Times*, "The evolution of [FAST] into a global enforcement arm reflects the United States' growing reach in combating drug cartels and how policy makers increasingly are blurring the line between law enforcement and military activities, fusing elements of the 'war on drugs' with the 'war on terrorism.'"[54] Described as "part special-forces, part detectives," FAST assists US-friendly governments battling narcotics-financed insurgent groups.[55] FAST was authorized in its current form by George W. Bush to help disrupt Afghan heroin production, but the logic behind the program traces back to the Reagan administration,[56] which developed paramilitary counternarcotics programs over years of deployments in Colombia, Bolivia, and Peru.[57] Reimagined and reauthorized by Bush and since expanded by Obama, FAST now counts some fifty military-trained commandos among its ranks, all under direction of a former Navy SEAL, Richard Dobrich.[58] According to Dobrich, the teams under his command "plan and conduct special enforcement operations; train, mentor, and advise foreign narcotics law enforcement units; collect and assess evidence and intelligence in support of US and bilateral investigations"; and support the DEA's "Drug Flow Attack Strategy," in order to "disrupt and seize shipments of drugs, precursor chemicals, and operating capital."[59] Whereas counterinsurgency pacification forces were deployed in the early stages of the Vietnam War purportedly to halt the expansion of communism,[60] FAST agents are deployed on missions of "geostrategic importance" and battles the growing narcoterror threat. As Dobrich describes,

The insurgency relies on drug trafficking as a significant source of revenue to fund transportation of fighters, training facilities, communications, weapons, and logistics; Operations and intelligence have proven that many narcotics traffickers and insurgents are one in the same; Narcotics trafficking feeds corruption and threatens the Afghan government's legitimacy and is a strategic threat to USG policy and goals in Afghanistan; Government legitimacy and stabilization depends on the rule of law.[61]

According to the journalist Josh Meyer, who reported on DEA operations in Afghanistan for the *St. Louis Post-Dispatch*, deployment of FAST was a recognition that the war in Afghanistan could not be "won with military force alone" and was crucial to the mission to "decapitate the Taliban-linked drug trafficking networks fueling the insurgency and corrupting the Afghan government." DEA operations in Afghanistan, according to Meyer, included all the hallmarks of counterinsurgency pacification programs, placing special emphasis on training Afghan authorities in how to investigate and prosecute suspected drug traffickers.[62] The DEA's counterinsurgency war in Afghanistan is perhaps best characterized by the May 2009 attack on Loy Choreh bazaar, dubbed "Operation Siege Engine Two." According to US officials, Loy Choreh bazaar was a Taliban front, serving as an opium collection and processing center and a staging area for Taliban and al-Qaeda operations. At the end of the four-day battle, which claimed the lives of sixty-five insurgents, the US-trained Counter Narcotics Police of Afghanistan and DEA FAST agents had "accomplished the largest narcotics seizure to date in Afghanistan along with discovery of substantial quantities of war material."[63]

In a related operation weeks later, FAST agents captured the purported "Afghan drug kingpin" Haji Bagcho. Bagcho was extradited to the US to stand trial in federal court, and Justice Department officials alleged that he "used a portion of his drug proceeds to provide cash, weapons and other supplies to the former Taliban governor of Nangarhar Province and two Taliban commanders responsible for insurgent activity in eastern Afghanistan, so that they could continue their 'jihad' against western troops and the Afghan government." Found guilty in 2012, Bagcho was sentenced to life in a US prison and forfeited $254,203,032 in drug proceeds and his property in Afghanistan to the US government.[64]

Figure 6.1. DEA FAST Agents on counternarcoterror operations in Afghanistan, 2008.

While the image in figure 6.1 of US law enforcement agents on counternarcotics operations in Afghanistan may again confound the lines between policing and war, we should resist seeing programs like FAST as
"fusing" the "war on drugs" with the "war on terrorism" or as necessarily
new developments born of the exceptionality and uncertainty of a post-
9/11 world. If we take seriously its stated goals of carrying out "special
operations," gathering intelligence, educating and training local police,
disrupting illicit trade, and seizing material and capital, all with the underlying goal of propping up US-friendly regimes and the "rule of law,"
we must understand FAST as a counterinsurgency pacification project
deployed around the globe in furtherance of US economic and security
interests under cover of "counternarcoterror." Helping "host-nation counterparts" like Haiti, Honduras, the Dominican Republic, Guatemala, and
Belize impose a particular understanding of social order on unruly narcoscapes,[65] FAST is not in the business of drug control but rather is an operative in a borderless war for security and capitalist order. As the former
DEA chief of operations Michael Braun argued in his testimony before the
US House of Representatives Committee on Homeland Security, FAST is
increasingly important to US national security interests as it helps bring
"permissive" and "ungoverned environments" under the rule of law:

FTOs [foreign terrorist organizations] and drug trafficking organizations [DTOs] both work hard to create permissive environments in which to operate, relying heavily on the hallmarks of organized crime, corruption, intimidation and ruthless violence, to carve out territory in certain regions of the world so that they can operate with impunity. Our military and intelligence community commonly refer to these areas as ungoverned or under-governed space. FTOs and DTOs thrive in permissive environments, and invest hundreds of millions of dollars a year to disrupt good governance in many areas of the world by relentlessly undermining the rule of law. . . . Let me put it more candidly: If you want to visualize ungoverned space or a permissive environment, I tell people to simply think of the bar scene in the first "Star Wars" movie. Operatives from FTOs and DTOs are frequenting the same shady bars, the same seedy hotels and the same sweaty brothels in a growing number of areas around the world. And what else are they doing? Based on over 37 years in the law enforcement and security sectors, you can mark my word that they are most assuredly talking business and sharing lessons learned.[66]

Braun offers an important window into the institutional imagination of FAST, the DEA, and "homeland security" more broadly. There are, as he would have it, countless dark and seedy spaces around the world where "FTO and DTO operatives" plan, organize, and carry out the business of narcoterror. In order to secure US interests and ultimately the homeland, the ungoverned must be governed—*pacified*. It is important to be clear, however, that the DEA's understanding of permissive, ungoverned narcoscapes is not necessarily based on local cultures or the "host-nation counterpart's" juridical frameworks but rather is structured by a decidedly Western and American conception of social order: the US government's desire to neutralize threats to its economic and security interests and thus to pacify certain territories and populations.

While FAST is clearly a heavily armed counterinsurgency force aimed at supporting and imposing the rule of law, like the military advisers deployed in the early days of the Vietnam War, the program's proponents argue that it serves strictly an intelligence-gathering and advisory role and that only in "exigent circumstances" is force authorized. Deployed along the La Moskitia coast of Honduras in May 2012 as part of an ongoing counternarcotics operation dubbed Anvil, ten FAST agents were at least present for such "circumstances," a dead-of-night jungle firefight supposedly initiated by cocaine traffickers. Alluding to but stopping just short of directly comparing the firefight to counterinsurgency pacification projects honed in the jungles of Vietnam, a Honduran security official admitted, "I don't want to say it was Vietnam-style, but it was typical of war action."[67] While FAST and Honduran agents did seize cocaine from a canoe adrift in a river, the "war action" was decidedly one-sided. Having failed to engage or even locate the traffickers, Operation Anvil personnel did shoot and kill several unarmed locals who happened to be moving up the river at the same time. And though FAST representatives insist that team members did not fire, they have refused to provide the weapons for ballistics comparison. By fall of 2012, public outrage over these killings—and over another, of an unarmed fifteen-year-old boy shot and killed for failing to stop at a military checkpoint by Honduran forces that had been trained at the Western Hemisphere Institute for Security Cooperation (School of the Americas)—had prompted the United States to withhold millions of dollars in aid while it investigated allegations of human rights violations.[68] Not long after, Lisa Kubiske, US ambassador to Honduras, announced a new educational program for La Moskitia's children funded by the US Agency for International Development (USAID), meant to "expand the basic education and skills training for at-risk youth and adults." Other services, which were provided to "develop life skills such as teamwork, communication, discipline and respect" and to educate Moskitian "youth on drug and alcohol abuse prevention" and "reproductive and sexual health," mirror USAID programs in India, Philippines, Colombia, Mexico, and Zambia.[69] Through elite military forces like FAST and programs to "train," "educate," and "discipline" native subjects, US counternarcoterror projects invoke and elide the power to wage war simultaneously.[70]

Mérida, Beyond Mérida, "Plan [Pacification] Mexico"

Because the Mexican government has long been leery of allowing "boots on the ground" forces like FAST to operate within its borders, US counterinsurgency pacification strategies there take on a different form than those deployed in Afghanistan, Colombia, Honduras, and Peru. As the geographer Joseph Nevins describes it, the US uses a broad collaborative policing project focused on drug traffickers, human smugglers, and migrant workers and aimed at "pacifying the border."[71] Whereas counternarcoterror projects in Colombia, Peru, and Honduras are almost exclusively focused on cocaine, methamphetamine control figures prominently in similar efforts in Mexico. As Nevins points out, under the guise of border control, the US government has used its considerable influence over its Mexican counterparts to create a "quasi-buffer zone" between itself and the rest of Central and South America. Which is to say that through antismuggling and border-patrol projects in Mexico, the United States is able to enact a broader security strategy and exert political influence over other Latin American nations.

The so-called Mérida Initiative, a multiyear plan devised by George W. Bush and Mexican president Felipe Calderón in March 2007, details further the many ways US influence operates through its drug-control projects.[72] Under Mérida, also called "Plan Mexico" by its critics, the United States promised $1.6 billion in new funding over three years to provide equipment, training, and technical assistance to aid counternarcotics and antismuggling efforts in Mexico, Belize, Costa Rica, El Salvador, Guatemala, Honduras, Nicaragua, and Panama.[73] Distributing funds across key program areas—counternarcotics, counterterrorism, and border security; public security and law enforcement; institution building and rule of law—$1.3 billion went to support Mexican counternarcotics, counterterrorism, and border-security efforts.[74] Transferring millions of dollars in American hardware (including helicopters, surveillance aircraft, x-ray and gamma-ray scanners, and night-vision equipment), helping to modernize Mexican immigration and criminal justice databases in order to improve the exchange of information between the two countries, to say nothing of the education, "training and technical assistance" programs provided by US advisers to Mexican and Central American partners, Mérida effectively extended the breadth of US counternarcoterror projects by proxy. Though Mérida was set to expire at the end of 2010, it evolved and expanded under the Obama administration, which provided some $2.35 billion to support Mexican counternarcoterror operations by the end of 2014.[75] As William Brownfield, assistant secretary of state for the Bureau of International Narcotics and Law Enforcement Affairs, explained to a congressional oversight committee, the program moved away from "big ticket equipment and into an engagement that reinforces progress by further institutionalizing Mexican capacity to sustain adherence to the rule of law and respect for human rights, build strong institutions, promote full civil society participation, transform the nature of our borders, and by providing intensive technical assistance and training."[76] The new plan, Mérida II or Beyond Mérida, implemented in 2011, is organized around areas or "pillars" of material support administered by USAID and supported by US Northern Command (USNORTHCOM) and its Joint Task Force North (JTF North), based at Biggs Army Airfield, Fort Bliss, Texas.[77] The following briefly summarizes the activities organized under the pillars of Mérida II.

Pillar 1: Disrupting the Operational Capacity of Organized Crime. While the first iteration of Mérida delivered nearly $600 million in Black Hawk helicopters, surveillance aircraft, and other hardware to assist Mexican security efforts, Mérida II includes a new emphasis on disrupting the proceeds of drug trafficking and building intelligence infrastructure. Since the advent of the program in 2007, the Mexican government increasingly views "DTOs as for-profit corporations" and has sought new methods to disrupt and seize the flow of drug proceeds between the two nations.[78] Mérida II funds supported a program to limit and track the amount of US currency exchanged and deposited in Mexican banks and, in 2012, helped implement a new compendium of money-laundering laws and establish a federal financial-crimes unit to enforce them. Mérida II has also allowed US intelligence agencies to share information gathered by its surveillance-drone program with Mexican authorities, built a $13 million cross-border telecommunications system for sister cities along the US-Mexico border, and helped Mexico establish five regional Fusion-type intelligence centers.[79]

Pillar 2: Institutionalizing Reforms to Sustain the Rule of Law and Respect for Human Rights in Mexico. According to the Congressional Research Service, reforming Mexico's corrupt and inefficient criminal justice system, or at least developing it in such a way that it more closely resembles the US system, "is widely regarded as crucial for combating criminality, strengthening the rule of law, and better protecting citizen security and human rights in the country."[80] Partnering with Mexico's National Police Training Program, US agents have trained city, state, and federal police from each of Mexico's thirty-two states. Reforms have also extended into Mexican prisons, with Mérida II funds helping to refurbish and expand facilities and provide American Correctional Association accreditation to at least thirteen state and federal institutions. Reform efforts engage nonstate organizations as well, with Mérida II funds supporting "civil society and human rights-related non-governmental organizations . . . in order to strengthen their ability to monitor police conduct and provide input on policing policies."[81]

Pillar 3: Creating a "Twenty-First-Century Border." Recognizing that in "an increasingly globalized world, the notion of a border is necessarily more complex than a physical line between two sovereign nations," efforts under Mérida II to create a twenty-first-century border have focused on "(1) enhancing public safety via increased information sharing, screenings, and prosecutions; (2) securing the cross-border flow of goods and people; (3) expediting legitimate commerce and travel through investments in personnel, technology, and infrastructure; (4) engaging border communities in cross-border trade; and (5) setting bilateral policies for collaborative border management."[82] Mérida II has also supported Mexico's efforts to secure its borders with Guatemala and Belize. In addition to training and equipping Mexican security forces, the US Department of Defense has assisted in the development of Mexico's air mobility and surveillance capabilities and provided more than $10 million in "Non-Intrusive Inspection Equipment" to capture the biometric and biographic data of people moving throughout southern Mexico.

Pillar 4: Building Strong and Resilient Communities. Pillar 4 is unique as it enables design and implementation of community-based programs in high-crime areas in cities near the US-Mexico border to "address the underlying causes of crime and violence, promote security and social development, and build communities that can withstand the pressures of crime and violence." One of the ways Mérida II aims to accomplish this is through so-called Culture of Lawfulness programs that engage "law enforcement, security forces, and other public officials; the media; schools; and religious and cultural institutions" in "top-down" and "bottom-up" approaches to educate all sectors of society on the importance of upholding the rule of law. Culture of Lawfulness programs funded by the USAID include an anonymous tip line, crime and violence mapping projects intent on identifying "hot spots" so that authorities can "respond with tailored prevention measures," and programs that "provide safe spaces, activities and job training programs for youth at-risk of recruitment to organized crime." Millions more in grant funding was administered by the USAID to support community groups promoting social cohesion, outreach to at-risk youth, improved citizen-police collaboration, partnerships with private-sector enterprises, with more than $10 million awarded to just "six civil society organizations for innovative crime prevention projects that engage at-risk youth and their families." Culture of Lawfulness programs also include a robust "Drug Demand Reduction" component that has trained at least 600 counselors on a new drug-treatment curriculum, supported research and clinical trials as to its effectiveness, and worked toward establishing drug-treatment courts throughout the country. Perhaps the most interesting piece of the Culture of Lawfulness initiative as it relates to counterinsurgency pacification is its school-based programs, which include a multiyear Crime and Violence Prevention program delivered by federal and state police to students in nine communities identified by the Mexican government. Mexico made another similar DARE-style school-based education program a required component of its standard middle-school curriculum, delivering it to more than 800,000 students during the 2013–2014 school year.[83]

Critics have charged that, like Plan Colombia, the militarized aid provided by Mérida exacerbated violence in Mexico. In fact, as in Colombia, Mexico's homicide rate began its much-publicized climb in 2008, the first full year of Mérida, increasing by 50 percent in 2009 and again in 2010.[84] Under the guise of rooting out corruption and professionalizing Mexico's military, Mérida funds have trained thousands of Mexican soldiers at the Western Hemisphere Institute for Security Cooperation (School of the Americas).[85] As we have seen across Central and South America, the results of this sort of training are sadly rather predictable. According to Mexico's National Human Rights Commission, between 2007 and 2012, the country saw a five-fold increase in complaints of human rights violations made against soldiers and federal police; crimes alleged include torture, rape, and execution.[86]

Even though elite politicians like Brownfield continue to insist that Mérida is simply a "foreign assistance program" and was not "intended to be, nor does it represent, a US operation to counter Mexican drug cartels or criminal actors," in the broader context of US counternarco-terror efforts and in relation to past programs like Plan Colombia, it is

hard to understand the program outside of the counterinsurgency pacification framework. Building the legal infrastructure to seize assets and
prosecute financial crimes, expanding criminal justice under the guise
of reform, training police, "accrediting" prisons, propping up a decidedly American legal system, forging a "twenty-first-century border" to
monitor and restrict human mobility, the Mexican state, military, police,
and prison system are entwined with or perhaps have become proxy
of the world's military superpower.[87] In coupling these programs with
education programs that focus on "at-risk youth" and local cultures to
promote "lawfulness," Mérida clearly promotes both police and military force and ideological programs meant to win the hearts and minds
of the Mexican people. This is pacification par excellence or, as Dawn
Paley describes, a "counterinsurgency war within a formal democratic
framework."[88]

This point is punctuated by what Brownfield and others offer as
evidence of the program's success. In his congressional testimony,
Brownfield proudly announced that Mérida funds helped to develop
Plataforma Mexico, "one of the largest integrated criminal information
databases in the world," which produced immediate and dramatic increases in seized drugs, cash, weapons, and *human beings*. Pointing out
that "only one high-level cartel member" had been arrested by Mexican
authorities in the six years prior to Mérida, Brownfield argued that training provided to "over 50,000 Mexican Federal police and government
officials," helicopters to carry out "anti-cartel operations," and "secure
information sharing" of Plataforma Mexico helped create the foundation of a strong and responsive federal police and security apparatus.
Anecdotally, he disclosed a December 2010 operation of more than 800
Mexican police personnel supported by DEA and "Mérida-provided air
assets" that "dealt a severe blow" to cartel La Familia Michoacána, killing
one of its founders and leaders. In another operation in September 2011,
Black Hawk helicopters provided by the US to elite special forces of the
Mexican navy raided a Zetas training base, making several arrests and
seizing a large quantity of weapons and ammunition.[89] Since 2009, according to Brownfield, thirty-three "high level priority targets" including "four of the top seven most wanted" were "removed or arrested" by
Mérida-supported Mexican forces.[90] Testifying at similar hearings a few
years later, the analyst Steven Dudley had the number at "25 of 37 des-

ignated kingpins" either killed or captured by Mexican authorities since the program's inception.[91] Touting the ability to kill or capture high-value targets, Mérida again echoes the early pacification programs of the Vietnam War and the notorious Phoenix program, which placed an emphasis on "neutralizing" (capturing, converting, or killing) members of the Viet Cong infrastructure.[92]

In addition to helping to build an operational foothold in Mexico, Mérida enhances US police power within its borders as well. In 2009, Mérida intelligence and infrastructure no doubt came to bear on "Operation Xcellerator," a twenty-one-month, multiagency investigation that culminated in the arrest of more than 750 members of the Sinaloa Cartel. According to the DEA administrator, Michele Leonhart, Xcellerator stretched from Washington State to Maine, "arresting U.S. cell heads and stripping them of more than $59 million in cash—and seriously impacted their Canadian drug operations as well."[93] Proudly announcing the ability to take out operatives on either side of the border and "strip them of cash" reveals how counternarcoterror projects embolden US police powers and do the work of pacification and primitive accumulation simultaneously.

Mérida, the Sinaloa Cartel, and the Hunt for "El Chapo"

US counternarcoterror pacification projects in Mexico are perhaps best understood through the hunt for and eventual capture of Joaquín Archivaldo Guzmán Loera, more commonly known as "El Chapo" (Shorty), leader of the Sinaloa Cartel. Describing Guzmán as "one of the world's most wanted men," then US attorney general Eric Holder charged that he "contributed to the death and destruction of millions of lives across the globe through drug addiction, violence, and corruption." While it is clear that the Sinaloa Cartel is a brutal organization and likely guilty of the bulk of the Mexican and US governments' allegations, I would like to focus on how the Sinaloa Cartel and El Chapo in particular symbolically reaffirm counternarcoterror projects. Here we can clearly see the methamphetamine imaginary at work, as Guzmán being made responsible for the "death and destruction of millions of lives" is linked not only to cartel violence but to the pain and misery of small American towns littered with burned-out buildings and degraded "meth heads."

Perhaps alluding to the extent of US involvement in the capture, Holder praised the operation, describing it as a "landmark achievement" that demonstrated the ability to "work effectively with Mexico through the cooperative relationship that U.S. law enforcement agencies have with their Mexican counterparts."[94]

Born to poor farmers in a small mountain village in Sinaloa, Guzmán rose through the ranks of the Amado Carrillo Fuentes organization, one of four groups identified by the DEA in 1996 as key methamphetamine traffickers, to command the multibillion-dollar empire. As Patrick Keefe of the *New Yorker* put it, "Guzmán has been characterized by the U.S. Treasury Department as the 'world's most powerful drug trafficker,' and after the killing of Osama bin Laden, three years ago, he became perhaps the most wanted fugitive on the planet."[95]

Sometimes called the biggest drug-trafficking organization in history, the Sinaloa Cartel is considered by the DEA as the world's foremost trafficker of cocaine, marijuana, heroin, and methamphetamine. Said to be responsible for nearly half of all illegal drugs brought into the US each year, the Sinaloa group is described by Keefe as having "more in common with a terrorist organization like Al Qaeda than with the antiquated hierarchies of the Cosa Nostra."[96] With Sinaloa being just one of three cartels that distribute methamphetamine and methamphetamine precursors, El Chapo and the cartel can be understood as the chief meth dealer and meth-producing organization in the Americas, invoking the kingpin imaginaries of Pablo Escobar and *Scarface* and the global distribution networks of Gustavo Fring, the Juárez Cartel, and Madrigal Electromotive in *Breaking Bad*.[97] Given the many comparisons made by Keefe and others, Guzmán and the Sinaloa Cartel might even be understood as the Osama bin Laden and al-Qaeda of methamphetamine. Making similar comparisons, the US government seemed to agree, though the $5 million bounty it placed on Guzmán was some ways off the $25 million it offered for the "kill or capture" of bin Laden.[98]

After El Chapo's escape from a Mexican prison in 2001, he evaded capture by moving between a dozen or so ranches on the Sierra Madre Occidentals until February 2014, when Mexican Special Forces of "Operation Gargoyle," backed by DEA intelligence and surveillance drones, caught up with him, holed up in a luxury hotel in the resort city of Mazatlán. Yet for all the self-congratulatory press releases issued by US and Mexican authorities, Operation Gargoyle seems to have been just the final, however anticlimactic, act in a years-long game of cloak and dagger, cat and mouse. The beginning of the end of El Chapo's run occurred in early 2012, when US officials identified and began to track the signal from his Blackberry. For years, Guzman had eschewed the satellite phones favored by Mexican traffickers for the Blackberry, erroneously assuming that US intelligence officials could not as easily compromise devices made in Canada. A series of near captures over the next year or so led El Chapo to alter his security practices. As Keefe describes, "Like bin Laden, he might have chosen to rely on couriers. But a courier system is too inefficient for the fast pace of the narcotics trade, and so, as US and Mexican authorities eventually discovered, Chapo devised an elaborate solution."[99] Chapo commanded that all communications be run through Blackberry's instant messaging service; "trusted lieutenants" then collected information from subordinates using public wireless networks that could not be easily traced by Mexican and US authorities. Messages were transmitted through public networks, transcribed and transmitted again, going through several iterations of this "mirror system" until they were finally taken offline and delivered for Guzman's eyes only. Messages from El Chapo followed the same path in reverse. The tactic proved successful until DEA agents, as did CIA agents in the hunt for bin Laden, captured a member of Chapo's inner circle. And as with the brutalities carried out by US personnel at blacksite prisons in the war on terror and in name of (national) security, torture seems to have played a roll in the hunt for El Chapo. Using torture to obtain confessions has been a common tactic of US-backed counterinsurgency squads in the Americas since the earliest days of USAID and Office of Public Safety intervention[100] and in Mexico since 2008, when Calderón modified the constitution to introduce *arraigo*, a provision allowing lengthy detention of suspects in order to permit authorities to gather more evidence.[101] This seems to be the case here, as an unnamed DEA agent reportedly told Keefe, "The marines [Mexican special forces] tortured these guys. . . . They would never have given it up, if not for that."[102]

El Chapo, who had innovated the use of smuggling tunnels at the US-Mexico boarder, used them to stay on the run for a few more months, moving between a series of safe houses as US drones circled overhead and Mexican forces closed in. Given the ways the hunt for El Chapo played out in popular discourse, it should come as no surprise that the final moments of Operation Gargoyle strike familiar comparisons to the Navy SEAL raid on bin Laden's Abbottabad compound. As Keefe describes,

> The commandos needed no battering ram as they crashed through a flimsy wooden door, shouting, "Marines!" . . . Guzmán had scrambled out of bed in his underwear, grabbed an assault rifle, and darted into a small bathroom. "Don't kill him!" [his wife pleaded]. "He's the father of my children!" The standoff lasted only a few seconds, with the marines bellowing and [his wife] screaming. Then Chapo shouted, "O.K., O.K., O.K., O.K.!" and extended his empty hands through the bathroom doorway. It had been a stunningly swift operation: less than three minutes after the marines stormed the apartment, Guzmán surrendered.

When the thirteen-year long hunt for the "world's most dangerous drug trafficker" finally came to its end, he was surrounded not by bodyguards, weapons, or mounds of cocaine but by his wife, children, their nanny, and their personal chef. Indeed, as Keefe remarked, "No one would have imagined such a legendary outlaw going out in anything but a firefight."[103] Yet even this is somehow reminiscent of the hunt for bin Laden, at least as imagined in the film *Zero Dark Thirty*. In the end, two of the world's most wanted and dangerous men—both surrounded by women and children—offered little resistance, one leaving in handcuffs, the other in a body bag.

Infrastructure built by Mérida aided in the hunt for El Chapo at every turn. From training and equipment provided to police and military, intelligence gathered by surveillance drones and shared through newly built databases, and the ideological work of Culture of Lawfulness programs, Mérida effectively extended US police power through Mexican proxies. In July 2015, after little more than a year in custody, Guzmán again worked free of authorities, making his escape through a tunnel engineered into a prison shower room. The DEA soon warned that Guzmán had reassumed leadership of the Sinaloa Cartel and hence "reestablished himself as the leader of the Mexican drug trade." And so, in a rather seamless fashion, US and Mexican authorities picked up where they had left off: the hunt for "the world's #1 fugitive and a Forbes-listed billionaire" began anew.[104] Of course, the sixteen or so months that El Chapo was sidelined in a Mexican prison did not have a significant impact on the drug trade, nor did it signal the end of counternarcoterror projects in Mexico.[105] Yet is important to consider how the ongoing hunt for El Chapo and the hunts yet to come do important political and cultural work on behalf of the US and Mexican governments and private corporations that benefit greatly from the drug war.

El Chapo, like Pablo Escobar, Haji Bagcho, and Osama bin Laden, is the threat, target, and enemy that the security state covets—its entire raison d'être. Like the first whispers of cartel violence brought into being with Escobar and jihad as put into practice by bin Laden and al-Qaeda, the combination of extreme violence, narco-refugees, the reverberating ills of the drug trade, and the specter of a failed state make the discourse of cartel wars a particularly powerful ideological message. Underlining the importance of this discourse to US security, if not business interests, Paul Rexton Kan of the US Army War College urges, "to admit an increasing number of asylum seekers into the United States undermines the message that Mexico is safe for American businesses and that the Mexican government is strong enough to prevail against the cartels."[106] Through "kingpin" or "decapitation" strategies that aim to deal with groups like the Sinaloa Cartel by neutralizing their leadership, the US and Mexican governments send an equally strong ideological reply: *Mexico is open for business*. Importantly, however, hidden within the message that capturing El Chapo has made Mexico safer for the public and capital is the concurrent reminder that police and state power prevail.

In order to more fully reckon the underlying economic incentives and the state's complicity in drug-war violence, as Dawn Paley insists, it is imperative to think outside the conceptual frame of the discourse of cartel wars and the assumption that counternarcoterror work is simply about arresting cartel violence.[107] As the drug war did in Colombia, the one in Mexico has helped produce a more welcoming environment for US businesses. Again, quite telling in this regard are Brownfield's remarks at another Mérida hearing. This time appearing before the House Foreign Affairs Subcommittee on the Western Hemisphere, he urged,

In every society, citizen security underpins economic stability and allows trade, investment, energy development, and education exchanges to flourish. The partnership forged between the United States and the Government of Mexico over the past six years under the Mérida Initiative exemplifies how strengthening citizen security supports these broader objectives. We have worked together to strengthen the capacity of Mexico's justice sector to counter organized crime and its violent and corrupting effects.[108]

Echoing John Walter's assertion that what is good for the economy is good for security, Brownfield admits the economic motives underlying US security projects. As in Colombia, US security contractors benefited greatly from Mérida. Some of the same private corporations—DynCorp, Northrup-Grumman—that were paid to support Plan Colombia and help put Iraq and Afghanistan back together are at work in Mexico's drug war, spraying crops and training police. Other military-connected subcontractors are doing the work of broad neoliberal reforms. For instance, Paley reports that in 2009, USAID awarded the Massachusetts-based ABT Associates more than $17 million to plan and implement the "Mexico Competitiveness Program," charged with the ambiguous task of "increasing private sector competitiveness," among others.[109]

While Mérida is certainly in keeping with the neoliberal rationality of opening and facilitating markets or promoting "citizen security," which underpins "economic stability," as Brownfield puts it, we should be careful not to overlook the ways counternarcoterror projects function very efficiently as primitive accumulation. For instance, in January 2015, the DEA announced indictments of sixty members of the Sinaloa Cartel, including its new leader, Ismael Zambada-Garcia "El Mayo," and Ivan Archivaldo Guzmán-Salazar, known as "Chapito," or "Little Chapo," El Chapo Guzmán's son. According to a DEA press release, the case emerged from what the agency thought to be a small-scale drug-distribution cell involving the "Deep Valley Bloods and the Deep Valley Crips street gangs" and morphed into a massive multinational, multistate probe of the Sinaloa Cartel that drew in police from California, Nevada, Texas, South Carolina, Delaware, Pennsylvania, Minnesota, Kentucky, Georgia, and cooperating agencies in Mexico, Canada, Colombia, Great Britain, the Philippines, Guatemala, and China. In addition to thousands of kilograms of methamphetamine, cocaine, heroin, and marijuana, the operation also allowed US authorities to seize more than "$14.1 million in narcotics proceeds, . . . 1982 Cessna Turbo 210 aircraft, a Lamborghini Murceilago luxury vehicle, and other vehicles and property."[110]

Incentive-based policing, or "policing for profit" as described by its critics, is a widespread practice authorized by most states and federal law. Even domestically, so widespread is civil-asset forfeiture that in 2008, for the first time, the US Justice Assets Forfeiture Fund held more than $1 billion. While individual accounting practices make it difficult to estimate, asset forfeiture at the state level is no doubt just as lucrative and perhaps even more so.[111] The billions in assets—cash, homes, vehicles—often seized with little proof of any wrongdoing, firmly position the drug war within the broader class war. In order to reproduce disparate class relations, the drug war regulates, by force, who can earn a living and how. Recalling the "Afghan heroin lord" Haji Bagcho—taken off the battlefield by DEA FAST forces, sentenced to life in a US prison, and ordered to surrender millions in cash and property to the US government—we can see how counternarcoterror projects neutralize economic and security threats simultaneously. El Chapo, the peasant farmer who rose to the heights of a multibillion-dollar empire, is no different. Guzmán, like all other Robin Hood figures who live outside the conventional bourgeois social order, represents a subject who refused his ascribed position, refused to remain poor, and thus refused to be governed. Writing on the logics of the manhunt, which underpinned the hunt for El Chapo, Grégoire Chamayou reasons that to bring order to disorder, there is but one recourse: "Violent hunting will be carried out in the form of war on men who, being born to be commanded, refuse to be commanded. In other words, the only thing left to do is to subjugate by force a prey that does not want to be a prey."[112] By "decapitating" the cartel, capturing its king, and bringing the "drug lord" to justice, the hunt for El Chapo aimed to reestablish by force the ontological order of ruler and ruled, the state's legitimacy, and the innate inequalities of capitalist life. To police the drug war is to police and thus reproduce the disparate social relations of life under late capitalism. *The king is dead! Long live the king!*

***

And so the hunt ensues and the drug war rages. Like the waves of dealers taken off street corners and open-air drug markets in the US interior, the work of counternarcoterror carries on, methodically identifying, locating, and eliminating new targets. As I finished writing this chapter, in fact, I received yet another emailed DEA press release announcing the capture of Servando Gómez-Martínez, also known as "La Tuta" (The teacher), leader of Knights Templar, "one of the world's most vicious and violent drug and criminal networks" and the latest in a bottom less reservoir of threats that will no doubt propel US counternarcoterror pacification projects into the coming years.

Epilogue

Endless (Drug) War

"You know what I say to people when I hear they're writing anti-war books?"

"No. What *do* you say, Harrison Starr?"

"I say, 'Why don't you write an anti-*glacier* book instead.'"

What he meant, of course, was that there would always be wars, that they were as easy to stop as glaciers. I believe that, too.

And even if the wars didn't keep coming like glaciers, there would still be plain old death.

—Kurt Vonnegut, *Slaughterhouse-Five*

I would like to return to my initial premise—what if we need the drug war? This question might seem absurd and in some respects quite insulting in the face of those who have spent decades working to end the drug war and pick up the pieces left in its wake. In no way is this theoretical provocation meant to dismiss these efforts. To be sure, not only do many people reject the drug war flatly, but increasingly some urge reformers to demand more than simply ending the drug war. Marie Gottschalk, for instance, has argued that if the US were to release every person presently serving time on drug charges, it would reduce state prison populations by only about 20 percent.[1] To seriously challenge mass imprisonment, Gottschalk urges activists to reprioritize their efforts and think beyond simply ending the drug war. While some like Gottschalk argue for refocused priorities, others hope to reframe or banish the drug war altogether. Shortly after Gil Kerlikowske assumed his post as director of National Drug Control Policy in 2009, he announced the Obama administration's desire to do away with the language of war, explaining, "Regardless of how you try to explain to people it's a 'war on drugs' or a 'war on a product,' people see a war as a war on them. We're not at war with people in this country."[2] Kerlikowske's declaration drew immediate praise from those on the political left who hoped the Obama administration would follow through on promises of shifting to a public-health model of drug control. Some hopeful academics even declared, "By that single statement, Kerlikowske changed the frame about illegal drugs in America; henceforth, instead of battling an enemy, our leaders would be offering treatment. Consider the consequences of this reframe: In place of militaristic imagery, the Office of National Drug Control Policy would use the langue of healing and restoration of 'sick' individuals. It was a dramatic shift in focus, with real world policy implications."[3] Even though the Obama administration commuted a number of particularly egregious drug sentences and reduced the notorious crack/cocaine sentencing disparity from 100:1 to 18:1, it did not succeed in rebranding or doing away with the "militaristic imagery" of the drug war, nor did it usher in more humane treatment for those pitiful souls pulled into its gears.

As American wars have come and gone, the drug war—its longest war—has endured, raging across sweltering mountain jungles, bombed-out city streets, and deserted country roads. And despite the many attempts at changing its course, the drug war has in fact kept coming like a glacier. Yet much like methamphetamine, a drug ubiquitous and illusory at once, the war itself is at times fleeting and hard to grasp. This is especially so for those privileged populations spared the incessant harassment of aggressive policing, the far-reaching consequences of a criminal record, and other costs of misguided practices carried out under the guise of safety and security. Yet consider Kerlikowske's facile claim that the drug war is not a "war with people" in relation to the following letter that appeared in the opinion column of a small Nebraska newspaper. Writing from county jail, the unnamed author pens a heart-wrenching "Dear John" letter to methamphetamine:

> Dear Meth,
> Due to my intense hatred toward you and everything you represent, I do not regret to inform you that I am writing this letter to finalize the end of our very sick and twisted relationship. We must conclude this love affair, part ways and never look back. I do not need, nor do I in any

way want you in my life. If ever I catch you lurking in the shadows of
my life again, I will hunt you down and rip your beating heart out and
let everyone around me watch as I lay your heart on the ground and
stomp on it, just as you have done with mine. Meth, do you remember
all of the amazing promises you made to me? The promise to make my
life better and enhance every aspect of my life? The promise to give me
more friends, more loyal friends? The promise to help me do better at
work and be more successful? Well, you are a damned liar, Meth. Lies
are all you told, and the biggest lie of all was that you wouldn't lie. You
are nothing but a coward and a hypocrite.

I am a strong man. I am declaring war against you. You caused a war
in me—a war against myself, and I almost lost.

But now the battle is against you and I will not lose this battle. I am
going to show the world that I am the winner and that you are the true
loser. You ain't nothing, Meth. You better recognize it. I will end this war
and I will come out on top as the victor.

I hate you, Meth. I wish you was dead. Now go to hell. I am never
again yours.[4]

The prisoner leaves no doubt: aimed by the state, police, and public
at users like him, the drug war rages. In fact, it may be that he best
embodies the drug war. Stewing in rage, humiliation, and self-loathing,
he fights the drug war as much within and against himself as against
methamphetamine.

No matter shifting prison demographics or tone-deaf attempts at rebranding, no matter how fleeting or hard to grasp, it is clear that the
drug war continues to haunt the lives of the most vulnerable. And so we
might see those things that cannot be recorded on a questionnaire or
codified as legislation—the imaginary—as its most insidious and harmful dimensions. While at the outset I explained how some people do in
fact see methamphetamine everywhere, to apprehend the drug war in
the contemporary everyday, particularly in light of those who hope to
deemphasize, reframe, or declare it "over" or lost, the target for radical
critique must be that which is often ignored by policy makers and orthodox scholarship. As we have seen, the drug war could not be a normalized, routine, livable part of everyday life if not for the immaterial and
transitory dimensions experienced through human culture and interac-

tion. From the vicarious violence of hit television shows, crime-control projects that (re)produce monstrous abjection and racial hierarchy, and newspaper politics that lay the groundwork for invasive legislation and perform the horror of murdered police, to the cultural work of small-town cops, best-selling novels, diagrams of drug flows, maps of meth lab homes, and global manhunts for narcoterrorists, the imaginary schematizes the wars on crime/drugs/terror as a livable background of everyday life. These wars are very much part of that which captivates and entertains, and we might say we encounter them first in the imagination and perhaps not at all otherwise.

For an example drawn from the contemporary moment, police in Florida continue their campaign against synthetic drugs, warning the public of "the dangers of a new drug called Flakka." In one particularly frightening news broadcast, a Broward County Sheriff's deputy cautioned, "If you come across somebody high on drugs, and it's a super strength drug and they have super strength and you try to detain them, talk to them and they get violent, it could be a bad situation." The segment included a local emergency-room physician who corroborated the deputy's account, adding, "They're hallucinating. They're on a psychotic state, they may have superhuman strength."[5] And though the surveillance footage offered as evidence showed a man allegedly "high on Flakka" angrily jerking on locked office doors, it hardly confirmed the old cliché of subjects granted "superhuman strength" by some "new" drug. This criticism matters little, however, for those who already position drugs as the catalyst of violent monstrosity. A report posted to the social media account of *American Police Beat Magazine*—with the caption, "WARNING! New drug on the streets can give people superhuman strength. Just what you need, right?"—elicited readers who commented, "wonderful, something else to deal with," "They are [sic] going to be alot [sic] of problems," "police will need bigger guns," and "shot guns would work good."[6]

Viewing the present through the past, we are reminded of how fetishizing drugs works to disavow and hence justify all manner of inequality and horrific violence. In 1914, the *New York Times* published the now-infamous article "Negro Cocaine 'Fiends' Are a New Southern Menace," by Edward Huntington Williams, M.D., which alleged that "murder and insanity [were] increasing among lower class blacks because the have taken to 'sniffing' since deprived of whisky by prohibition." Williams went on to suggest that cocaine could "make the 'fiend' a peculiarly dangerous criminal" by providing resistance to the "knock down effects" of standard police firearms. As evidence, Williams offered the case of a "cocaine sniffing negro" in Asheville, North Carolina, who while "running amuck in a cocaine frenzy" attempted to stab a storekeeper. When police confronted the "hitherto inoffensive negro," a scuffle ensued, prompting the "him or me" mantra still used to justify policing killings today. Pressing the "muzzle over the negro's heart," the officer fired, "intending to kill him right and quick," but the shot, followed by another, "did not even stagger the man." The policeman, worried he would need his remaining ammunition for the "gathering mob of infuriated negroes," "finished the man with his club" and the next day "exchanged his revolver for one of heavier calibre."[7] As the criminologist Doris Marie Provine and others have observed, simply the suggestion that cocaine could transform a "hitherto inoffensive negro" into a violent, unstoppable "fiend" was all that was necessary to arm southern police with weapons of greater "shocking power" and to further license the extermination of blacks, whether intoxicated or otherwise.[8] It is important to reassert that this case is not simply early drug-war propaganda but part of complex history put to work by everyday people in order to understand their own present. Given the long-standing myth of people, particularly black people, transformed into monsters by cocaine, "Flakka," and so on, we are better able to understand why when attempting to justify the killing of Michael Brown, Officer Darren Wilson said, "[Brown] had the most intense aggressive face. The only way I can describe it, it looks like a demon, that's how angry he looked."[9] Whether Brown was intoxicated or not, in order for Wilson to justify his actions, he needed only to invoke the demonic so as to access the already-existing cultural imaginary of transformation, dehumanization, and monstrosity. Police, Egon Bittner has written, are in the business of fighting monsters or, more plainly, eradicating threats. Yet it is the imagination from which threats emerge, and it is the public that gives the monsters names.[10]

The ways that we go about naming our monsters has, of course, been the abiding concern in this book. In a drug imagined as the near-exclusive domain of poor, isolated, rural people, we glimpse hidden dimensions of a starkly racialized carceral system. If we are to understand the drug war as a project of accumulation, as argued in chapter 6, life sentences handed down for simply selling the drug, child-endangerment laws aimed at derelict mothers, and police killings of unarmed suspects "high on meth"[11] provide powerful evidence of the ways in which poor "white trash" are also subjects of the political economy of punishment and mass imprisonment. This is a critical point made by Jonathan Simon, who urges critical academics and activists not to assume that mass imprisonment befalls only racial minorities.[12] Similarly and much as I have argued here, Gottschalk also suggests that methamphetamine has opened up a "new front" of the war on drugs "in rural predominately white areas," which may account for the declining disparity between black and white drug arrests.[13]

Whether the drug war does or does not operate as an engine of mass imprisonment still does not quite address my initial provocation—what if we need the drug war? As I have proposed, the drug war may help some people cope with the pervasive anxieties of contemporary social life, what Jock Young, borrowing from Anthony Giddens, has dubbed "ontological insecurity." For Young, discontinuities of personal biography, social disembeddedness, and economic precariousness create for some people an identity crisis, a deeply felt sense of existential aimlessness and insecurity. From this precariousness of being spring forth all manner of punitive sentiments and the social divisions marking self and other.[14]

Without disagreeing with Young, we might add that the certainty of human mortality generates social anxieties far more timeless and unmoving than those furnished by the bustle of late modernity. In fact, the criminologists Fenna Van Marle and Shadd Maruna have observed that Young's understanding of ontological insecurity is highly compatible with a large body of empirical research in terror management theory (TMT), first derived from anthropologist Ernest Becker's Pulitzer Prize–winning *The Denial of Death*.[15] As Becker wrote, "The idea of death, the fear of it, haunts the human animal like nothing else; it is a mainspring of human activity—activity designed largely to avoid the fatality of death, to overcome it by denying in some way that it is the final destiny for man."[16] For the contemporary proponents of TMT Sheldon Solomon, Jeff Greenberg, and Tom Pyszcynski, the cultural worldview that imbues everyday life with order, meaning, and permanence, though often taken for granted, is quite fragile and thus must be perpetually reproduced and defended. This is particularly so when individuals are confronted with an event that reminds them of the precariousness of their particular social system and, more importantly, of the impermanence of their own lives. Numerous TMT studies provide convincing evidence suggesting that when confronted with the terror of death, in order to reaffirm the security of life as meaningful and eternal, human beings tend to "react generously" to that which reinforces their values and lash out at "anyone or anything that calls those beliefs into question."[17]

Put in dialogue with Žižek's fetishistic disavowal, ontological insecurity, the denial of death, and terror management theory lend some clarity to decades of repeated drug-war failures. Here individuals beset by the existential insecurities of late-modern life are permitted to reject the drug war as a failure and cite its many deleterious effects, while still clinging to the system through which it is authorized. Again, this is not to suggest simple denial or willful ignorance but rather a ruse helping to disown the often-dire circumstances of our own lives and the unassailable march toward death. As the famed writer and critic James Baldwin wrote in *The Fire Next Time*,

> Life is tragic simply because the earth turns and the sun inexorably rises and sets, and one day, for each of us, the sun will go down for the last, last time. Perhaps the whole root of our trouble, the human trouble, is that we will sacrifice all the beauty of our lives, will imprison ourselves in totems, taboos, crosses, blood sacrifices, steeples, mosques, races, armies, flags, nations, in order to deny the fact of death, the only fact we have. It seems to me that one ought to rejoice in the fact of death—ought to decide, indeed, to earn one's death by confronting with passion the conundrum of life. One is responsible for life: It is the small beacon in that terrifying darkness from which we come and to which we shall return.[18]

It may be that drugs and the drug war are but two more of the many totems erected in order to deny, however so briefly, the fact of death. And so what Baldwin, Young, Becker, and Žižek all seem to be pointing toward is the disjuncture between our everyday practices and our innermost beliefs, the things that we do and say, regardless of what we believe to be true, the *je sais bien, mais quand-même* (I know very well, but nevertheless) muttered under our breath.

As with the perpetually recycled drug panics of the interior, decades of international drug policy are driven by the same existential insecurities. Recently, the long-standing California senator and chairperson of the powerful Senate Intelligence Committee Diane Feinstein joined the cause, invoking the imaginary to sound alarm bells over the "dramatic" increase in "Mexican meth" traveling across the border south of San Diego and a supposed spike in meth-linked deaths. Recapitulating the same tired policies, Feinstein urged for more funding for police and HIDTA task forces and paid lip service to "treatment." Most urgent, however, was her insistence on increased cooperation with "international partners," in which one could not help but be reminded of "cooperation" in the form of Plan Colombia and Mérida. In addition to roundly praising the strength of the US partnership with Mexico, Feinstein interestingly drew a new player into the conversation and thus the methamphetamine imaginary:

> China is one of the largest suppliers of meth precursor chemicals, and we must redouble our efforts to encourage the Chinese government to stop these shipments. Our legislative and law enforcement efforts have done a great deal to combat domestic meth production, but drug traffickers have adapted. To ensure previous successes aren't reversed, we need to address these new challenges quickly and effectively. We must prevent meth from infiltrating our borders and confront its deadly consequences.[19]

Reading Feinstein's warnings through a history of drug-war projects and the increasingly relentless onslaught of news headlines like "Chinese Meth Bust Smells a Lot like Breaking Bad"[20] or "Flakka, Florida's Latest Drug Scourge, Can Easily Be Purchased Online in China,"[21] one cannot help but anticipate how China's alleged role in US drug problems might in the near future serve as the ideological basis for new drug-control, perhaps counternarcoterror projects, aiming not toward the Global South but eastward at China.

It is this sort of discursive work that greases the gears of the much-larger ideological machinery undergirding international drug control. Rendering threats knowable, the methamphetamine and drug-war imaginaries are the connective tissue in a broader politics of security linking the internal, external, foreign, domestic, global, and local. It is worth restating that the importance of the imaginary to these broader security projects is not a theoretical abstraction or simply speculation. As early as 2004, mainstream publications such as the *Washington Post*[22] began reporting on a number of government programs working to imagine the range of potential threats from foreign terrorists, domestic radical groups, state-sponsored adversaries, and labor-union activists, later described as the "universal adversary."[23] One program, called Analytic Red Cell or simply Red Cell, adds the input of novelists and screenwriters to the typical roster of homeland-security personnel to provide "independent and alternative assessments intended to provoke thought and stimulate discussion."[24] In other words, the US security state relies on novelists and Hollywood screenwriters to imagine new and impossible threats to the "homeland" and prepare accordingly. As one participant in universal adversary planning described for the *New York Times*, "There are almost limitless forms of terrorist attacks, but many of them will employ the same kinds of trade craft. Knowing the trade craft helps a great deal as it can allow you to stay one step ahead of the terrorist."[25] Because such programs are predicated on thinking the unthinkable in order to know the unknowable, "insurgent narcoterrorists" no doubt figure in prominently. In testimony before the Senate Homeland Security and Governmental Affairs Committee on "southern border violence" in 2009, then secretary of Department of Homeland Security Janet Napolitano described how "planning contingencies for worst-case scenarios" were a fundamental aspect national security: "I believe the United States can effectively help to suppress the violence in Mexico, by both doing our part on our side of the border and providing assistance to Mexican authorities. However, this does not mitigate our need to plan for worst-case scenarios, even if they are unlikely—and not only scenarios where the United States encounters significant spillover violence, but also other situations where DHS capabilities could be strained as a result of ongoing violence."[26]

In scenarios in which Mexican cartels team up with jihadists to smuggle weapons of mass destruction into the US and in which cartel violence and waves of "narco-refugees" spill across the southern border, the methamphetamine and drug-war imaginaries are clearly at work within a reciprocal system of cultural production, where the screen actively scripts the actions of police and state power.[27] Indeed the relationship between screenwriters and the security state goes both ways in coordinated efforts to "get the right ideological message across not only to Americans, but also to the Hollywood public around the globe," providing, as Žižek describes, the "ultimate empirical proof that Hollywood does in fact operate as an 'ideological state apparatus.'"[28]

While we might be able to see the many ways that the methamphetamine imaginary is at work with a longer history of state violence, this still does not quite address my initial proposition—what if we need the drug war? This book has deliberately operated at the level of the cultural, ideological, and imaginary, in order to identify and critique the oft-ignored background that sustains and propels the drug war, but only as a symptom of the broader system. An anticipated criticism of this approach might be that writing of this sort is often long on critique and rather short on alternatives. Admittedly, a way forward in terms of concrete policy has not been a central concern of this book. Yet this does not suggest nonintervention or postpolitical apathy but rather a more deliberate strategy. Far more modest than actually "doing away with the drug war," my goal has been to identify and confront it in its most mundane forms and to position it within the terrain of a much-larger symbolic order.

So in some ways, I might agree with those who argue for deemphasizing the drug war if only to avoid fetishizing it. It may be that a better question is, What would happen if the drug war ended? Žižek offers a possible answer, when in *Welcome to the Desert of the Real!* he argues that those who hope to expose the state's impotence by assailing it with impossible demands also expose their own insincerities:

> For example, when "radical" academics demand full rights for immigrants and opening of the borders, are they aware that the direct implementation of this demand would, for obvious reasons, inundate developed Western countries with millions of newcomers, thus provoking a violent working-class racist backlash which would then endanger the privileged position of these very academics? Of course they are, but they count on the fact that their demand will not be met in this way, they can hypocritically retain their clear radical conscience while continuing to enjoy their

privileged position. . . . In both cases, the gesture is that of calling the other's bluff, counting on the fact that what the other really fears is that one will fully comply with his or her demand.[29]

The dual purpose of this "game of hysterical provocation," as he calls it, is to challenge the master while producing and maintaining a position of radical conscience and a place in the larger order of things. If the drug war is indeed in service of the capitalist order, would doing away with it not also require doing away with the system that authorizes it? Is this possibility too unfathomable?

Here it might be useful to return to the Althusserian understanding of ideology, whereby state power and authority interpellates the individual as subject. Inverting this order, the theorist Jodi Dean argues that bourgeois ideology interpellates the subject as individual. So rather than a theory of subjection, she proposes that ideological interpellation actually makes more sense as a theory of individuation. Dean offers the Protestant Reformation as an example of bourgeois ideology's interpellation of the subject as individual, arguing that in the break from Catholic communality, Protestant theologies fashion believers as wholly responsible for their own salvation. As she would have it, being hailed by the police or addressed by power is to be singled out from the crowd, called forth and singularized in relation to a background. Through ideological interpellation, what was once a crowd becomes a loose collection of separable individuals.[30] Here Dean sets out the individual as a form of enclosure, a once-communal entity claimed, privatized, and put into the service of capitalism. Interpellation of the social subject as individual helps conceptualize agency only as the exercised will of the actor, freedom to that which can only be understood as individual experience and property to that which is singularly possessed. Accordingly, ideological individuation schematizes the social as a primitive form prone to groupthink and irrational, if not violent, behavior. Dean elaborates, "It is bourgeois ideology that treats conditions that are collective and social, embedded in histories of violence and systems of exploitation, as if they were relationships specific to an individual, as if states arose through individual consent, as if politics were a matter of individual choice, and as if desires and capacities, affects and will naturally originate from and reside in an individual form."[31]

At the beginning of the book, I set out my aim of describing a few of the many ways in which individuals imagine themselves and their relations to one another through methamphetamine and the drug war. Interlaced with or conditioned by bourgeois ideology, the methamphetamine and drug-war imaginaries help to individualize the most fundamental of social relations. Interpellating the social subject as enclosed individual erases these revolutionary possibilities and instead encourages the recognition and treatment of others as "trash," "monsters," and "animals."

Drawing on Frederic Jameson, the criminologists Simon Winlow and Steve Hall have argued that in the contemporary moment, when political will and social solidarity are in short order, it may in fact be easier to imagine the end of the world than a better one.[32] In this respect, the drug war is perhaps most necessary for those who fashion their identities and earn their livings railing against it. This might seem like a highly contradictory statement given the book's apparent subject matter. Yet this is precisely my point: what I hope I have written is not a book about methamphetamine or the drug war but a critique of the politics, culture, and ideology that underpin and animate both. In *The Magic of the State*, Michael Taussig writes that "fear drives you to reduce something strange into something familiar so you no longer marvel at it."[33] This is precisely a function of the drug war, as the fear and insecurity that structure it disown and disavow the many strange contradictions of the present social order and our shared fates as finite beings. Meanwhile, laws are passed, careers are made, race and class divisions are reborn, and bodies pile up. If the drug war can be understood as a death wish, then it manifests as a compulsion to repeat, a surrogate social world chosen and a future preferred over others. To produce another world, we cannot begin by simply ending the drug war. More modestly, we must engage the imaginary in such a way that we may begin to believe that a better world is possible.

NOTES

INTRODUCTION

1. KFVS12.com (2014).
2. McLaughlin (2014).
3. US Attorney's Office, Northern District of Georgia (2015).
4. Data provided by the Kansas Department of Corrections TOADS database (February 15, 2011) include all drug tests recorded in the TOADS system from 2004–2010 and indicate that meth use among intensive probationers is in on par with cocaine (2.7 percent) and about half as frequent as marijuana (5.9 percent).
5. Detailed tables on meth-lab seizure statistics can be found at www.accesskansas.org/kbi/de/stats_meth.shtml.
6. Tzanelli and Yar (2014).
7. C. Taylor (2004), 23.
8. My formulation of the methamphetamine imaginary also shares some overlap with Raymond Williams's "structures of feeling" (1975).
9. For an excellent discussion of the cultural production of cyberspace, see Yar (2014a).
10. Proclamation 5562, Crack/Cocaine Awareness Month, October 1986. In 1986, President Ronald Reagan named October Lupus Awareness Month, American Liver Foundation National Liver Awareness Month, National Down Syndrome Month, National Spina Bifida Month, Polish American Heritage Month, *and* Crack/Cocaine Awareness Month.
11. Following William Garriott's (2011) use of the term, *narcopolitics* describes the drug war as a distinct governing strategy animated across the social, cultural, and political fields, rather than simply being a disparate collection of policies and political rhetoric.
12. A note on the use of "drug war" versus "war on drugs": whenever possible, "drug war" is used in this book, as "drugs," much like "terror," are an illusory object against which war cannot be waged. Further, "war on drugs" is misleading and disingenuous, as the "war" has never been on drugs but on those marginalized and superfluous populations with which they are associated. Finally, as the drug was employs similar tactics and costs countless lives, it should be understood as a literal war, not necessarily in the conventional sense but as a war fought on the terrain of class relations. Therefore, in order to name it for what it is, whenever possible, we should draw direct links to recognizable wars, such as the Vietnam War, the Iraq War, etc.

13. Balko (2014b).
14. Alexander (2010).
15. Proclamation 8086, National Methamphetamine Awareness Day, 2006, http://www.presidency.ucsb.edu/ws/?pid=24335.
16. Bush speaking to a group of schoolchildren, parents, and teachers, September 17, 2002, Nashville, Tennessee.
17. Frydl (2013).
18. Žižek (2009b).
19. Žižek (2009b), 53.
20. Žižek (2009a), 299–300.
21. See, for instance, Wirth (1928). However, following Small (2008), use of "ghetto" here should be understood as a stereotype hastily applied to inner-city neighborhoods by popular discourse and academic research and thus should be viewed critically.
22. Frydl (2013).
23. Marx (1970), 131.
24. Sexton (2011). The US Department of Justice (2000) defines methamphetamine as a synthetic psychostimulant that produces intoxication, dependence, and psychosis. Methamphetamine has mood-altering effects, behavioral effects such as increased activity and decreased appetite, and a high lasting eight to twenty-four hours. Although there is an initial general sense of well-being, methamphetamine use has been associated with both long- and short-term problems such as brain damage, cognitive impairment and memory loss, stroke, paranoia, anorexia, hyperthermia, hepatitis, HIV transmission, and violence. Methamphetamine is a Schedule II drug, available only through a highly restricted prescription procedure. Medical uses include treatment for narcolepsy, attention deficit disorder, and obesity.
25. Hart et al. (2012), 586–608.
26. Jenkins (1994).
27. Schumer (2006).
28. Hendricks (2012).
29. Brisman (2006), 1273.
30. Bogazianos (2012).
31. *The House I Live In* (2012).
32. See National Survey on Drug Use and Health reports and data files at www.samhsa.gov.
33. Erceg-Hurn (2008).
34. On "the police power" versus "police power," with the addition of the article *the*, I am following an academic convention (for instance, see Neocleous 2014a) to denote a distinct quality—the power to regulate social life—possessed by a wide range of agencies, not just the police.
35. Garriott (2011), 8.
36. Neocleous (2000).
37. Ayres and Jewkes (2012).

38. CDC (2015).
39. Scott (1998).
40. Neocleous (2008).
41. Brisman (2006).
42. Brownstein, Mulcahy, and Huessy (2014), 12.
43. Brownstein, Mulcahy, and Huessy (2014), 86.
44. Swidler (1986).
45. Brownstein, Mulcahy, and Huessy (2014), 87.
46. Rafter (2007), 417.
47. Ferrell (2013).
48. Ferrell, Hayward, and Young (2015), 6–7.
49. Yar (2014b), 194.
50. Althusser (2014).
51. Žižek (2009a), 113.
52. Žižek (2009a), 114.
53. Žižek (1993), 234.
54. Žižek (2011), 3.
55. P. Taylor (2014).

CHAPTER 1. WALTER WHITE'S DEATH WISH

1. KLTV (2012).
2. J. Cohen (2013).
3. Zimmerman (2012).
4. Wiggin (2011).
5. HuffPost Crime (2013).
6. HuffPost Crime (2013).
7. *Vice* (n.d.).
8. Jenkot (2008).
9. *KCPD Chief's Blog* (2010).
10. Hayward and Young (2004), 259.
11. Season 2, episode 7.
12. *Narcocorridos* are a variant of traditional Mexican folk music (ballads), focusing on the drug trade.
13. Hatsukami and Fischman (1996).
14. As the neuroscientist Carl Hart and his colleagues recently put it, "to punish crack users more harshly than powder cocaine users is analogous to punishing those who are caught smoking marijuana more harshly than those caught eating marijuana-laced brownies." Hart, Ceste, and Habibi (2014), 3.
15. *Frontline* 2006.
16. "P2P" refers to a more elaborate distillation process that was common among "outlaw" motorcycle gangs in the 1960s–1970s. This differs from the "Red P" (red phosphorous) method, which was common to most "mom-and-pop" clandestine labs. For a detailed history of P2P meth markets, see Jenkins (1994).

17. Interestingly, Blue Sky makes an appearance on another popular AMC program, *The Waking Dead*, briefly shown in the white supremacist Merle Dixon's drug stash.
18. Kotulak (1980), 94.
19. *Sydney Morning Herald* (2014).
20. She is also credited as "Spooge's Lady." The character is played by Dale Dickey, who has also played a violent meth dealer in *Winter's Bone* and an imprisoned drug dealer in *Justified*.
21. Season 4, episode 1.
22. Linnemann, Wall, and Green (2014).
23. Hallsworth (2013), 69. See also Hallsworth and Young (2008).
24. US House of Representatives (2012b).
25. State of South Carolina v. Andres Antonio Torres, no. 26904 (Supreme Court of South Carolina, December 13, 2010), Final Brief of Respondents.
26. Hart et al. (2012).
27. Hart et al. (2008).
28. Hart et al. (2000).
29. Atlanta, GA, Chicago, IL, Denver, CO, New York, NY, Sacramento, CA.
30. Because subtotals are approximations based on weighted samples, estimations are rounded up. ADAM II report available at http://www.whitehouse.gov.
31. Thompson (2010), 204.
32. Thompson (2010).
33. Ronell (2004), 59.
34. Adams (2012).
35. J. Young (2007), 42.
36. Segal (2011), emphasis added.
37. Yar (2014b).
38. J. Young (2003).
39. US House of Representatives (2004a), emphasis added.
40. US House of Representatives (2004a), emphasis added.
41. Bittner (1970), 7.
42. Neocleous (2014a).
43. Hobbes (1889).
44. Hobbes (1928).
45. Nietzsche (2003), 102.

CHAPTER 2. THIS IS YOUR RACE ON METH

1. KOCO (2013).
2. Drawing on Mirzoeff (2006) and others, the term *visuality* refers to the ways in which vision, seeing things, is subject to the dominant social order: "how we see, how we are able, allowed, or made to see." Mirzoeff (2006), 55. Recognition of the primacy of the visual does not preclude critique or a countervisuality.
3. Bonilla-Silva (2012).

4. Linnemann (2010).
5. Oklahoma Senate Communications Division (1999).
6. Fields and Fields (2012).
7. *Variety* (1999).
8. Rock (2002).
9. Wray (2013), emphasis added.
10. Hartigan (1999).
11. According to Wray and Newitz (1997), 2, Mitford Matthews's *A Dictionary of Americanisms on Historical Principles* (1951) dates the earliest usage to 1833.
12. The OED cites an earlier appearance in 1831 but does not indicate location.
13. Allen (2012), 91–114.
14. Allen (2012), 32.
15. And according to Jacqueline Zara Wilson (2002), it was a competition among Celtic peoples—the indigenous inhabitants of Wales, Ireland, and the Scottish Highlands, of the British Isles—more generally.
16. Ignatiev (2009).
17. Adolph Reed (2013) suggests that Irish laborers may in fact have been lower down the social hierarchy than black slaves, because slaves had monetary value to their masters. As evidence, Reed offers the monument to the nearly 30,000 Irish laborers who died constructing the New Basin Canal.
18. Ignatiev (2009), 3.
19. Ignatiev (2009), 47.
20. Ignatiev (2009), 49.
21. Yan and Schwartz (2011). In late 2011, then GOP presidential hopefuls Michelle Bachman and Rick Santorum signed the so-called Marriage Vow, which contained this curious reference to slavery and the state of African American families: "Slavery had a disastrous impact on African-American families, yet sadly a child born into slavery in 1860 was more likely to be raised by his mother and father in a two-parent household than was an African American baby born after the election of the USA's first African-American President."
22. Harkins (2003), 110.
23. Rafter (2001), 71; Rafter (2014).
24. Goddard (1912).
25. Gould (1996), 171.
26. Gould (1996), 171.
27. Bishop (1989).
28. Murray (1993).
29. Fraser (1995), 6.
30. Murray (1993).
31. DiIulio (1995).
32. Murray (2013), 12.
33. Hayward and Yar (2006). See also Jones (2012).
34. Hayward and Yar (2006), 14.

35. As James Keller (2003) suggests, the use of white trash by Marshall Mathers (aka Eminem) as a form of masculine protest is not confined to the script of *8 Mile*. The theme appears throughout the rapper's lyrics, style, and public persona.
36. Hartigan (1999).
37. Sweeney (1997), 250.
38. Sweeney (1997).
39. In a review of the film *Zero Dark Thirty*, Slavoj Žižek (2013b) makes a similar point about depictions of torture, in which he suggests quite plainly that to depict neutrally is to endorse.
40. For the full interview and an image of the character, see O'Connor (2014).
41. Wray and Newitz (1997).
42. Wolters (2014).
43. Burke (2011).
44. Hayward (2010), 1.
45. Days before the *Breaking Bad* series finale, the drug-culture standard *High Times Magazine* published a list of its favorite slang names for the drug, one of which, "Okie Coke," is particularly relevant here. Gibson (2013).
46. Stern (2006).
47. Michelle Brown (2009).
48. Michelle Brown (2014).
49. Lynch (2004).
50. Butler (1993), 16. This excerpt is also discussed in Kilby (2013).
51. Mirzoeff (2006).
52. Lee (2012).
53. Useful here is Judith Butler's (2009) discussion of framing, when she suggests that to frame is also to "set up" a person, as in the "framing" of someone for a crime he or she did not commit.
54. A. Young (1996), 1–2.
55. Shafer (2005b).
56. Kristeva (1982).
57. Kristeva (1982), 4.
58. Linnemann and Wall (2013), 325.
59. Valier (2002), 324.
60. Linnemann and Wall (2013).
61. Butler (2006).
62. J. Young (2007), 42.
63. Žižek (2011), 8.
64. Biber (2006), 136.
65. S. Anderson (2012), 13–14.
66. Webster (2008), 308.
67. Carney (2010), 31.
68. Linnemann and Wall (2013), 329.
69. Casper and Moore (2009), 14.

70. View all ads at www.themethproject.org.
71. Stebner (2011).
72. Greer, Ferrell, and Jewkes (2007).
73. NIDA (1997).
74. O'Malley and Palmer (1996).
75. Carlen (2008).
76. From the project website's "About Us" page: http://foundation.methproject.org/About-Us/.
77. STRIDE data 2011, www.dea.gov.
78. Nicosia et al. (2009).
79. Meth Project (2007).
80. D. Anderson (2010).
81. Erceg-Hurn (2008).
82. Lilienfeld (2007).
83. Ferrell (2012), 1.
84. Manderson (1995).
85. Zernike (2006).
86. Zernike (2006).
87. Zernike (2006).
88. Tony Kaye (*American History X*), Darren Aronofsky (*Requiem for a Dream, Black Swan*), Alejandro González Iñárritu (*21 Grams*), and Wally Pfister (*The Dark Knight*).
89. Siebel and Mange (2009), 4.
90. Mirzoeff (2006), 55.
91. Michelle Brown (2009), 23.
92. Morales, Wu, and Fitzsimons (2012).
93. Wyoming Meth Project (2012).
94. Bush-Baskette and Smith (2012).
95. In order to confront the complexities of TMP imagery, I took basic inventory of the ads' context, format, and content. Treating each of TMP's twenty-nine print advertisements as a single case, I reviewed the ads, noting basic stylistic elements and presentation. Attempting to ignore textual information and focus only on the image sharpened the analysis to the particular aesthetics of each advertisement. First noted was that almost every advertisement featured a subject or character that a meth user or the drug itself was acting on—the message imparting "what meth does to you." So, for instance, the "15 bucks" advertisement features the scene of what appears to be a young white woman in a physical struggle with a white man. The gaunt skin and blank stare of the young woman evokes not terror but a subjectivity more akin to a lamb led to slaughter. Perhaps playing off the supposed blue-collar appeal of "poor man's cocaine," the man's clothing suggests that he is working class. In this sense, staged emotionality, dark imagery, and distinct race and class cues help imagine meth crimes as a white, working-class phenomenon. Though aesthetically stunning, the advertisement is even more power-

ful and grim when coupled with the caption, "15 bucks for sex isn't normal. But on meth it is." Viewed through its text, ambiguity falls away, and the photographic message and its preferred reading are clear: the sex-work rape of a young woman, undoubtedly born of meth addiction. The young woman is the victim of both meth and an attacker, and her blank stare communicates a hardened emotionality, in which a fifteen-dollar sex-work transaction is "normal" consequence of meth addiction. For vulnerable young women, as the caption warns, meth use makes the unknowable terror of rape knowable. I followed this convention to develop four conceptual themes instructing what "meth does to you." On a cursory level, I found that the advertisements feature women and young girls more than men and boys, and in keeping with meth's racialization, all advertisements display what appear to be white bodies. It is important to acknowledge that while I focused on finding the most obvious "message" or the preferred reading of each advertisement, I in no way suggest that these complex productions advance a single message. Concerned with spectators' engagement with the images, while also aware of the difficulty in locating a singular meaning, I developed a process to explore the advertisements' pedagogical instructions further: 107 students from three different undergraduate "Crime, Media, Society" courses responded to the format of TMP's website and ten advertisements selected at random. First, volunteers were shown a screen-shot image (taken that day) of the project's website and asked to respond to the following open-ended question: "Based on the information on the website, who produces the Meth Project?" Of the 107 volunteers, 98 believed the website was an official state project, with the rest reporting that a private entity produced the website. This is an important starting point for the analysis, as the presentation and appearance of TMP as an official state project certainly speaks to the affective force of its images. Next, volunteers responded to ten advertisements for content and theme. Focusing on the main character or subject of the advertisement, I simply asked volunteers, "What is the race of this person?" and "What is the sex of this person?" Resoundingly, volunteers confirmed my previous assertions of the advertisements' overt racialization. With 107 responses for each of the ten images (1,070), nearly all (1,059) believed the advertisements featured "white" people, with just 11 responding with "Hispanic" or "Latino." In fact, in all but two of the ten images, respondents were in total agreement with the whiteness of the subject. The perceived sex of the subjects was even clearer, with all 1,070 responses in agreement with my reading and with each other. Next, volunteers identified the "message" of each advertisement, by completing the sentence, "According to the advertisement, meth use leads to . . ." Volunteers were provided a document with the themes and asked to mark any they felt appropriately represented the advertisement. I also encouraged volunteers to write in a description if they believed an image conveyed a message not represented by the themes. Tallying by theme, I used the category with the most responses as an approximation of consensus. For each of the ten advertisements, volunteers most often selected the theme in agreement with the analysis, and none wrote in an alternative reading. While this is certainly not "proof" of audience reception, I view the volunteers' readings as some support for my themes. Additionally, the process demonstrated the consistent theme of instant addiction, characterized by the tag line "Meth: not even once," and I refocused my attention to this important aspect of the campaign. See Linnemann, Hanson, and Williams (2013).

96. Murakawa (2011).
97. Montana Meth Project (2007).
98. Associated Press (2011).
99. Siebel Foundation (2012).
100. Hall, Winlow, and Ancrum (2005), 108.
101. Schept (2014).

CHAPTER 3. GOVERNING THROUGH METH

1. Skelton (2014).
2. *Smurfing* describes the circuitous process of collecting cold medicine for methamphetamine production. Smurfing is often taken up by groups that trade cold pills with pill brokers for cash or other drugs.
3. Balko (2014a).
4. Ingraham (2014).
5. Drug Policy Alliance (2014).
6. Reiss (2014), 1, emphasis added.
7. Simon (2007).
8. For related arguments on liberal complicity in mass imprisonment, see Murakawa (2014) and Schept (2015).
9. Neocleous (2011), 192.
10. Neocleous (2011), 198.
11. Meth Watch home page: www.kdheks.gov/methwatch/.
12. The collection of articles the private contractor put together from 2003 to 2010 is superior to those that could be gathered by LexisNexis and similar search engines, as it includes small, local papers that do not appear in electronic databases. All simply are clipped from the print pages as they appear, also an advantage over electronic databases. These articles show a significant increase in coverage beginning in late 2004, hinting at important developments in the public discussion of methamphetamine. My sampling frame was from December 2004 to December 2005. I examined hard copies of each article in a subsample of every third article in the frame. Rather than focusing on keywords to fit texts to existing categories, I stressed grounded reflexivity and comparison, allowing categories and narratives to emerge organically. To construct analytic categories along lines of content and theme warranted several full reads of each article. Many of the articles are typical "police blotter" reports of arrests and summaries of prosecutions for methamphetamine-related crimes. These are generally brief and do not provide much information beyond the relative frequency of meth cases locally. The most fruitful category includes editorials, press releases, and commentary from politi-

cians and law enforcement. Another includes community commentary, editorials not from government or law enforcement sources, and announcements regarding meth-awareness groups, funding, letters to the editor, and so on. Once subcategories were located, they form a timeline mapping meth's shifting narrative throughout the year. Using monthly summaries, I fit the rest of the articles to the timeline. After coding all the articles, it was not necessary to alter the timeline or categories further, confirming its validity.

13. From December 2004 to December 2005, there were 3,181 articles published by Kansas newspapers making some mention of methamphetamine. From July 2004 to August 2009, there were 8,902 articles. By comparison, the service collected data on the keywords "Kansas court system" and "smoking and tobacco," yielding 10,738 and 1,981 articles, respectively. See Linnemann (2013).

14. Access Kansas (2005).

15. Linnemann (2013), 46.

16. Sebelius (2005).

17. DEA Methamphetamine Lab Incidents Archives, 2004–2009, www.dea.gov.

18. Sebelius (2005).

19. Neocleous (2008), 73.

20. Reuter and Caulkins (2003).

21. *Emporia Gazette* (2005).

22. Rothschild (2005).

23. Hanna (2005).

24. *Wichita Eagle* (2005).

25. Toplikar (2005).

26. Simon (2007), 101.

27. Puriton (2005), 6.

28. Ferrell (2003).

29. Forty Kansas law enforcement agencies did not report standard Uniform Crime Reports data in 2005.

30. Associated Press (2005a).

31. *Sterling Bulletin* (2005), 3.

32. *Emporia Gazette* (2005).

33. State of Kansas (2005).

34. Associated Press (2005b).

35. Manning (2005a).

36. Manning (2005b).

37. Finger (2005a).

38. Finger (2005a).

39. Finger (2005a).

40. Probst (2005).

41. State of Kansas (2007).

42. Schmidt (2010).

43. Schmidt (2011).

44. Schmidt (2014); Schmidt (2013).
45. Kansas Task Force Addressing Methamphetamine and Illegal Drugs (2010), emphasis added.
46. City of Parsons, Kansas (2011).
47. Robert Albertini, email to the author, June 8, 2011.
48. KSA 21–3608a.
49. KSA 22–4902.
50. Casey (2005).
51. Stemen and Renfigo (2009).
52. Tiger (2012).
53. Hallsworth and Lea (2011).
54. White House (2006).
55. Neocleous (2007).
56. Finger (2005b).
57. NATO (2002).
58. Neocleous (2011), 202.
59. *Lindsborg News-Record* (2005).
60. Žižek (2014), 11.
61. Žižek (2009b), 53.

CHAPTER 4. THE WAR OUT THERE

1. Google Scholar returns over 4,000 hits on the keywords "Mayberry policing."
2. James Kimbrell, Barney Fife Need Not Apply. *The Junction City Daily Union* , (2004, October 15), 7.
3. Fernandez (2008); Lovell (2009).
4. Loader (1997), 3.
5. Loader and Mulcahy (2001), 41, 42.
6. C. Wilson (2000).
7. Sim (2000).
8. Steinert (2003).
9. Loader and Mulcahy (2001).
10. Chambliss (2001).
11. Marx (1907), 15.
12. Payne, Berg, and Sun (2005).
13. Neocleous (2011), 202.
14. Loader (1997), 3.
15. This chapter draws on thirty-seven in-depth, issue-focused interviews with municipal police officers in four Kansas communities, conducted in 2010 and 2011. Following a basic schedule, interviews typically lasted about an hour and were transcribed verbatim. I also completed more than fourteen hours of "ride-along" observations with police and spent fifteen days in study communities. The chosen urban site (1) is the state's largest city and boasts a police department with over 600 sworn officers. This city is more racially diverse than the state on average,

and when its suburbs and bedroom communities are included, its population nears 700,000. The rural locations (2, 3, 4) are in the southeast corner of the state, within close proximity of one another. While no more than ninety miles separate the rural communities, each is in a different county. Communities 2 and 3 can be characterized as small "farm towns" where the primary vocation is agriculture, supplemented by light manufacturing. Though quite similar to communities 2 and 3, the dynamics of community 4 are influenced by a small state university and some extractive industry. Though all three rural communities are more racially homogeneous than the state on average, it is important to note that communities 2 and 3 are more than 90 percent white, non-Hispanic, according to the latest census data. The aim of the interviews was to pay special attention to the dynamic moments when meaning is constructed, negotiated, and reproduced, what Jeff Ferrell (1997) calls criminological *verstehen*. See Linnemann and Kurtz (2014).

Location	Population	% white	Sworn officers	2010 crime rate per 1,000			Seized labs
				Violent	Property	Drug	
1	376,880	69.8	643	8.1	48.5	4.10	0
2	5,704	91.5	16	3.7	41.4	6.8	0
3	1, 341	94.3	3	3.0	14.2	0	0
4	19,817	88.5	38	3.8	58.0	4.10	6
State	2,815,460	77.8	6,826	3.7	31.2	3.8	61

16. For drug-use data, see Substance Abuse and Mental Health Services Administration (2010). On the variance of meth and crack use by urban and rural locations, Weisheit and Wells (2010) suggest that more racially diverse large cities are also able to support more diverse drug markets, hence the cultural script that "white culture has moved more towards the meth" and "black culture seems like they stay with crack cocaine."
17. KBI (2011).
18. Owen (2007), 203.
19. Sibley (1995).
20. Neocleous (2000), 20.
21. Capote (2013), 3.

CHAPTER 5. IMAGINING METHLAND
1. Howell (1998).
2. M. Bell (2007), 404.
3. DeKeseredy and Donnermeyer (2012), 207–208, emphasis added, quoting Sampson et al. (1998), 1.
4. DeKeseredy, Muzzatti, and Donnermeyer (2014), 179.
5. Doing just this, the US Census Bureau and the US Office of Management and Budget (OMB) provide two of the most commonly cited definitions of *urban* and *rural*. On the one hand, the US Census Bureau somewhat simply asserts

that a "territory, population and housing units not classified urban constitute rural," defining *urban* as settlement areas with more than 2,500 residents (2010b). On the other hand, the OMB defines "rural areas" as a jurisdiction that is not located in a metropolitan statistical area (MSA) but in a county that has a population less than 50,000. "Rural states," according to the OMB, are states with a population density of fifty-two or fewer persons per square mile or a state in which the largest county has fewer than 150,000 people (US Census Bureau 2010a).

6. Tunnell (2011).
7. Ferrell (2013).
8. Campbell (2012), 401.
9. Hayward (2012).
10. Kaylen and Pridemore (2013).
11. Kaylen and Pridemore (2013), 918.
12. Hall and Winlow (2007); Ferrell (2007).
13. For a thoughtful discussion of carceral habitus, see Schept (2013).
14. Ferrell, Hayward, and Young (2015), 5.
15. Bell, Lloyd, and Vatovec (2010), 209.
16. Butterfield (2014).
17. See, for instance, Boeri (2013).
18. Ulaby (2011).
19. Miller (1991).
20. Season 1, episode 1.
21. The book won the following awards: Friends of American Writers Chicago Adult Literature Award, 2010 Hillman Prize for Book Journalism, 2009 *Chicago Tribune* Heartland Prize for Non-Fiction, *New York Times* 100 Notable Books 2009, *Seattle Times* Best Books of 2009, *Los Angeles Times* Favorites 2009, *St. Louis Post-Dispatch* Favorites 2009, *San Francisco Chronicle* 100 Best Nonfiction 2009.
22. E. Anderson (2009).
23. Reding (2010), 6.
24. NPR (2009).
25. R. Williams (1975).
26. D. Bell (1997).
27. D. Bell (2006).
28. Reding (2010), 18.
29. Garland (2002).
30. Frank (2007), 5.
31. Bettmann (1974), 54.
32. M. Bell (2007), 404.
33. Bageant (2007), 4.
34. M. Bell (1997).
35. Benedict Anderson (1992).
36. Butterfield (2014).

37. See detailed crime data at the Nebraska Commission on Law Enforcement and Criminal Justice: www.ncc.state.ne.us.
38. Mackinder (1919), 186.
39. Blouet (2004).
40. US House of Representatives (2004a).
41. Bonné (2013).
42. Kaplan (2003), 88.
43. Kiernan (2008).
44. White House (2001).
45. Reding (2010), 22.
46. Reding (2010), 29.
47. Reding (2010), 26, emphasis added.
48. Reding (2010), 29.
49. Reding (2010), 30.
50. KBI meth-lab statistics found at www.accesskansas.org.
51. Reding (2010), 30.
52. Reding (2010), 30–31.
53. Reding (2010), 35.
54. *Courier* (2005).
55. Reding (2010), 35.
56. Reding (2010), 35.
57. Reding (2010), 36.
58. Reding (2010), 36.
59. Reding (2010), 39.
60. Reding (2010), 183.
61. Egan (2009).
62. Wilbur (2009).
63. Žižek (2013a).
64. Wilbur (2009).
65. Cresswell (2005).
66. Stein (2008).
67. Williamson (2016).
68. Murray (1993).
69. Foucault (1995), 197–198.
70. D. Bell (2006).
71. Cowen and Siciliano (2011); Wall (2009).
72. Bell, Lloyd, and Vatovec (2010) describe the material and symbolic as rural power and the power of the rural, respectively.
73. Fields and Fields (2012), 121.
74. Foucault (1995), 198.
75. Hall (2009).
76. Rafter (1988), 2.
77. Wells (1898), 169.

78. Smarsh (2014).
79. Murakawa (2011).
80. Bassiouny (2013).
81. Smarsh (2014).
82. View the registry at www.justice.gov.
83. Christie (2013).
84. Iowa Governor's Office of Drug Control Policy (2013), 16.
85. El Paso Intelligence Center (2011).
86. WATE (2013).
87. Easter (2010).
88. Shafer (2005a).
89. Potter (2013).
90. Easter (2010).
91. Christie (2013). Locating and cleaning up "meth lab homes" is big business for companies like Meth Lab Cleanup, which booked more than 1,500 jobs inspecting and decontaminating homes in 2012.
92. If 5 percent is 84,000, then the estimated number of labs, discovered and undiscovered, is 1,680,000.
93. Ferrell (1996).
94. Deleuze and Guattari (2011), 172.
95. Rentschler (2011) uses the term "physiognomy of urban crime" to describe how crime can stick to a particular neighborhood or street.
96. J. Young (1971).
97. R. Williams (1975), 302.

CHAPTER 6. DRUG WAR, TERROR WAR, STREET CORNER, BATTLEFIELD

1. Survey data in the author's possession.
2. S. Cohen (2015).
3. US Senate (2007), 1.
4. US Senate (2007), 2.
5. At this time, the DEA named the Arellano-Felix, Amado Carrillo-Fuentes, Amecua-Contreras, and Caro-Quintero organizations as the primary Mexican organizations trafficking methamphetamine into the United States.
6. US Department of Justice (1996).
7. Gootenberg (2009), 24.
8. Drug-war and terror-war actors (1) are involved in illegal activities and frequently need the same supplies; (2) exploit excessive violence and the threat of violence; (3) commit kidnappings, assassinations, and extortions; (4) act in secrecy; (5) challenge the state and the laws (unless they are state funded); (6) have backup leaders and foot soldiers; (7) are exceedingly adaptable, open to innovations, and flexible; (8) threaten global security; and (9) enact deadly consequences for former members who have quit the group. Kan (2012), 10.

9. Björnehed (2004).
10. Walker (2015).
11. Dodd (n.d.).
12. Gomis (2015).
13. Paglen (2010).
14. Payan (2006).
15. McCaffrey and Scales (2011).
16. Perry (2005).
17. Kan (2008).
18. Paley (2014).
19. Kan (2011).
20. Paley (2014), 34–36.
21. Kleiman (2004).
22. Democracy Now! (2014).
23. Michaels and Wall (2015).
24. Obama (2014).
25. Agamben (2005).
26. Žižek (2015).
27. Neocleous (2000), 118–119.
28. Neocleous (2014b), 13.
29. Neocleous (2000).
30. Neocleous (2014b), 14.
31. Council on Foreign Relations (2010).
32. K. Williams (2011).
33. K. Williams (2011), 82.
34. Neocleous (2014b), 38.
35. Neocleous (2011), 199.
36. Gülden and Rigakos (2014).
37. Machuca ([1599] 2008).
38. Kienscherf (2011), 519.
39. Kuzmarov (2012).
40. Neocleous (2011), 200.
41. Platt et al. (1975).
42. Frydl (2013), 415.
43. US House of Representatives (2004b).
44. InSight Crime (n.d.).
45. Paley (2014), 58.
46. Paley (2014), 53.
47. US House of Representatives (2004b).
48. US House of Representatives (2004b).
49. Colectivo de Abogados José Alvear Restrepo (2008).
50. Paley (2014), 16.
51. Kienscherf (2011); K. Williams (2011).

52. Saborio (2013).
53. Brian Anderson (2013).
54. Savage (2011).
55. Schwartz (2014).
56. The Defense Authorization Act of 1982 first authorized military force in counternarcotics operations.
57. Marcy (2010).
58. Schwartz (2014).
59. Dobrich (2014).
60. Hunt (1998).
61. Dobrich (2014).
62. Meyer (2009).
63. US Department of Defense (2009).
64. US Department of Justice (2012).
65. Cabañas (2014).
66. US House of Representatives (2012a).
67. Savage (2011).
68. Associated Press (2012).
69. Children International (2014).
70. Neocleous (2014b), 9.
71. Nevins (2010).
72. Cook and Seelke (2008).
73. Olson and Wilson (2010).
74. Paley (2014), 87.
75. Paley (2014), 87.
76. US House of Representatives (2011).
77. "Joint Task Force North (JTF North), based at Biggs Army Airfield, Fort Bliss, Texas, is the Department of Defense (DOD) organization tasked to support our nation's federal law enforcement agencies in the interdiction of suspected transnational threats within and along the approaches to the continental United States. Transnational threats are those activities conducted by individuals or groups that involve international terrorism, narco-trafficking, alien smuggling, weapons of mass destruction, and the delivery systems for such weapons that threaten the national security of the United States. JTF North was originally established in 1989 as Joint Task Force Six (JTF-6), in response to President George H. W. Bush's declaration of the 'War on Drugs.' On Sept. 28, 2004, JTF-6 was renamed JTF North and its mission was expanded to include providing support to the nation's federal law enforcement agencies." US Northern Command (2013).
78. Seelke and Finklea (2014), 13.
79. Monahan (2010).
80. Seelke and Finklea (2014), 14–19.
81. Seelke and Finklea (2014), 19–22.
82. Seelke and Finklea (2014), 14.

83. Seelke and Finklea (2014), 22–24.
84. Paley (2014), 114.
85. Witness for Peace (2015).
86. Witness for Peace (2015).
87. Paley (2014), 88.
88. Paley (2014), 85.
89. US House of Representatives (2011), 5.
90. US House of Representatives (2011), 5. At similar hearings a few years later, Brownfield reported that fifty high-value targets had been captured by the Mexican government. US House of Representatives (2013).
91. US House of Representatives (2013).
92. Andrade and Willbanks (2008).
93. US Department of Justice (2009).
94. US Department of Justice (2014a).
95. Keefe (2014).
96. Keefe (2014).
97. US Department of Justice (2011), 2–7.
98. US Department of State (n.d.).
99. Keefe (2014).
100. Langguth (1978).
101. Paley (2014), 105.
102. Keefe (2014).
103. Keefe (2014).
104. US Department of Justice (2015).
105. US Department of Justice (2014b).
106. Kan (2011), 29.
107. Paley (2014), 34–36.
108. US House of Representatives (2013); also quoted in Paley (2014), 87–88.
109. Paley (2014), 92.
110. DEA (2015).
111. Williams et al. (2010).
112. Chamayou (2012), 8.

EPILOGUE

1. Gottschalk (2014), 130.
2. Fields (2009).
3. Simons and Jones (2012), 180.
4. *Kearney Hub* (2015).
5. WFLA (2015).
6. www.facebook.com/AmericanPoliceBeat/.
7. E. Williams (1914).
8. Provine (2008).
9. NPR (2014).

10. Bittner (1970).
11. Matthew Brown (2015).
12. Simon (2007), 19–22.
13. Gottschalk (2014), 6.
14. J. Young (1999), 15.
15. Van Marle and Maruna (2010).
16. Becker (1973), xvii.
17. Solomon, Greenberg, and Pyszczynski (2015), 9–15.
18. Baldwin (2013), 91.
19. Feinstein (2015).
20. Hunwick (2014).
21. Timmons (2015).
22. Mintz (2004).
23. FEMA (2009); Neocleous (2015).
24. US Department of Homeland Security (2005).
25. Lipton (2005).
26. US Department of Homeland Security (2009).
27. McCaul (2016).
28. Žižek (2002), 16.
29. Žižek (2002), 6.
30. Dean draws on the work of Warren Montag, who argues that Althusser specified ideological hailing as a gesture that singles out individuals from an undifferentiated mass and endows them with a unique identity. Montag (2013), 137.
31. Dean (2014).
32. Winlow and Hall (2013).
33. Taussig (1997), 9.

REFERENCES

Access Kansas. 2005, February 15. Media release: Final 2004 meth statistics in Kansas. www.accesskansas.org/kbi.

Adams, Genetta. 2012, July 12. "Breaking Bad": From Mr. Chips to Scarface in 10 easy steps. www.cnn.com.

Agamben, Giorgio. 2005. *State of Exception*. Translated by Kevin Attell. Chicago: University of Chicago Press.

Alexander, Michelle. 2010. *The New Jim Crow: Mass Incarceration in the Age of Colorblindness*. New York: New Press.

Allen, Theodore. 2012. *The Invention of the White Race*. Vol. 1, *Racial Oppression and Social Control*. London: Verso.

Althusser, Louis. 2014. *On the Reproduction of Capitalism: Ideology and Ideological State Apparatuses*. London: Verso.

Anderson, Benedict. 1992. *Imagined Communities: Reflections on the Origin and Spread of Nationalism*. London: Verso.

Anderson, Brian. 2013, February 17. What Rio's favela "pacification" program looks like from the streets. Motherboard, *Vice*. www.motherboard.vice.com.

Anderson, D. Mark. 2010. Does information matter? The effect of the Meth Project on meth use among youths. *Journal of Health Economics*, 29, 732–742.

Anderson, Elijah. 2000. *Code of the Street: Decency, Violence, and the Moral Life of the Inner City*. New York: Norton.

Anderson, Eric. 2009, July 22. Iowa meth town no myth. *Daily Iowan*. www.dailyiowan.com.

Anderson, Scott Thomas. 2012. *Shadow People: How Meth-Driven Crime Is Eating at the Heart of Rural America*. Folsom, CA: Coalition for Investigative Journalism.

Andrade, Dale, and James Willbanks. 2008. *CORDS/Phoenix: Counterinsurgency Lessons from Vietnam for the Future*. Washington, DC: Army Center of Military History.

Associated Press. 2005a, February 21. Meth lab stats understate actual busts. *Topeka Capital-Journal*.

———. 2005b, April 2. Bill to curb methamphetamine production goes to governor. *Lawrence Journal-World*.

———. 2011, November 3. Report: Grandmother sold meth while baby-sitting. *Lawrence Journal-World*.

———. 2012, November 15. Killing of Honduran teenager could jeopardize U.S. aid. *New York Times*.

Ayres, Tammy, and Yvonne Jewkes. 2012. The haunting spectacle of crystal meth: A media-created mythology? *Crime, Media, Culture, 8*(3), 315–332.

Bageant, Joseph. 2007. *Deer Hunting with Jesus: Dispatches from America's Class War.* New York: Random House.

Baldwin, James. 2013. *The Fire Next Time.* New York: Vintage.

Balko, Radley. 2014a, October 14. As it turns out, meth laws have unintended consequences. *The Watch* (blog), *Washington Post.*

———. 2014b. *Rise of the Warrior Cop: The Militarization of America's Police Forces.* New York: Perseus Books.

Bassiouny, Mohammed. 2013. Dental erosion due to abuse of illicit drugs and acidic carbonated beverages. *General Dentistry, 61*(2), 38–44.

Becker, Ernest. 1973. *The Denial of Death.* New York: Free Press.

Bell, David. 1997. Anti-idyll: Rural horror. In *Contested Countryside Cultures: Otherness, Marginalisation, and Rurality*, edited by Paul Cloke and Jo Little, 94–108. New York: Psychology Press.

———. 2006. Variations on the rural idyll. In *Handbook of Rural Studies*, edited by Paul Cloke, Terry Marsden, and Patrick Mooney, 149–160. London: Sage.

Bell, Michael. 1997. The ghosts of place. *Theory and Society, 26*(6), 813–836.

———. 2007. The two-ness of rural life and the ends of rural scholarship. *Journal of Rural Studies, 23*, 402–415.

Bell, Michael, Sarah Lloyd, and Christine Vatovec. 2010. Activating the countryside: Rural power, the power of the rural and the making of rural politics. *Sociologia Ruralis, 50*(3), 205–224.

Bettmann, Otto. 1974. *The Good Old Days—They Were Terrible!* New York: Random House.

Biber, Katherine. 2006. The spectre of crime: Photography, law, and ethics. *Social Semiotics, 16*(1), 133–149.

Bishop, Katherine. 1989, September 16. Fear grows over effects of a new smokable drug. *New York Times.*

Bittner, Egon. 1970. *The Functions of the Police in Modern Society.* Chevy Chase, MD: National Institute of Mental Health, Center for Studies of Crime and Delinquency.

Björnehed, Emma. 2004. Narco-terrorism: The merger of the war on drugs and the war on terror. *Global Crime, 6*(3–4), 305–324.

Blouet, Brian W. 2004. The imperial vision of Halford Mackinder. *Geographical Journal, 170*(4), 322–329.

Boeri, Miriam. 2013. *Women on Ice: Methamphetamine Use among Suburban Women.* New Brunswick, NJ: Rutgers University Press.

Bogazianos, Dimitri. 2012. *Five Grams.* New York: NYU Press.

Bonilla-Silva, Eduardo. 2012. The invisible weight of whiteness: The racial grammar of everyday life in contemporary America. *Ethnic and Racial Studies, 35*(2), 173–194.

Bonné, Jon. 2013. Scourge of the heartland: Meth takes root in surprising places. NBC-News.com.

Brisman, Avi. 2006. Meth chic and the tyranny of the immediate: Reflections on the culture-drug/drug-crime relationships. *NDL Review, 82*, 1273.

Brown, Matthew. 2015, January 7. Killing of unarmed Montana man by police found justified. Associated Press. http://news.yahoo.com.

Brown, Michelle. 2009. *The Culture of Punishment: Prison, Society, and Spectacle.* New York: NYU Press.

———. 2014. Visual criminology and carceral studies: Counter-images in the carceral age. *Theoretical Criminology, 18*(2), 176–197.

Brownstein, Henry H., Timothy M. Mulcahy, and Johannes Huessy. 2014. *The Methamphetamine Industry in America: Transnational Cartels and Local Entrepreneurs.* New Brunswick, NJ: Rutgers University Press.

Burke, David. 2011, January 27. Actress-comic uses theater to create Etta May. *Quad-City Times.* http://qctimes.com.

Bush-Baskette, Stephanie, and Vivian Smith. 2012. Is meth the new crack for women in the war on drugs? Factors affecting sentencing outcomes for women and parallels between meth and crack. *Feminist Criminology, 7*(1), 48–69.

Butler, Judith. 1993. Endangered/endangering: Schematic racism and white paranoia. *Reading Rodney King/Reading Urban Uprising,* 15–22.

———. 2006. *Precarious Life: The Powers of Mourning and Violence.* New York: Verso.

———. 2009. *Frames of War.* New York: Verso.

Butterfield, Fox. 2014, January 4. Across rural America, drug casts grim shadow. *New York Times.*

Cabañas, Miguel. 2014. Imagined narcoscapes: Narcoculture and the politics of representation. *Latin American Perspectives, 41*(?), 3–17.

Campbell, Elaine. 2012. Landscapes of performance: Stalking as choreography. *Environment and Planning D: Society and Space, 30*(3), 400–417.

Capote, Truman. 2013. *In Cold Blood.* New York: Random House.

Carlen, Pat. 2008. *Imaginary Penalities.* London: Willan.

Carney, Phil. 2010. Crime, punishment and the force of the photographic spectacle. In Hayward and Presdee, *Framing Crime,* 17–35.

Casey, James. 2005, June 9. Editorial. *Madison (KS) News,* 2.

Casper, Monica, and Lisa Jean Moore. 2009. *Missing Bodies: The Politics of Visibility.* New York: NYU Press.

CDC (US Centers for Disease Control). 2015. Epidemiology glossary. www.cdc.gov.

Chamayou, Grégoire. 2012. *Manhunts: A Philosophical History.* Princeton, NJ: Princeton University Press.

Chambliss, William. 2001. *Power, Politics and Crime.* Boulder, CO: Westview.

Children International. 2014, July 14. U.S. ambassador to Honduras, Lisa Kubiske, visits Children International to see success of USAID-supported programs and recognize "community heroes." Press release. www.children.org.

Christie, Les. 2013, February 12. My home was a former meth lab. CNN Money. http://money.cnn.com.

City of Parsons, Kansas. 2011, April 5. Parsons becomes first Kansas city to adopt pseudoephedrine by prescription only ordinance. City of Parsons, Kansas, official Facebook page.

Cohen, Jason. 2013, January 21. Breaking sad: East Texas chemistry teacher busted for selling meth. *Texas Monthly*. www.texasmonthly.com.

Cohen, Sharon. 2015, January 15. "Not Mayberry anymore": Oil patch cops scramble to keep up. Associated Press. *Washington Times*.

Colectivo de Abogados José Alvear Restrepo. 2008, February 4. Private security transnational enterprises in Colombia. www.colectivodeabogados.org.

Cook, Colleen, and Christine Seelke. 2008, July. *Mérida Initiative: Proposed US Anticrime and Counterdrug Assistance for Mexico and Central America*. Washington, DC: Congressional Research Service, Library of Congress.

Council on Foreign Relations. 2010, September 8. A conversation with U.S. Secretary of State Hillary Rodham Clinton. www.cfr.org.

Courier. 2005, February 17. Mount Pleasant schools to ban homemade cookies, fearing drugs. www.wcfcourrier.com.

Cowen, Deborah, and Amy Siciliano. 2011. Surplus masculinities and security. *Antipode*, 43(5), 1516–1541.

Cresswell, Timothy. 2005. Moral geographies. In *Cultural Geography: A Critical Dictionary of Key Ideas*, edited by David Atkinson, Peter Jackson, David Sibley, and Neil Washbourne, 128–135. New York: I. B. Tauris.

DEA (US Drug Enforcement Administration). 2015, January 16. Dozens of alleged members of Sinaloa Cartel charged: List includes kingpin "El Mayo," his sons and other top leaders. www.dea.gov.

Dean, Jodi. 2014, December 2. Enclosing the subject. *Political Theory*.

DeKeseredy, Walter, and Joseph Donnermeyer. 2012. Thinking critically about rural crime: Toward a new left realist perspective. In *New Directions in Crime and Deviancy*, edited by Simon Winlow and Rowland Atkinson, 206–222. Abingdon, UK: Routledge.

DeKeseredy, Walter, Stephen Muzzatti, and Joseph Donnermeyer. 2014. Mad men in bib overalls: Media's horrification and pornification of rural culture. *Critical Criminology*, 22(2), 179–197.

Deleuze, Gilles, and Félix Guattari. 1988. *A Thousand Plateaus: Capitalism and Schizophrenia*. Translated by Brian Massumi. New York: Bloomsbury.

Democracy Now! 2014, August 15. Cops or soldiers? Pentagon, DHS helped arm police in Ferguson with equipment used in war. www.democracynow.org.

DiIulio, John. 1995. The coming of the super predators. *Weekly Standard*, 1(11), 23–30.

Dobrich, Richard. 2014. Foreign-deployed advisory support teams. NDIA/LIC Symposium, Drug Enforcement Administration.

Dodd, Brian. n.d. The nexus between drugs and terrorism. US Drug Enforcement Administration, Counter-Narcoterrorism Operations Center, Special Operations Center.

Drug Policy Alliance. 2014, March 26. The new Jim Crow: What's next? A talk with Michelle Alexander and DPA's asha bandele. www.drugpolicy.org.

Easter, Michael Glenn. 2010, April 29. Are you living in a former meth lab? *Scientific American*. www.scientificamerican.com.

Egan, Timothy. 2009, July 21. Methland vs. Mythland. *Opinionator* (blog), *New York Times*.

El Paso Intelligence Center. 2011. *Seizures by state—Summary and details.* www.accesskansas.org.

Emporia Gazette. 2005, February 26. Schmidt proposes anti-methamphetamine bill.

Erceg-Hurn, David. 2008. Drugs, money, and graphic ads: A critical review of the Montana Meth Project. *Prevention Science*, 9(4), 256–263.

Feinstein, Dianne. 2015, March 18. Funding needed to combat influx of meth crossing the border. *San Diego Union-Tribune*. www.utsandiego.com.

FEMA (Federal Emergency Management Agency). 2009. *Fact Sheet: Universal Adversary Program.* www.fema.gov.

Fernandez, Luis. 2008. *Policing Dissent: Social Control and the Anti-globalization Movement.* New Brunswick, NJ: Rutgers University Press.

Ferrell, Jeff. 1996. *Crimes of Style: Urban Graffiti and the Politics of Criminality.* Boston: Northeastern University Press

———. 1997. Criminological *verstehen*: Inside the immediacy of crime. *Justice Quarterly*, 14(1), 3–23.

———. 2003. Speed kills. *Critical Criminology*, 11(3), 185–198.

———. 2007. For a ruthless cultural criticism of everything existing. *Crime, Media, Culture*, 3(1), 91–100.

———. 2012. Crime and the visual: Critical criminology and the photodocumentary tradition. *Critical Criminologist*, 21(1), 1.

———. 2013. Cultural criminology and the politics of meaning. *Critical Criminology*, 21(3), 257–271.

Ferrell, Jeff, Keith Hayward, and Jock Young. 2015. *Cultural Criminology: An Invitation.* 2nd ed. London: Sage.

Fields, Barbara, and Karen Fields. 2012. *Racecraft: The Soul of Inequality in American Life.* London: Verso.

Fields, Gary. 2009, May 14. White House czar calls for end to "war on drugs." *Wall Street Journal.* www.wsj.com.

Finger, Steven. 2005a, February 1. Mother details life of slaying suspect: Years of drug abuse led up to night sheriff was killed, Scott Cheever's mother says. *Wichita Eagle*, 1.

———. 2005b, February 15. Public offered class on terror spotting. *Wichita Eagle*, 1B.

Foucault, Michel. 1995. *Discipline and Punish: The Birth of the Prison.* Translated by Alan Sheridan. New York: Random House. Originally published in 1977.

Frank, Thomas. 2007. *What's the Matter with Kansas? How Conservatives Won the Heart of America.* New York: Macmillan.

Fraser, Steven. 1995. *The Bell Curve Wars.* New York: Basic Books.

Frontline. 2006, February 14. "The Meth Epidemic." PBS. TV documentary.

Frydl, Kathleen. 2013. *The Drug Wars in America, 1940–1973.* Cambridge: Cambridge University Press.

Garland, David. 2002. *The Culture of Control: Crime and Social Order in Contemporary Society*. Chicago: University of Chicago Press.

Garriott, William. 2011. *Policing Methamphetamine: Narcopolitics in Rural America*. New York: NYU Press.

Gibson, Mary Jane. 2013, September 27. 12 names for meth on Breaking Bad. *High Times*. www.hightimes.com.

Goddard, Henry Herbert. 1912. *The Kallikak Family: A Study in the Heredity of Feeble-Mindedness*. New York: Macmillan.

Gomis, Benoit. 2015, May. Demystifying "narcoterrorism." Policy brief 9. Global Drug Policy Observatory.

Gootenberg, Paul. 2009. Talking about the flow: Drugs, borders, and the discourse of drug control. *Cultural Critique*, *71*(1), 13–46.

Gottschalk, Marie. 2014. *Caught: The Prison State and the Lockdown of American Politics*. Princeton, NJ: Princeton University Press.

Gould, Stephen Jay. 1996. *The Mismeasure of Man*. New York: Norton.

Greer, Chris, Jeff Ferrell, and Yvonne Jewkes. 2007. It's the image that matters: Style, substance and critical scholarship. *Crime, Media, Culture*, *3*, 5–8.

Gülden, Ören, and George Rigakos. 2014. Pacification. In *The Wiley-Blackwell Encyclopedia of Globalization*, 1–4. edited by George Ritzer. Los Angeles: Wiley.

Hall, Rachel. 2009. *Wanted: The Outlaw in American Visual Culture*. Charlottesville: University of Virginia Press.

Hall, Steve, and Simon Winlow. 2007. Cultural criminology and primitive accumulation: A formal introduction for two strangers who should really become more intimate. *Crime, Media, Culture*, *3*(1), 82–90.

Hall, Steve, Simon Winlow, and Craig Ancrum. 2005. Radgies, gangstas, and mugs: Imaginary criminal identities in the twilight of the pseudo-pacification process. *Social Justice*, *32*(1), 100–112.

Hallsworth, Simon. 2013. *The Gang and Beyond: Interpreting Violent Street Worlds*. London: Palgrave Macmillan.

Hallsworth, Simon, and John Lea. 2011. Reconstructing Leviathan: Emerging contours of the security state. *Theoretical Criminology*, *15*(2), 141–157.

Hallsworth, Simon, and Tara Young. 2008. Gang talk and gang talkers: A critique. *Crime, Media, Culture*, *4*(2), 175–195.

Hanna, John. 2005, January 31. Panel can't agree on anti-meth legislation. *Topeka Capital-Journal*.

Harkins, Anthony. 2003. *Hillbilly: A Cultural History of an American Icon*. Oxford: Oxford University Press.

Hart, Carl, Joann Ceste, and Don Habibi. 2014. *Methamphetamine: Fact vs. Fiction and Lessons from the Crack Hysteria*. New York: Open Society Foundation.

Hart, Carl, Eric Gunderson, Audrey Perez, Matthew Kirkpatrick, Andrew Thurmond, Sandra Comer, and Richard Foltin. 2008. Acute physiological and behavioral effects of intranasal methamphetamine in humans. *Neuropsychopharmacology*, *33*(8), 1847–1855.

Hart, Carl, Mark Haney, Richard Foltin, and Marian Fischman. 2000. Alternative reinforcers differentially modify cocaine self-administration by humans. *Behavioral Pharmacology*, 11(1), 87–91.

Hart, Carl, Caroline Marvin, Rae Silver, and Edward Smith. 2012. Is cognitive functioning impaired in methamphetamine users? A critical review. *Neuropsychopharmacology*, 37(3), 586–608.

Hartigan, John. 1999. *Racial Situations: Class Predicaments of Whiteness in Detroit*. Princeton, NJ: Princeton University Press.

Hatsukami, Dorothy, and Marian Fischman. 1996. Crack cocaine and cocaine hydrochloride: Are the differences myth or reality? *JAMA*, 276(19), 1580–1588.

Hayward, Keith. 2010. Opening the lens: Cultural criminology and the image. In Hayward and Presdee, *Framing Crime*, 1–16.

———. 2012. Five spaces of cultural criminology. *British Journal of Criminology*, 52(3), 441–462.

Hayward, Keith, and Mike Presdee. 2010. *Framing Crime: Cultural Criminology and the Image*. Abingdon, UK: Routledge.

Hayward, Keith, and Majid Yar. 2006. The "chav" phenomenon: Consumption, media and the construction of a new underclass. *Crime, Media, Culture*, 2(1), 9–28.

Hayward, Keith, and Jock Young. 2004. Cultural criminology: Some notes on the script. *Theoretical Criminology*, 8(3) 259–274.

Hendricks, Mike. 2012, July 21. A matter of life and meth: Drug has tragic consequences. *Kansas City Star*.

Hobbes, Thomas. 1889. *Behemoth, or the Long Parliament*. Chicago: University of Chicago Press.

———. 1928. *Leviathan, or the Matter, Forme and Power of a Commonwealth Ecclesiasticall and Civil*. New Haven, CT: Yale University Press.

House I Live In, The. 2012. Dir. Eugene Jarecki.

Howell, Phillip. 1998. Crime and the city solution: Crime fiction, urban knowledge, and radical geography. *Antipode*, 30(4), 357–378.

HuffPost Crime. 2013, May 24. Real-life Walter White? Stephen Doran, Massachusetts tutor with cancer, charged with trafficking meth. *Huffington Post*. www.huffingtonpost.com.

Hunt, Richard. 1998. *Pacification: The American Struggle for Vietnam's Hearts and Minds*. Boulder, CO: Westview.

Hunwick, Robert F. 2014, December 5. Chinese meth bust smells a lot like "Breaking Bad." *USA Today*. www.usatoday.com.

Ignatiev, Noel. 2009. *How the Irish Became White*. New York: Routledge.

Ingraham, Christopher. 2014, October 14. The marijuana industry could be bigger than the NFL by 2020. *Wonkblog, Washington Post*.

InSight Crime. n.d. Colombia. www.insightcrime.org. Accessed April 2015.

Iowa Governor's Office of Drug Control Policy. 2013, November 1. *Iowa Drug Control Strategy*. www.publications.iowa.gov.

Jenkins, Philip. 1994. "The ice age": The social construction of a drug panic. *Justice Quarterly*, 11(1), 7–31.

Jenkot, Robert. 2008. "Cooks are like gods": Hierarchies in methamphetamine-producing groups. *Deviant Behavior*, 29(8), 667–689.

Jones, Owen. 2012. *Chavs: The Demonization of the Working Class*. London: Verso.

Kan, Paul Rexton. 2008. *Drug Intoxicated Irregular Fighters: Complications, Dangers and Responses*. Carlisle, PA: Strategic Studies Institute.

———. 2011. *Mexico's "Narco-Refugees": The Looming Challenge for US National Security*. Army War College, Strategic Studies Institute, Carlisle Barracks, PA.

———. 2012. *Cartels at War: Mexico's Drug-Fueled Violence and the Threat to US National Security*. Potomac Books.

Kansas Task Force Addressing Methamphetamine and Illegal Drugs. 2010. *Rural Law Enforcement Methamphetamine Initiative State Strategic Plan Kansas*. Washington, DC: SAI.

Kaplan, Amy. 2003. Homeland insecurities: Some reflections on language and space. *Radical History Review*, 85(1), 82–93.

Kaylen, Maria T., and William A. Pridemore. 2013. Social disorganization and crime in rural communities: The first direct test of the systemic model. *British Journal of Criminology*, 53(5), 905–923.

KBI (Kansas Bureau of Investigation). 2011, June 30. *Adult Arrests by Agency 2010*. http://www.accesskansas.org.

KCPD Chief's Blog. 2010, July 21. New color, same old meth. http://kcpdchief.blogspot.com.

Kearney Hub. 2015, March 7. From cell, prisoner declares war on meth. www.kearney-hub.com.

Keefe, Patrick. 2014, May 5. The hunt for El Chapo: How the world's most notorious drug lord was captured. *New Yorker*.

Keller, James. 2003. Shady Agonistes: Eminem, abjection, and masculine protest. *Studies in Popular Culture*, 25(3), 13–24.

KFVS12. 2014, February 13. Suspected meth lab turns out to be sweet maple syrup. www.kfvs12.com.

Kienscherf, Marcus. 2011. A programme of global pacification: US counterinsurgency doctrine and the biopolitics of human (in)security. *Security Dialogue*, 42(6), 517–535.

Kiernan, Ben. 2008. *Blood and Soil: A World History of Genocide and Extermination from Sparta to Darfur*. New Haven, CT: Yale University Press.

Kilby, Jane. 2013. The visual fix: The seductive beauty of images of violence. *European Journal of Social Theory*, 16(3), 326–341.

Kimbrell, James. 2004, October 15. Barney Fife need not apply. *Junction City Daily Union*, 7.

Kleiman, Mark A. 2004, April. *Illicit Drugs and the Terrorist Threat: Causal Links and Implications for Domestic Drug Control Policy*. Washington DC: Congressional Research Service, Library of Congress.

KLTV. 2012, September 12. ETX teacher arrested for selling meth in school parking lot. www.kltv.com.

KOCO. 2013, September 26. Woman faces charges after child tests positive for meth. www.koco.com.

Kotulak, Robert. 1980, February 20. The zombie murderers. *Montreal Gazette*, 94.

Kristeva, Julia. 1982. *Powers of Horror: An Essay on Abjection*. New York: Columbia University Press.

Kuzmarov, Jeremy. 2012. *Modernizing Repression: Police Training and Nation-Building in the American Century*. Amherst: University of Massachusetts Press.

Langguth, A. J. 1978. *Hidden Terrors*. New York: Pantheon.

Lee, Baldwin. 2012. *Portraits of Black Americans 1987–1990*. Photographic exhibit. Chrysler Museum of Art, Norfolk, VA.

Lilienfeld, Scott. 2007. Psychological treatments that cause harm. *Perspectives on Psychological Science*, 2, 53–70.

Lindsborg News-Record. 2005, Janurary 27. County rentals are prime locations. 2.

Linnemann, Travis. 2010. Mad men, meth moms, moral panic: Gendering meth crimes in the Midwest. *Critical Criminology*, 18(2), 95–110.

———. 2013. Governing through meth: Local politics, drug control and the drift toward securitization. *Crime, Media, Culture*, 9(1), 39–61.

Linnemann, Travis, Laura Hanson, and L. Susan Williams. 2013. "With Scenes of Blood and Pain": Crime Control and the Punitive Imagination of the Meth Project. *British Journal of Criminology*, 53(4), 605–623.

Linnemann, Travis, and Donald L. Kurtz. 2014. Beyond the ghetto: Police power, methamphetamine and the rural war on drugs. *Critical Criminology*, 22(3), 339–355.

Linnemann, Travis, and Tyler Wall. 2013. "This Is Your Face on Meth": The punitive spectacle of "white trash" in the rural war on drugs. *Theoretical Criminology*, 17(3), 315–334.

Linnemann, Travis, Tyler Wall, and Edward Green. 2014. The walking dead and killing state: Zombification and the normalization of police violence. *Theoretical Criminology* 18(4), 506–527.

Lipton, Eric. 2005, March 26. Fictional doomsday team plays out scene after scene. *New York Times*. www.nytimes.com.

Loader, Ian. 1997. Policing and the social: Questions of symbolic power. *British Journal of Sociology*, 48(1), 1–18.

Loader, Ian, and Aogan Mulcahy. 2001. The power of legitimate naming: Part I—Chief constables as social commentators in post-war England. *British Journal of Criminology*, 41(1), 41–55.

Lovell, Jarret. 2009. *Crimes of Dissent: Civil Disobedience, Criminal Justice, and the Politics of Conscience*. New York: NYU University Press.

Lynch, Mona. 2004. Punishing images: Jail cam and the changing penal enterprise. *Punishment & Society*, 6(3), 255–270.

Machuca, Bernardo. (1599) 2008. *The Indian Militia and Description of the Indies*. Edited by Kris Lane. Translated by Thomas F. Johnson. Durham, NC: Duke University Press.

Mackinder, Halford John. 1919. *Democratic Ideals and Reality: A Study in the Politics of Reconstruction*. New York: Holt.

Manderson, Desmond. 1995. Metamorphoses: Clashing symbols in the social construction of drugs. *Journal of Drug Issues*, 25, 799–816.

Manning, Carl. 2005a, September 25. KBI: Law cuts meth labs. *Topeka Capital-Journal*. http://cjonline.com.

———. 2005b, September 29. Meth raids in state down 64 percent. *Southwest Daily Times*, 1.

Marcy, William. 2010. *The Politics of Cocaine: How US Foreign Policy Has Created a Thriving Drug Industry in Central and South America*. Chicago: Chicago Review Press.

Marx, Karl. 1907. *The Eighteenth Brumaire of Louis Bonaparte*. Chicago: Charles H. Kerr.

———. 1970. *Critique of Hegel's "Philosophy of Right."* Edited by J. O'Malley. Cambridge: Cambridge University Press.

Matthews, Mitford M. 1951. *A Dictionary of Americanisms on Historical Principles*. Chicago: University of Chicago Press.

McCaffrey, Barry, and Richard Scales. 2011, September 20. *Texas Border Security: A Strategic Military Assessment*. Colgen LP. www.texasagriculture.gov.

McCaul, Michael. 2016. *Failures of Imagination: The Deadliest Threats to Our Homeland—and How to Thwart Them*. New York: Crown Forum.

McLaughlin, Eliott C. 2014, October 7. No indictments for Georgia SWAT team that burned baby with stun grenade. CNN.com.

Meth Project. 2007, Summer. Newsletter.

Meyer, Josh. 2009, July 26. U.S. expands Afghan drug fight: DEA agents enter fray as ties between drug traffickers and insurgent fighters have grown closer, officials say. *St. Louis Post-Dispatch*. www.stltoday.com.

Michaels, Christopher, and Tyler Wall. 2015. Militarization is not the problem: Police power, capitalist order, and pacification. Unpublished manuscript.

Miller, Wilbur. 1991. *Revenuers and Moonshiners: Enforcing Federal Liquor Law in the Mountain South, 1865–1900*. Chapel Hill: University of North Carolina Press.

Mintz, John. 2004, June 18. Homeland Security employs imagination. *Washington Post*. www.washingtonpost.com.

Mirzoeff, Nicholas. 2006. On visuality. *Journal of Visual Culture*, 5, 53–78.

Monahan, Torin. 2010. The future of security? Surveillance operations at homeland security fusion centers. *Social Justice*, 37(2–3), 84–98.

Montag, Warren. 2013. *Althusser and His Contemporaries: Philosophy's Perpetual War*. Durham, NC: Duke University Press.

Montana Meth Project. 2007, March 7. Montana Meth Project kicks off new campaign with ads by critically acclaimed director Darren Aronofsky. Press release.

Morales, Andrea C., Eugenia C. Wu, and Gavin Fitzsimons. 2012. How disgust enhances the effectiveness of fear appeals. *Journal of Marketing Research*, 49, 383–393.

Murakawa, Naomi. 2011. Toothless. *Du Bois Review: Social Science Research on Race*, 8(01), 219–228.

———. 2014. *The First Civil Right: How Liberals Built Prison America*. New York: Oxford University Press.

Murray, Charles. 1993, October 29. The coming white underclass. *Wall Street Journal*.

———. 2013. *Coming Apart: The State of White America, 1960–2010*. New York: Crown.

NATO. 2002, June 6. Press conference by US Secretary of Defense Donald Rumsfeld. www.nato.int.

Neocleous, Mark. 2000. *The Fabrication of Social Order: A Critical Theory of Police Power*. London: Pluto.

———. 2007. Security, commodity, fetishism. *Critique*, 35(3), 339–355.

———. 2008. *Critique of Security*. Montreal: McGill-Queen's University Press.

———. 2011. "A brighter and nicer new life": Security as pacification. *Social & Legal Studies*, 20(2), 191–208.

———. 2014a. The monster and the police: Dexter to Hobbes. *Radical Philosophy*, 185(May–June), 8–18.

———. 2014b. *War Power, Police Power*. Edinburgh: Edinburgh University Press.

———. 2015. *On the Universal Adversary: Security, Capital and "The Enemies of All Mankind."* London: Routledge.

Nevins, Joseph. 2010. *Operation Gatekeeper and Beyond: The War on "Illegals" and the Remaking of the US-Mexico Boundary*. London: Routledge.

Nicosia, Nancy, Rosalie Liccardo Pacula, Beau Kilmer, Russell Lundberg, and James Chiesa. 2009. *The Economic Costs of Methamphetamine Use in the United States, 2005*. Santa Monica, CA: RAND.

NIDA (National Institute on Drug Abuse). 1997. *Drug Abuse Prevention: What Works*. Washington, DC: National Institutes of Health.

Nietzsche, Friedrich. 2003. *Beyond Good and Evil*. New York: Penguin.

NPR (National Public Radio). 2009, July 8. Author paints small town's struggle in "Methland."

———. 2014, November 25. Ferguson documents: Officer Darren Wilson's testimony. *The Two-Way* (blog). www.npr.org.

Obama, Barack. 2014, August 18. Statement by the president. Whitehouse.gov.

O'Connor. Keith. 2014, April 29. Etta May to bring "southern fried comedy" to CityStage. MassLive. www.masslive.com

Oklahoma Senate Communications Division. 1999, November 12. Senator asks governor to apologize for racial comments, Dickerson calls Keating statements inappropriate, offensive. www.oksenate.gov.

Olson, Eric, and Christopher Wilson. 2010. Beyond Mérida: The evolving approach to security cooperation. Woodrow Wilson International Center for Scholars.

O'Malley, Pat, and Darren Palmer. 1996. Post-Keynesian policing. *Economy and Society*, 25(2), 137–155.

Owen, Frank. 2007. *No Speed Limit: The Highs and Lows of Meth*. New York: Macmillan.

Paglen, Trevor. 2010. *I Could Tell You but Then You Would Have to Be Destroyed by Me: Emblems from the Pentagon's Black World*. New York: Melville House.

Paley, Dawn. 2014. *Drug War Capitalism*. Oakland, CA: AK.

Payan, Tony. 2006. *The Three US-Mexico Border Wars*. Westport, CT: Praeger Security.

Payne, Brian, Bruce Berg, and Ivan Sun. 2005. Policing in small town America: Dogs, drunks, disorder and dysfunction. *Journal of Criminal Justice*, 33(1), 31–41.

Perry, Tony. 2005, January 13. Fallujah insurgents fought under influence of drugs, marines say. *Los Angeles Times*, 1.

Platt, Tony, Ray Gerda, Richard Schauffler, Larry Trujillo, Lynn Cooper, Elliott Currie, and Sidney Harring. 1975. *The Iron Fist and the Velvet Glove: An Analysis of the US Police*. San Francisco: Crime and Social Justice Associates.

Potter, Dan. 2013, February 13. Tulsa is proven meth capital of nation. KRMG.com.

Probst, Jason. 2005, November 13. Crack cocaine numbers rise. *Hutchinson News*, 1.

Provine, Doris Marie. 2008. *Unequal under Law: Race in the War on Drugs*. Chicago: University of Chicago Press.

Puriton, Cait. 2005, May 7. State salutes fallen sheriff: Sebelius: "Recognize daily the sacrifices made." *Topeka Capital-Journal*.

Rafter, Nicole. 1988. Introduction to *White Trash: The Eugenic Family Studies, 1877–1919*, 1–31. Boston: Northeastern University Press.

———. 2001. Seeing and believing: Images of heredity in biological theories of crime. *Brooklyn Law Review*, 67, 71.

———. 2007. Crime, film and criminology: Recent sex-crime movies. *Theoretical Criminology*, 11(3), 403–420.

———. 2014. Introduction to "Visual Culture and the Iconography of Crime and Punishment." Special issue, *Theoretical Criminology*, 18(2), 127–133.

Reding, Nick. 2010. *Methland: The Death and Life of an American Small Town*. New York: Bloomsbury.

Reed, Adolph, Jr. 2013, February 25. *Django Unchained*, or, *The Help*: How "cultural politics" is worse than no politics at all, and why. *Nonsite.org*.

Reiss, Suzanna. 2014. *We Sell Drugs: The Alchemy of US Empire*. Berkeley: University of California Press.

Rentschler, Carrie. 2011. An urban physiognomy of the 1964 Kitty Genovese murder. *Space and Culture*, 14(3), 310–329.

Reuter, Peter, and Jonathan Caulkins. 2003. Does precursor regulation make a difference? *Addiction*, 98, 1177–1179.

Rock, Chris. 2002. *Bring the Pain*. DreamWorks Records Home Video.

Ronell, Avital. 2004. *Crack Wars: Literature, Addiction, Mania*. Urbana: University of Illinois Press.

Rothschild, Scott. 2005, February 1. Senate slows work on anti-meth bill. *Lawrence Journal World*.

Saborio, Sebastian. 2013. The pacification of the favelas: Mega events, global competitiveness, and the neutralization of marginality. *Socialist Studies/Études socialistes*, 9(2), 130–145.

Sampson, Robert J., Stephen W. Raudenbush, and Felton Earls. 1998. *Neighborhood Collective Efficacy—Does It Help Reduce Violence?* US Department of Justice, Office of Justice Programs, National Institute of Justice.

Savage, Charlie. 2011, November 6. D.E.A. squads extend reach of drug war. *New York Times*.

Schept, Judah. 2013. "A lockdown facility . . . with the feel of a small, private college": Liberal politics, jail expansion, and the carceral habitus. *Theoretical Criminology*, 17(1), 71–88.

———. 2014. (Un)seeing like a prison: Counter-visual ethnography of the carceral state. *Theoretical Criminology*, 18(2), 198–223.

———. 2015. *Progressive Punishment: Job Loss, Jail Growth, and the Neoliberal Logic of Carceral Expansion.* New York: NYU Press.

Schmidt, Derek. 2010. Derek Schmidt attorney general 2010. www.DerekSchmidt.com.

———. 2011, April 18. A new electronic weapon in the war on meth. Press release. www. as.kg.gov.

———. 2013, May 3. AG's office sends 35 to prison for meth in 2012. Press release. www. as.kg.gov.

———. 2014, February 8. Independence man sentenced to 6 years for manufacturing meth. Press release. www.as.kg.gov.

Schumer, Charles. 2006, October 30. Schumer: New stats show crystal meth quickly becoming the new crack: Seizures in New York up 31% over last year. Press release. http://schumer.senate.gov.

Schwartz, Mattathias. 2014, January 6. A mission gone wrong. *New Yorker.*

Scott, James. C. 1998. *Seeing like a State: How Certain Schemes to Improve the Human Condition Have Failed.* New Haven, CT: Yale University Press.

Sebelius, Kathleen. 2005, January 10. State of the State speech. http://kslib.info.

Seelke, Clare, and Kristine Finklea. 2014, April 8. *US-Mexican Security Cooperation: The Mérida Initiative and Beyond.* Washington, DC: Congressional Research Service, Library of Congress.

Segal, David. 2011, July 6. The dark art of "Breaking Bad." *New York Times.* www. nytimes.com.

Sexton, Rocky. 2011. Methamphetamine. In *Encyclopedia of Drug Policy*, vol. 1, edited by Mark A. Kleiman and James E. Hawdon. London: Sage.

Shafer, Jack. 2005a, August 4. Where, exactly, is the meth capital of the world? *Slate.* www.slate.com.

———. 2005b, August 29. The meth-mouth myth: Our latest moral panic. *Slate.* www. slate.com.

Sibley, David. 1995. *Geographies of Exclusion.* London: Routledge.

Siebel, Thomas, and Steven Mange. 2009. The Montana Meth Project: "Unselling" a dangerous drug. *Stanford Law & Policy Review*, 20, 405–416.

Siebel Foundation. 2012. *2011 Siebel Foundation Annual Report.*

Sim, Joe. 2004. The victimized state and the mystification of social harm. In *Beyond Criminology: Taking Harm Seriously*, edited by Paddy Hillyard, Christina Pantazis, Steve Tombs, and Dave Gordon. London: Pluto.

Simon, Jonathan. 2007. *Governing through Crime: How the War on Crime Transformed American Democracy and Created a Culture of Fear.* New York: Oxford University Press.

Simons, Herbert W., and Jean Jones. 2011. *Persuasion in Society*. 2nd ed. New York: Routledge.

Skelton, Alissa. 2014, October 13. Mexican cartel picks up slack after Nebraska curtails meth trade. *Omaha World-Herald*.

Small, Mario Luis. 2008. Four reasons to abandon the idea of "the ghetto." *City & Community*, 7(4), 389–398.

Smarsh, Sarah. 2014, October 23. Poor teeth. *Aeon*. https://aeon.co.

Solomon, Sheldon, Jeff Greenberg, and Tom Pyszczynski. 2015. *The Worm at the Core: On the Role of Death in Life*. New York: Random House.

Stahl, Jerry. Bad. In *The Speed Chronicles*, edited by Joseph Mattson. New York: Akashic Drug Chronicles, 2011.

State of Kansas. 2005, February 17. *Journal of the Senate*, 28th day. www.kansas.gov.

———. 2007, January 25. Morrison commends drop in meth lab seizures calls for further action. www.ksag.org.

Stebner, Beth. 2011, December 9. "She couldn't say no": The shocking state date-rape ad pulled amid over suggestions that drunken victims are to blame. *Daily Mail Online*. www.dailymail.co.uk.

Stein, Sam. 2008, November 7. Palin explains what parts of country not "pro-America." *Huffington Post*. www.huffingtonpost.com.

Steinert, Heinz. 2003. The indispensable metaphor of war: On populist politics and the contradictions of the state's monopoly of force. *Theoretical Criminology*, 7(3) 265–291.

Stemen, Don, and Andres Renfigo. 2009. Mandating treatment for drug possessors: The impact of Senate Bill 123 on the criminal justice system in Kansas. *Journal of Criminal Justice*, 37(3), 296–304.

Sterling Bulletin. 2005, February 24. Shame on us!

Stern, Seth. 2006, June 5. Meth vs. crack: Different legislative approaches. *CQ Weekly*.

Substance Abuse and Mental Health Services Administration. 2010. *National Survey on Drug Use and Health*.

Sweeney, Gael. 1997. The king of white trash culture: Elvis Presley and the aesthetics of excess. In *White Trash: Race and Class in America*, edited by Matt Wray and Annalee Newitz, 249–266. New York: Routledge.

Swidler, Ann. 1986. Culture in action: Symbols and strategies. *American Sociological Review*, 51(2), 273–286.

Sydney Morning Herald. 2014, May 2. Seven things you might not know about Breaking Bad. www.smh.com.au.

Taussig, Michael. 1997. *The Magic of the State*. New York: Psychology Press.

Taylor, Charles. 2004. *Modern Social Imaginaries*. Durham, NC: Duke University Press.

Taylor, Paul. 2014. Fetish/fetishistic disavowal. In *The Žižek Dictionary*, edited by Rex Butler, 93–96. New York: Acumen.

Thompson, Hunter S. 2010. *Fear and Loathing in Las Vegas: A Savage Journey to the Heart of the American Dream*. New York: Vintage.

Tiger, Rebecca. 2012. *Judging Addicts: Drug Courts and Coercion in the Justice System*. New York: NYU Press.

Timmons, Heather. 2015, April 16. Flakka, Florida's latest drug scourge, can easily be purchased online in China. *Quartz*. http://qz.com.

Toplikar, David. 2005, February 24. Samuels Act makes it harder to get Sudafed. *Valley Falls Vindicator*.

Tunnell, Kenneth. 2011. *Once upon a Place*. Bloomington, IN: Xlibris.

Tzanelli, Rodanthi, and Majid Yar. 2014, July 10. *Breaking Bad*, making good: Notes on a televisual tourist industry. *Mobilities*, 1–19.

Ulaby, Neda. 2011, August 18. On location: The frozen Ozarks of "Winter's Bone." NPR. org.

US Attorney's Office, Northern District of Georgia. 2015, July 22. Former Habersham County deputy sheriff charged for her role in flash bang grenade incident. www.fbi. gov.

US Census Bureau. 2010a. Metropolitan and micropolitan statistical areas main. www. census.gov.

———. 2010b. 2010 Census urban and rural classification and urban area criteria. www. census.gov.

US Department of Defense. 2009, May 31. Afghanistan subject: Afghanistan counternarcotics: Narco-insurgency hub decimated by Afghan and U.S. forces. Kabul. www.wikileaks.org.

US Department of Homeland Security. 2005, July 21. *Red Cell Report: Thinking beyond Mass Transit for the Next Homeland Attack*. https://info.publicintelligence.net.

———. 2009, March 25. Testimony of Secretary Janet Napolitano before Senate Homeland Security and Governmental Affairs Committee, Southern Border Violence: Homeland Security Threats, Vulnerabilities, and Responsibilities. www.dhs.gov.

US Department of Justice. 1996. *Methamphetamine Situation in the United States*. Drug Enforcement Administration, Domestic Unit of the Strategic Intelligence Section.

———. 2000, January. *Methamphetamine Interagency Task Force: Final Report*. www. ncjrs.gov.

———. 2009, February 25. Hundreds of alleged Sinaloa Cartel members and associates arrested in nationwide takedown of Mexican drug traffickers. Press release.

———. 2011, August. *2011 Drug Threat Assessment*. National Drug Intelligence Center. www.justice.gov.

———. 2012, June 12. Haji Bagcho sentenced to life in prison on drug trafficking and narco-terrorism charges. Press release. www.justice.gov.

———. 2014a, February 22. Attorney General Eric Holder. Dept. of Justice statement on the arrest of Joaquin "El Chapo" Guzman Loera. Press release. www.dea.gov.

———. 2014b, November. *2014 Drug Threat Assessment*. National Drug Intelligence Center. www.dea.gov.

———. 2015, August 5. DEA announces tip line, wanted poster for Chapo. www.dea.gov.

US Department of State. n.d. Narcotics Rewards Program: Joaquin Guzman-Loera. www.state.gov.

US House of Representatives. 2004a, February 6. *Fighting Methamphetamine in the Heartland*. Committee on Government Reform, Subcommittee on Criminal Justice,

Drug Policy and Human Resources. 109th Cong., 1st sess. Serial No. 108–179. Washington, DC: US Government Printing Office.

———. 2004b, July 17. *The War against Drugs and Thugs: A Status Report on Plan Colombia Successes and Remaining Challenges.* Committee on Government Reform. 108th Cong. Serial No. 18–214. Washington, DC: US Government Printing Office.

———. 2011, October 4. *Mérida Part II: Insurgency and Terrorism in Mexico.* Foreign Affairs Subcommittee on the Western Hemisphere and House Homeland Security Subcommittee on Oversight, Investigations and Management, US Department of State. Washington, DC: US Government Printing Office.

———. 2012a, May 21. *Iran, Hezbollah and the Threat to the Homeland.* Committee on Homeland Security.112th Cong., 1st sess. Washington, DC: US Government Printing Office.

———. 2012b, July 24. *Meth Revisited: Review of State and Federal Efforts to Solve the Domestic Methamphetamine Production Resurgence: Hearing before the Subcommittee on Health Care, District of Colombia, Census and the National Archives of the Committee on Oversight and Government Reform, House of Representatives.* 112 Cong., 2nd sess. Serial no. 112–189. Washington, DC: US Government Printing Office.

———. 2013, May 13–23. *U.S-Mexico Security Cooperation: An Overview of the Mérida Initiative 2008–Present.* House Foreign Affairs Subcommittee on the Western Hemisphere. 113th Cong., 1st sess. Washington, DC: US Government Printing Office.

US Northern Command. 2013, May 16. Joint Task Force North. www.northcom.mil.

US Senate. 2007, September 27. *Breaking the Methamphetamine Supply Chain: Meeting Challenges at the Border.* Committee on Finance. 110th Cong., 1st sess. Washington, DC: US Government Printing Office.

Valier, Claire. 2002. Punishment, border crossings and the powers of horror. *Theoretical Criminology*, 6(3), 319–337.

Van Marle, Fenna, and Shadd Maruna. 2010. "Ontological Insecurity" and "Terror Management": Linking Two Free-Floating Anxieties." *Punishment & Society*, 12(1), 7–26.

Variety. 1999, July 8. Review of *Bigger and Blacker*. http://variety.com.

Vice. n.d. The real Walter White. www.vice.com.

Walker, Margath. 2015. Borders, one-dimensionality, and illusion in the war on drugs. *Environment and Planning D*, 33(1), 84–100.

Wall, Tyler. 2009. War-nation: Military and moral geographies of the Hoosier homefront. PhD diss., Arizona State University.

WATE. 2013, July 22. BCSO: 2 "one pot" meth labs found at Maryville motel. www.wate.com.

Webster, Colin. 2008. Marginalized white ethnicity, race and crime. *Theoretical Criminology*, 12(3), 298–312.

Weisheit, Ralph, and L. Edward Wells. 2010. Methamphetamine laboratories: The geography of drug production. *Western Criminology Review*, 11, 9.

Wells, Samuel. 1898. *New Physiognomy: Or Signs of Character, as Manifested through Temperament and External Forms and Especially in "the Human Face Divine."* New York: Kessinger.

WFLA. 2015, April 10. Florida police warn of dangerous drug Flakka, causes superhuman strength. www.wfla.com.

White House. 2001, October 8. Gov. Ridge sworn-in to lead Homeland Security. www.whitehouse.gov.

———. 2006, March 9. The PATRIOT Act. http://georgewbush-whitehouse.archives.gov.

Wichita Eagle. 2005, January 20. Ks. sheriff shot dead serving warrant.

Wiggin, Katie. 2011, December 5. Boston professor charged with running meth lab, police say. CBS News. www.cbsnews.com.

Wilbur, Ash. 2009, July 17. Town split over portrayal in "Methland." *Star Tribune.* www.startribune.com.

Williams, Edward H. 1914, February 8. Negro cocaine "fiends" are a new southern menace. *New York Times,* 12.

Williams, Kristian. 2011. The other side of the COIN: Counterinsurgency and community policing. *Interface,* 3(1), 81–117.

Williams, Maria, Jefferson Holcomb, Tomislav Kovandzic, and Scott Bullock. 2010, March. *Policing for Profit: The Abuse of Civil Asset Forfeiture.* Arlington, VA: Institute for Justice.

Williams, Raymond. 1975. *The Country and the City.* Oxford: Oxford University Press.

Williamson, Kevin. 2016, March 28. The father-führer. *National Review.* www.nationalreview.com.

Wilson, Christopher. 2000. *Cop Knowledge: Police Power and Cultural Narrative in Twentieth-Century America.* Chicago: University of Chicago Press.

Wilson, Jacqueline. 2002. Invisible racism: The language and ontology of white trash. *Critique of Anthropology,* 22(4), 387–401.

Winlow, Simon, and Steve Hall. 2013. *Rethinking Social Exclusion: The End of the Social?* London: Sage.

Wirth, Louis. 1928. *The Ghetto.* Vol. 7. New Brunswick, NJ: Transaction.

Witness for Peace. 2015, February 27. Fact sheet: The Mérida Initiative / Plan Mexico. www.witnessforpeace.org.

Wolters, Eugene. 2014, May 9. Bell hooks dancing to Beyonce's "Drunk in Love" is the most adorable thing you'll see all day. *Critical Theory* (blog). www.critical-theory.com.

Wray, Matt. 2013, June 21. White trash: The social origins of a stigmatype. *Society Pages.*

Wray, Matt, and Annalee Newitz. 1997. Introduction to *White Trash: Race and Class in America,* edited by Matt Wray and Annalee Newitz. New York: Routledge.

Wyoming Meth Project. 2012, March 7. New research cites Meth Project ads as effective. http://wyoming.methproject.org.

Yan, Holly, and Gabriella Schwartz. 2011, July 11. GOP candidates caught in slavery controversy. *Political Ticker* (blog), CNN. http://politicalticker.blogs.cnn.com.

Yar, Majid. 2014a. *The Cultural Imaginary of the Internet: Virtual Utopias and Dystopias.* London: Palgrave Macmillan.

———. 2014b. Imaginaries of crime, fantasies of justice: Popular criminology and the figure of the superhero. In *The Poetics of Crime: Understanding and Researching*

Crime and Deviance through Creative Sources, edited by Michael Hviid Jacobsen, 193–208. Farnham, UK: Ashgate.

Young, Alison. 1996. *Imagining Crime*. London: Sage.

Young, Jock. 1971. The role of the police as amplifiers of deviancy, negotiators of reality and translators of fantasy. In *Images of Deviance*, edited by Stanley Cohen, 27–61. Harmondsworth, UK: Penguin.

———. 1999. *The Exclusive Society: Social Exclusion, Crime and Difference in Late Modernity*. London: Sage.

———. 2003. Merton with energy, Katz with structure: The sociology of vindictiveness and the criminology of transgression. *Theoretical Criminology*, 7(3), 388–414.

———. 2007. *The Vertigo of Late Modernity*. London: Sage.

Zernike, Kate. 2006, February 26. With scenes of blood and pain, ads battle methamphetamine in Montana. *New York Times*.

Zimmerman, Neetzan. 2012, September 17. Life imitates Breaking Bad—again—as Texas chemistry teacher charged with cooking, selling meth. *Gawker*. http://gawker.com.

Žižek, Slavoj. 1993. *Tarrying with the Negative: Kant, Hegel, and the Critique of Ideology*. Durham, NC: Duke University Press.

———. 2002. *Welcome to the Desert of the Real! Five Essays on September 11 and Related Dates*. London: Verso.

———. 2009a. *In Defense of Lost Causes*. London: Verso.

———. 2009b. *Violence: Six Sideways Reflections*. New York: Profile.

———. 2011. *Living in the End Times*. London: Verso.

———. 2013a. *Enjoy Your Symptom! Jacques Lacan in Hollywood and Out*. London: Routledge.

———. 2013b, January 25. *Zero Dark Thirty*: Hollywood's gift to American power. *Guardian*. www.theguardian.com.

———. 2014. *Event: A Philosophical Journey through a Concept*. New York: Melville House.

———. 2015, March 9. Divine violence in Fergusson. *European Magazine*. www.theeuropean-magazine.com.

INDEX

ABOUT THE AUTHOR

Travis Linnemann is Assistant Professor of Justice Studies at Eastern Kentucky University.